Neuro-linguistic Programming

FOR

DUMMIES®

2ND EDITION

by Romilla Ready and Kate Burton

WILEY

A John Wiley and Sons, Ltd, Publication

Neuro-linguistic Programming For Dummies®, 2nd Edition
Published by
John Wiley & Sons, Ltd
The Atrium
Southern Gate
Chichester
West Sussex
PO19 8SQ
England

E-mail (for orders and customer service enquires): cs-books@wiley.co.uk

Visit our Home Page on www.wiley.com

For general information on our other products and services, please contact our Customer Care Department within the U.S. at 877-762-2974, outside the U.S. at 317-572-3993, or fax 317-572-4002.

For technical support, please visit www.wiley.com/techsupport.

Wiley also publishes its books in a variety of electronic formats. Some content that appears in print may not be available in electronic books.

British Library Cataloguing in Publication Data: A catalogue record for this book is available from the British Library

ISBN 978-0-470-66543-5 (hardback), ISBN 978-0-470-66610-4 (ebk),

ISBN 978-0-470-66609-8 (ebk), ISBN 978-0-470-97843-6

Printed and bound in China, by 1010 International Ltd

About the Authors

Romilla Ready is the creator and architect of Relationship Wizardry®, her own brand of training and coaching, which combines the two potent technologies of Neuro-linguistic Programming and Huna (the ancient knowledge from Hawai'i). Relationship Wizardry® evolved from the realisation that the common denominator in any interaction, be it one that causes distress or one that gives pleasure, is people and the way they think and communicate. Her product offerings are:

- Relationship Wizardry®, which is aimed at people (usually singletons) who want to create their perfect relationship.

- Relationship Wizardry® in Business, which helps companies build profitable stakeholder relationships through improved employee and customer engagement as well as through enhanced salesmanship.

- Relationship Wizardry® Coaching, which enables time paupers to experience fast, powerful, life-enhancing results in their personal and business lives.

- Applied NLP for Business Results™ networking events, where business owners discover how to apply NLP to create the specific results they want for their business.

Romilla has worked in high-stress, customer-facing environments for multi-national companies and across cultural boundaries, has provided training in the UK, Europe, and Africa, and is the MD of her company, Ready Solutions Ltd.

Kate Burton is an international NLP master coach, author, and workshop leader who challenges individuals and organisations to create successful lives that are sustainable and fun. Her business career began in corporate advertising and marketing with Hewlett-Packard. Since then she has worked with varied businesses across industries and cultures on how they can be great communicators.

What Kate loves most is delivering custom-built coaching programmes. She thrives on supporting people in boosting their motivation, self-awareness, and confidence. Her belief is that people all have unique talents, abilities, and core values. The skill is about honouring them to the full.

In addition to co-authoring *Neuro-linguistic Programming For Dummies* and the *Neuro-linguistic Programming Workbook For Dummies* with Romilla, Kate co-authored *Building Self-Confidence For Dummies* with Brinley Platts. Her latest book, *Live Life, Love Work,* is published by Capstone (a Wiley imprint) and she is currently writing *Coaching with NLP For Dummies.*

Authors' Acknowledgements

From Romilla: The thrill of finding *Neuro-linguistic Programming For Dummies* in the bookshops is as fresh now as when it first published. The fulfillment of this dream wouldn't have been possible without the help and support of a raft of wonderful people, to all of whom I wish to offer my heartfelt thanks. My 'partner in crime', Kate Burton: I am so glad you agreed to collaborate on this project when I rather nonchalantly asked you if you'd like to write a book on NLP with me. Thank you, mum, for all your love, support, and ideas – keep them coming; Angela, my sister, has always been there in times of trouble and celebration, and has done a grand job of being the first 'test dummy' for our book and making sure I didn't split my infinitives! Oswyn for being the perfect grandfather to 'brattus', my son, Derwent, who bails me out when I come a-cropper with technology and won't let me give up; Rintu who continues to help me learn and stretch; my Yoga teacher, Swami Ambikananda Saraswati, for her patience in the face of all my questions; David, my NLP trainer, who gave me another rung in the ladder for personal change. Last but not least, I'd like to thank the terrific team at Wiley for all their help and support.

Derek, 'the wind beneath my wings', is gone but I will cherish memories of our life together.

From Kate: When Romilla and I set out to write the original book, our intention was to learn and have some fun; we never anticipated the pleasure this book would bring. So my thanks to Romilla that we continue to enjoy such a deep understanding and friendship. All my family, especially Bob, Rosy, and Jessica have my thanks for your unconditional love and unfailing ability to nurture me while I focus on writing more books. To my special friends, thank you for your patience and grounding in common sense. I thank Ian, Robert, Penny, and James, and many other amazing NLPers for sharing their knowledge with such integrity; I remain in awe of your skill and commitment. Thanks to Jan for demonstrating the sheer joy of masterful NLP coaching at its finest. To my clients and colleagues, I appreciate the endless opportunities to learn and practice NLP with you. To the fabulous professionals at Wiley for shaping ideas into reality; you certainly demonstrate the power of belief. What we had not expected was that *Neuro-linguistic Programming For Dummies* would be such a runaway best seller with so many international translations, and the workbook and CDs following on from it, so our thanks above all go to our readers for your support and good wishes. This book sprang to life because we wanted to enthuse others with the power of NLP and I hope you'll continue to be intrigued and inspired as there's so much to learn and to apply.

Publisher's Acknowledgements

We're proud of this book; please send us your comments through our Dummies online registration form located at www.dummies.com/register/.

Some of the people who helped bring this book to market include the following:

Commissioning, Editorial, and Media Development

Project Editor: Steve Edwards
(Previous Edition: Daniel Mersey, Amie Tibble)

Content Editor: Jo Theedom

Commissioning Editor: Nicole Hermitage

Assistant Editor: Ben Kemble

Copy Editor: Andy Finch

Technical Editor: Lynne Cooper

Proofreader: Jamie Brind

Production Manager: Daniel Mersey

Cover Photos: verre d'eau © cdrcom

Cartoons: Rich Tennant
(www.the5thwave.com)

Composition Services

Project Coordinator: Lynsey Stanford

Layout and Graphics: Nikki Gately, Joyce Haughey, Christin Swinford

Proofreader: Laura Albert

Indexer: Ty Koontz

Publishing and Editorial for Consumer Dummies

    Diane Graves Steele, Vice President and Publisher, Consumer Dummies

    Joyce Pepple, Acquisitions Director, Consumer Dummies

    Kristin A. Cocks, Product Development Director, Consumer Dummies

    Michael Spring, Vice President and Publisher, Travel

    Kelly Regan, Editorial Director, Travel

Publishing for Technology Dummies

    Andy Cummings, Vice President and Publisher, Dummies Technology/General User

Composition Services

    Gerry Fahey, Vice President of Production Services

    Debbie Stailey, Director of Composition Services

Contents at a Glance

Table of Contents

Part VI: The Part of Tens *335*

Introduction

Welcome to the second edition of *Neuro-linguistic Programming For Dummies*, which is packed with ideas and tips to increase your success and happiness. Most likely, you're reading this book because you've heard neuro-linguistic programming (NLP throughout this book) mentioned as you go about your daily life – in companies, colleges, and coffee shops. We wrote the original version of this book because our experience of NLP transformed our own lives. We wanted to ignite the spark of curiosity in others about what's possible with NLP. We also believed that the time had come for NLP to move away from academic- and business-speak to real-life plain English, and be used by all people who want to make improvements in their lives.

In recent years, we've witnessed NLP growing ever more popular. Part of this popularity is because NLP offers enlightening 'aha!' moments, and part is because it simply makes sense. Yet the name itself can be off-putting and the associated jargon may present a barrier to non-NLP professionals. So a little explanation is required:

- ✔ **Neuro** relates to what's happening in your mind.
- ✔ **Linguistic** refers not only to the words you use in your communication, but also your body language and how you use it.
- ✔ **Programming** tackles the persistent patterns of behaviour that you learn and then repeat.

Some people describe NLP as 'the study of the structure of subjective experience'; others call it 'the art and science of communication'. We prefer to say that NLP enables you to understand what makes you tick: how you think, how you feel, and how you make sense of everyday life in the world around you. Armed with this understanding, your whole life – work and play – can be renewed.

It's hard to believe that six years have passed since the first edition of this book was published. The first edition of *Neuro-linguistic Programming For Dummies* presented us with opportunities, which came primarily in the form of amazing clients who've shared their lives, problems, and successes with us. We have incorporated some of the lessons from this more recent work to bring a fresh perspective to you.

In particular, you have the benefit of two new chapters. The first one (Chapter 19) is about modelling. NLP began with modelling, an approach that enables you to enhance your skills. The second new chapter (Chapter 20) is focused on making change easier. Given that change is a given in the frenetic world in which we live, you'll find new ideas here to help you mitigate the negative effects of stress, and the application of favourite tools out of the NLP toolkit.

About This Book

This book aims to entrance anyone fascinated by people. Through its experiential approach, NLP encourages people to take action to shape their own lives. It attracts those willing to 'have a go' and open their minds to new possibilities.

We try to make NLP friendly, pragmatic, accessible, and useful for you. We expect you to be able to dip into the book at any chapter and quickly find practical ideas on how to use NLP to resolve issues or make changes for yourself.

In displaying the NLP 'market stall', our choice of content is selective. We aim to offer an enticing menu if you're a newcomer. And for those with more knowledge, we hope this book helps you to digest what you already know as well as treat you to some new ideas and applications. To that end, we make finding information such as the following easy for you:

- How to discover what's important to you to pursue your goals with energy and conviction.
- What the main NLP presuppositions are and why they're important to you.
- What the best ways are to understand other people's style, helping you to get your own message heard.
- When to build rapport and when to break it.
- How to get your unconscious mind to work together with your conscious mind to make a strong team.

In addition, because the best way to discover NLP is to experience it, take full opportunity of playing with all the exercises we provide. Some of the ideas and exercises in this book may be quite different from your normal style of behaviour, but don't be put off. The NLP approach is about setting aside your disbelief, having a go, and realising your potential.

Conventions Used in This Book

To help you navigate throughout this book, we set up a few conventions:

- *Italic* is used for emphasis and to highlight new words or terms that are defined.
- **Boldfaced** text is used to indicate the action part of numbered steps.
- Monofont is used for website addresses.

What You're Not to Read

We've written this book so that you can easily understand what you want to discover about NLP. And although after all this writing on our part we'd like to believe that you want to hang on our every last word between these yellow and black covers, we make identifying the 'skippable' material easy. This information is the stuff that, although interesting and related to the topic at hand, isn't essential for you to know:

- ✔ **Text in sidebars:** The sidebars are the shaded boxes that appear here and there. They share personal stories and observations, but aren't essential reading.

- ✔ **The stuff on the copyright page:** No kidding. You find nothing here of interest unless you're inexplicably enamoured by legal language and reprint information!

Foolish Assumptions

In this book, we make a few assumptions about you. We assume that you're a normal human being who wants to be happy. You're probably interested in learning and ideas. You may have heard the term NLP mentioned, you may already work with the concepts, or perhaps it's just new and intriguing for you. You need no prior knowledge of NLP, but this book is for you if any of the following situations ring a bell:

- ✔ You're tired or fed-up with the way some things are for you now.

- ✔ You're interested in how to take your living experience to new levels of achievement, happiness, adventure, and success.

- ✔ You're curious about how you can influence others ethically and easily.

- ✔ You're somebody who loves learning and growing.

- ✔ You're ready to turn your dreams into reality.

How This Book Is Organised

We divide this book into seven parts, with each part broken into chapters. The table of contents gives you more detail on each chapter, and we even throw in a cartoon at the start of each part for your amusement.

Part I: Introducing NLP

A wise person said that 'If you always do what you've always done, you'll always get what you always got.' Remember these great words of wisdom as you begin the journey into NLP territory for yourself. In this part, you start to get a feel for what NLP can do for you. As you begin, bear one thing in mind: suspend your disbelief or assumptions that may get in the way of your learning. In this part, we invite you to think about the best NLP question of all, which is 'What do I want?', and then to delve into what's happening behind the scenes in your brain and your unconscious thinking. Interesting stuff, we hope you agree.

Part II: Winning Friends and Influencing People

Ever considered how easy life would be if others just did what you wanted them to do? We're not claiming to be magicians – that we can make your worst enemies smooth putty in your hands – but rapport is such a key theme in NLP that the heart of this book explores it hand-in-hand with you. In this part, we give you tools for understanding other people's points of view. We show you how to take responsibility for making changes in how you connect with the key people in your life, and how to discover becoming more flexible in your own behaviour.

Part III: Opening the Toolkit

The heart of NLP opens up before you in this part, as we let you loose on the core NLP toolkit. Loads of practical stuff is here for you to keep coming back to. You discover how you can adapt and manage your own thinking to tackle situations that you find difficult, plus how you can get the resources to change habits that no longer help you. You also whiz into the future and work with concepts of time to resolve old issues and create a more compelling path ahead of you.

Part IV: Using Words to Entrance

This part focuses on how the language you use doesn't just describe an experience, but has the power to create it. Just imagine how great you'd feel to have an audience eating out of your hands. Building on the skills and styles of powerful communicators, we explain how to get audiences coming back with an appetite for more, and if you consider that life can be described as a series of stories, you find out how to write your own winning narrative.

Part V: Integrating Your Learning

In this part we encourage you to bring together what you read and experiment within the book, and apply it to your own life. You find out about modelling and how to learn from your choice of role model to achieve excellence in your chosen field. In addition, we take a look at what happens in times of change and how you can move forward with grace and ease.

Part VI: The Part of Tens

If you're impatient to get your answers about NLP sorted quickly, start here. This part takes you straight to some top ten tips and lists, such as applications of NLP, the resources and books to guide you, plus more besides. We design this part for those of you who always like to read the end of a book first and to understand the meaty stuff inside.

Part VII: Appendixes

In the appendixes we include an NLP resource list of useful addresses and websites, plus the two most important templates to use every day to achieve the following ends:

- ✔ Making your desired outcomes real – we explain more in Chapter 4.
- ✔ Building rapport with other people – we explore this aspect in Chapter 7.

Icons Used in This Book

The icons in this book help you to find particular kinds of information that may be of use to you.

This icon highlights NLP terminology that may sound like a foreign language but which has a precise meaning in the NLP field.

This icon suggests ideas and activities to give you practice of NLP techniques and food for thought.

This icon contains practical advice to put NLP to work for you.

This icon is a friendly reminder of important points to note.

This icon indicates real-life experiences of NLP in action. Some are real, some people have had their names changed, and others are composite characters.

This icon marks things to avoid in your enthusiasm to try out NLP skills on your own.

Where to Go From Here

You don't have to read this book from cover to cover, but you benefit greatly if you capture everything at the pace and in the order that's right for you. Use the table of contents to see what grabs your interest. For example, if you're keen to understand someone else, first try Chapter 7. Or if you want to know what makes you tick, turn to Chapter 6 and discover the power of your senses. Feel free to dip and dive in.

When you've read the book and are keen to discover more, we recommend that you experience NLP more fully through workshops and coaching with others. We include a resource section in the Part of Tens to help you on your journey.

Part I
Introducing NLP

The 5th Wave
By Rich Tennant

"My thinking has changed a little this year."

In this part . . .

You find out what NLP stands for and why people are talking about it. From seeing how it all started with some smart people in California, to getting you to think about your own assumptions, we help you to set off in the right direction to get what you want out of your life. Very soon you'll be delving behind the scenes into what's happening in your brain and unconscious thinking, the part of you that has your best interests at heart.

Chapter 1

Getting to Know NLP

*H*ere's a little Sufi tale about a man and a tiger.

A man being followed by a hungry tiger, turned in desperation to face it and cried: 'Why don't you leave me alone?' The tiger answered: 'Why don't you stop being so appetising?'

In any communication between two people, or in this case between human and beast, more than one perspective always exists. Sometimes people just can't grasp that fact because they don't know to change their behaviour to communicate in a way that gets them what they want.

Neuro-linguistic Programming (NLP) is one of the most sophisticated and effective methodologies currently available to help you communicate effectively. NLP centres on communication and change. These days everybody needs the skills to develop personal flexibility. Tricks and gimmicks aren't enough: everyone needs to get real.

So welcome to the start of the journey: in this chapter you get a quick taster of the key themes of NLP.

Introducing NLP

All able-bodied humans are born with the same basic neurological system.

Your *neurological system* transmits the information you receive from your environment through your senses to your brain. Your *environment*, in this context, is everything external to you, but also includes your organs, such as your eyes, ears, skin, stomach, and lungs. Your brain processes the information and transmits messages back to your organs. With your eyes, for example, the result of this may be that you blink. The information can also create emotions, and you may feel joy, cry, or laugh. In short, you behave in a certain way.

Your ability to do anything in life – whether swimming the length of a pool, cooking a meal, or reading this book – depends on how you respond to the stimuli on your nervous system. Therefore, much of NLP is devoted to discovering how to think and communicate more effectively within yourself and with others.

Here's how the term *Neuro-linguistic Programming* breaks down:

- ✔ **Neuro** concerns your neurological system. NLP is based on the idea that you experience the world through your senses and translate sensory information into thought processes, both conscious and unconscious. Thought processes activate the neurological system, which affects physiology, emotions, and behaviour.

- ✔ **Linguistic** refers to the way you use language to make sense of the world, capture and conceptualise experience, and communicate that experience to others. In NLP, linguistics is the study of how the words you speak and your body language influence your experience.

- ✔ **Programming** draws heavily from learning theory and addresses how you code or mentally represent your experiences. Your personal programming consists of your internal processes and strategies (thinking patterns) that you use to make decisions, solve problems, learn, evaluate, and get results. NLP shows you how to recode your experiences and organise your internal programming so that you can get the outcomes you want.

To see this process in action, begin to notice how you think. Imagine a hot summer's day. You're standing in your kitchen at the end of the day holding a lemon you've taken from the fridge. Look at the outside of it, its yellow waxy skin with green marks at the ends. Feel how cold it is in your hand. Raise it to your nose and smell it. Mmmm. Press it gently and notice the weight of the lemon in the palm of your hand. Now take a knife and cut it in half. Hear the juices start to run and notice that the smell is stronger now. Bite deeply into the lemon and allow the juice to swirl around in your mouth.

Words. Simple words have the power to trigger your saliva glands. Hear the one word 'lemon' and your brain kicks into action. The words you read told your brain that you had a lemon in your hand. You may think that words only describe meanings, but in fact they create your reality. You find out much more about this truth as you read this book.

A few quick definitions

NLP can be described in various ways. The formal definition is that NLP is 'the study of the structure of our subjective experience'. Here are a few more ways of answering the elusive question 'what is NLP?':

- ✔ The art and science of communication
- ✔ The key to learning
- ✔ The way to understand what makes you and other people tick
- ✔ The route to get the results you want in all areas of your life
- ✔ The way to influence others with integrity
- ✔ The manual for your brain
- ✔ The secret of successful people
- ✔ The method of creating your own future
- ✔ The way to help people make sense of their reality
- ✔ The toolkit for personal and organisational change

Where NLP started and where it's going

NLP began in California in the early 1970s at the University of Santa Cruz. Richard Bandler, a master's level student of information sciences and mathematics, and Dr John Grinder, a professor of linguistics, studied people who they considered to be excellent communicators and brilliant at helping their clients change. They were fascinated by how some people defied the odds to get through to so-called difficult or very ill people where others failed miserably to connect.

So, NLP has its roots in a therapeutic setting thanks to three world-renowned psychotherapists that Bandler and Grinder studied: Virginia Satir (developer of Conjoint Family Therapy), Fritz Perls (the founder of Gestalt Psychology), and Milton H Erickson (largely responsible for the advancement of Clinical Hypnotherapy).

In their work, Bandler and Grinder also drew upon the skills of linguists Alfred Korzybski and Noam Chomsky, social anthropologist Gregory Bateson, and psychotherapist Paul Watzlawick.

From those early days, the field of NLP exploded to encompass many disciplines in many countries around the world. We can't possibly name all the great teachers and practitioners in NLP today. In Appendix A, you can find resources for more guidance on extending your knowledge of NLP.

In the 1980s, Grinder became dissatisfied with some early coding work done in collaboration with Bandler, which he now refers to as Classic Code. Together with Judith DeLozier, he initiated some new models known as New Code (documented in his book *Whispering in the Wind*) and he continues this work with Carmen Bostic St.Clair.

So what's next for NLP? The discipline has certainly travelled a long way from Santa Cruz in the 1970s, and since we wrote the first edition of this book the interest in NLP shows no sign of waning. So many more pioneers have picked up the story and taken it forward – making it practical and helping to transform the lives of real people. The literature and applications of NLP are prolific, as any Google search demonstrates. Today you can find NLP applications among doctors and nurses, taxi drivers, salespeople, coaches, accountants, teachers, animal trainers, parents, workers, retired people, and teenagers alike. In Chapter 21, we list just a few such practical applications.

Each generation is going to take the ideas that resonate in its field of interest, sift and refine them, and chip in its own knowledge experiences. Much of the development of NLP today is around the applications rather than core models; people who are experts in one field incorporate NLP tools and take them into their own field. If NLP encourages new thinking and new choices and acknowledges the positive intention underlying all action, all we can say is the future remains bright with possibilities. The rest is up to you.

A note on integrity

You may hear the words integrity and manipulation associated with NLP, and so we want to put the record straight now. You influence others all the time. When you do so consciously to get what you want, the question of integrity arises. Are you manipulating others to get what you want at their expense?

Therefore, when you're in, for example, a selling situation, ask yourself a simple question: what is your positive intention for the other person – whether that's an individual or a company? If your intention is good and to benefit the other party, you have integrity – a win/win situation. And if not, you're manipulating. When you head for win/win, you're on track for success. And as you know, what goes around comes around.

Encountering the Pillars of NLP: Straight Up and Straightforward

The first thing to understand is that NLP is about four things, known as the pillars of NLP (check out Figure 1-1). These four foundations of the subject can be described as follows:

✔ **Rapport:** How you build a relationship with others and with yourself is probably the most important gift that NLP gives you. Given the pace at which most humans live and work, one big lesson in rapport is how you can say 'no' to all the requests for your time and still retain friendships or professional relationships. To find out more about rapport – how to build it and when to break it off – head to Chapter 7.

✔ **Sensory awareness:** Have you noticed how when you walk into someone else's home the colours, sounds, and smells are subtly different from yours? Or that a colleague looks worried when he talks about his job. Maybe you notice the colour of a night sky or the fresh green leaves as spring unfolds. Like the famous fictional detective Sherlock Holmes, you begin to notice that your world is so much richer when you pay attention to all your senses. Chapter 6 tells you all you need to know about how powerful your sensory perceptions are and how you can use your natural sight, sound, touch, feelings, taste, and smell capabilities to your benefit.

✔ **Outcome thinking:** You're going to hear the word 'outcome' mentioned throughout this book. This term connects to beginning to think about what you want, instead of getting stuck in a negative problem mode of thinking. The principles of an outcome approach can help you make the best decisions and choices – whether that's about what you're going to do at the weekend, running an important project at work, or finding out the true purpose of your life. Head to Chapter 4 to get the results you deserve.

✔ **Behavioural flexibility:** This term means discovering how to do something different when what you're currently doing isn't working. Being flexible is key to practising NLP, and you can find tools and ideas for this developing aspect in every chapter. We help you find fresh perspectives and build these into your repertoire. You may want to head to Chapter 5 for starters on how you can maximise your own flexibility.

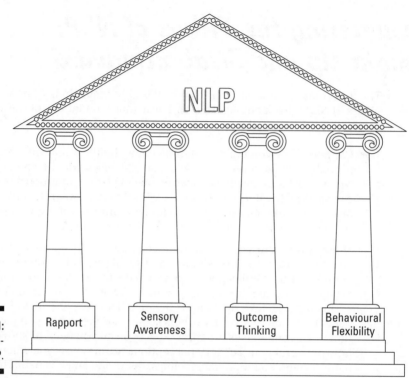

Figure 1-1:
The four pil-
lars of NLP.

Here's an example of what these four pillars may mean to you in an everyday event. Suppose that you order a software package by post to store all your names, addresses, and phone numbers of friends or clients. You load it onto your computer, use it a few times, and then mysteriously it stops working. A bug is in the system, but you've already invested many hours in the installation and entering all your contacts. You phone up the supplier and the customer service people are unhelpful to the point of rudeness.

You need to bring out all your skills in building *rapport* with the customer service manager before anyone listens to your complaint. You need to *engage your senses* – particularly your ears as you listen carefully to what the supplier says – and notice how to control your feelings and decide on your best response. You need to be very clear about your desired *outcome* – what do you want to happen after you make your complaint? For example, do you want a full refund or replacement software? And finally, you may need to be *flexible in your behaviour* and consider different options if you don't achieve what you want the first time.

Discovering Models and Modelling

As we describe in the earlier section 'Where NLP started and where it's going', NLP began as a model of how people communicate and grew out of studies of some great communicators. Therefore, the concept of models and modelling is at the heart of NLP.

The NLP premise begins as follows: if you can find someone who's good at something, you can then model how that person does that thing and learn from them. You can discover how to model anyone you admire – top business leaders or sports personalities, the waitress at your favourite restaurant, or your hugely energetic personal fitness trainer. You can find out more about modelling in Chapter 19.

Employing the NLP communication model

The NLP model describes how you process the information that comes at you from the outside. According to NLP, you move through life not by responding to the world around you, but by responding to your model or map of that world. The model is explained with examples in Chapter 5.

A fundamental assumption of NLP is that 'the map is not the territory' and that each individual has different maps of how the world operates. This insight means that you and another person may experience the same event and yet do so differently.

Imagine that you go to a party – you have a good time, meet lots of friendly people, enjoy good food and drinks, and perhaps watch some entertainment. Yet, if the next day we ask you and another person at the same party to recount what happened, you'd both have a different story to tell. The differences are because internal representations that people make about an outside event are different from the event itself: 'the map is not the territory'.

Or imagine that you're suddenly transported to a completely different culture on the other side of the world. The thoughts and assumptions that your new-found neighbours construct of how life operates are going to be very different from your own.

NLP doesn't change the world – it simply helps you change the way that you observe/perceive your world. NLP allows you to build a different or more detailed map that helps you to be more effective.

John is an architect who rents expensive office space in a central city location. He used to moan frequently that the offices weren't cleaned to a high enough standard, the staff were lazy, and he never got any satisfaction from the office manager. On meeting John in his office, we discovered that he worked in chaos, leaving the office with plans and design ideas on every available surface and not tidying anything away. He frequently worked late into the evening and was grumpy if interrupted, and so the cleaners came and went without daring to disturb him.

Through coaching, John came to recognise that he hadn't considered anyone else's point of view or noticed what a difficult task the cleaners had cleaning his office around him. His map of reality was completely different from that of the office management team and the cleaners. He subsequently built a new map that incorporated the reality of what life in the office was like for his colleagues, and he became more considerate towards them. By changing this one map of his experience, other aspects of his life also improved, and he grew more aware of the effect of his general untidiness. For example, now he feels more comfortable inviting girlfriends to his neater flat.

Modelling excellence

Modelling excellence is a theme much discussed in this book, because so much of NLP is future orientated and applied to creating change for the better – whether that's a better qualified individual, a better quality of life, or a better world for the next generation.

The NLP approach is that you learn best by finding someone else who already excels at whatever you want to learn. By modelling other people, you can break your discovering into its component parts. This perspective is empowering, and an encouragement to convert large overwhelming projects into lots of small ones and discover people who've already been there and can show you the way.

Using NLP to Greater Effect

As you discover throughout this book, the practical application of NLP is about increasing your options, instead of falling into the trap of being restricted by your experience and saying, 'this is the way I do things, and this is how it has to be'. In order to get the benefit of NLP, you need to be open and give yourself and others the benefit of questioning and challenging your norms in a supportive way. This section provides a few tips to remind you how to do so.

Understanding that attitude comes first

At its essence NLP brings a positive attitude about life and possibilities rather than dwelling on problems. NLP also provides the 'how' to achieve what you want with the tools and support to change anything about your life that doesn't reflect who you want to be today. So much more is possible when you have the mindset and attitudes to support your success; you tap into your natural human resourcefulness. If your attitudes don't support you in living a richly rewarding life, you may want to consider changing them. Changing your mind and attitude really does change your life.

Many people spend a lot of time looking at the negatives in their lives – how they hate their jobs, or don't want to smoke or be fat. By conditioning yourself to concentrate on what you *do* want, positive results can be achieved very quickly.

Being curious and confused are good for you

Here are two helpful attributes to bring with you: *curiosity* – accepting that you don't know all the answers – and a *willingness to be confused*, because as the great hypnotherapist Milton H Erickson said, 'enlightenment is always preceded by confusion.'

If you find that ideas in this book make you feel confused, thank your unconscious mind because confusion is the first step to understanding. Take the sense of confusion as a sign that you're processing information to sift and to find the way forward, and that you intuitively know more than you realise consciously.

Changing is up to you

Gone are the days when you need to stay stuck in a downward spiral of repetitive behaviours and responses that are tedious and ineffective. Today NLP is all about producing measurable results that enhance the quality of people's lives without a lengthy and painful journey into the past.

As you read the chapters in this book, you discover the experiential nature of NLP – that it's about trying things out, having a go. Test out the ideas for yourself – don't take our word for it.

The responsibility for change lies with you, and this book is the facilitator. If you aren't open to change, you aren't going to get the most from the book. So we encourage you to do the exercises, note your new process, and then teach and share with others, because to teach is to learn twice. By the time you complete the book, you may be surprised at how much you've already changed.

Having fun on the way!

When Clint Eastwood was interviewed on British TV by Michael Parkinson he offered sound advice: 'let's take the work seriously, and not ourselves seriously.' NLP involves much fun and laughter. If you set yourself up to become perfect, you put enormous and unrealistic pressure on yourself. So pack a sense of your own playfulness as you travel and try to make sense of a changing world: learning is serious work that's serious fun.

Chapter 2

Some Basic Assumptions of NLP

*B*renda has a much loved, only daughter, Mary. By the age of ten, Mary was a little spoiled because she arrived after Brenda and her husband had given up hope of ever having a child. Mary was prone to throwing tantrums the likes of which you're extremely fortunate not to experience. Mary thrashed about on the floor, screaming and flailing her arms and legs.

Brenda made no progress with Mary's tantrums until one day, when Mary was on the floor exercising her lungs with total abandonment, the long-suffering Brenda took some metal pans out of a cupboard and joined Mary on the floor. Brenda banged the pots on the wooden floor and kicked and screamed even better and louder than Mary. Guess what? Mary lay still in stunned astonishment, staring at her mother. She decided there and then that her mother was the more expert 'tantrummer' and that she would lose the tantrum contest every time. She realised that pursuing this particular course of action was futile and the tantrums stopped from that moment. Brenda took control of her interaction with Mary by displaying the greater flexibility of behaviour.

This little anecdote illustrates that 'the person with the most flexibility in a system influences the system'. This statement isn't the result of some experiment conducted in a laboratory. Instead, it's an NLP *presupposition* (or assumption), which, if practised and adopted, can help to ease your journey through life. Brenda's story illustrates just one of several presuppositions – also called convenient beliefs – which form the basis of NLP.

Introducing NLP Presuppositions

NLP presuppositions are no more than generalisations about the world that can prove useful to you when you act as if they're true. In the following sections, we describe some of the presuppositions that we consider to be most influential out of several that the founders of NLP developed.

The map is not the territory

One of the first presuppositions is that 'the map is not the territory'. This statement was published in *Science and Sanity* in 1933 by Korzybski, a Polish count and mathematician. Korzybski was referring to the fact that you experience the world through your senses (sight, hearing, touch, smell, and taste) – the territory. You then take this external phenomenon and make an internal representation (IR) of it within your brain – the map.

This internal map that you create of the external world, shaped by your experiences, is never an exact replica of the map made by someone else perceiving the same surroundings as you. In other words, what's outside can never be the same as what's inside your brain.

Take the following analogy. If you ask a botanist what Belladonna means, they may give you the Latin name for the plant and describe the flowers and slight scent while making a picture of the plant in their head. Whereas a homoeopath may explain its uses in treating certain symptoms and see a picture of a patient they treated. If you ask a murder-mystery writer about Belladonna, they may say that it's a poison.

Or try another analogy: if you're driving in London, with your London street map, the 'roads' shown on the map are completely different from the roads you're actually driving along. For a start the tube stations you drive past are in three dimensions and in colour, whereas they are shown as a blue circle with a red line through it on the map.

The point is that depending on the context and someone's background, different people make different IRs of the same thing.

Putting perceptions through your own personal filter

Your senses bombard you with millions of different bits of information every second, and yet your conscious mind can deal with only a handful of individual pieces at any given moment: as a result, an awful lot of information is filtered out. This filtration process is influenced by your values and beliefs, memories, decisions, experiences, and your cultural and social background, to allow in only what your filters are tuned to receive.

When you're with another person or other people, choose something in your surroundings and have each of you write a short description of what you observe: for example, the view from a window. Notice that people's descriptions are individually tailored by their own life experiences.

Some Europeans and North Americans experience a major culture shock when visiting countries such as India or Mexico. Because of their cultural background, they may be shocked by the level of poverty in some areas whereas local people accept the poverty as part of life. People accept the familiarity of their own landscape.

Travelling down another person's map: Unfamiliar territory

The result of this personal filter is that everyone has a very individual map of the world. To make communication easier, a really useful exercise is to at least attempt to understand the IR or map of the person with whom you're communicating.

Romilla was buying some fish and chips for supper and was asked to complete a short form about the quality, service, and value-for-money of the food. The women serving behind the counter were very upset because the man who had just left had declined, quite rudely, to fill in the form. Romilla asked the ladies whether they had considered how the poor man may have felt if he was illiterate, and that perhaps he was rude because he was embarrassed. The change in the two ladies was phenomenal: 'I never even thought about that,' said one. Their demeanour changed immediately from one of anger and resentment to one of sympathy. They also felt much better in themselves and were able to let go of all the negative feelings.

The following short exercise helps you to find tolerance, or at least gain some understanding, when you find yourself in a situation where another person's response or behaviour surprises you, irritates you, or just leaves you puzzled:

1. **Count all the blessings in your life.**

2. **With examples of your own good fortune rattling around in your brain, put on your most generous hat.**

3. **Ask yourself what may be going on in this other person's world that would warrant the behaviour.**

When you begin to master this process, you may find that not only are you happier with your lot, but also you accept people and their idiosyncrasies with greater ease.

A child's map of the world

A child's map of the world can sometimes make an adult think again! This truth is neatly illustrated by the following delightful snippet.

A policeman was sitting in his police van with his canine partner when he noticed a little boy staring in at them. The boy asked if that was a dog in the van. The policeman confirmed that the other occupant of the van was indeed a dog. The little boy got extremely puzzled and asked, 'What's he done to get arrested?'

People respond according to their map of the world

Like all humans, you respond in accordance with the map of the world you hold in your head. This map is based on what you believe about your identity and on your values and beliefs as well as your attitudes, memories, and cultural background.

Sometimes, the map of the world from which one person operates may not make sense to you. However, a little understanding and tolerance can help to enrich your life.

When Dr Diwan was a junior doctor, she used to visit a psychiatric hospital. One of the patients was a very well-spoken, highly educated professor of English. One of the professor's little foibles was to walk around at night with an open umbrella. He was convinced that the rays of the moon would give him 'moon madness'. However, the professor took great delight in sharing his passion for English literature with members of staff, whose lives were certainly enriched by their daily interactions with him.

If the staff had been intolerant of the 'mad professor' and ignored or sidelined him, they may not have realised but their lives would have been impoverished without the richness of his literary stories and his sense of humour – he often referred to himself as the 'impatient patient'.

There is no failure, only feedback

This presupposition is a very powerful one by which to live your life. Everyone makes mistakes and experiences setbacks. You have a choice between allowing yourself to be waylaid by your undesirable results or taking on-board the lessons that present themselves, dusting yourself off, and having another shot at jumping the hurdle.

Romilla attended a course run by a wonderful Hawaiian Kahuna, Serge Kahili King, during which he said that he never made mistakes. This statement caused a few chuckles because none of the delegates believed him and the twinkle in his eyes belied the deadpan expression on his face. He then added that he may not always get the results he wants, but he never makes mistakes.

One of the messages we took away from listening to entrepreneur and top marketeer Liz Jackson, MBE, at an International Women's Day event, is not to be afraid of failure. Liz has herself had to adapt to the challenge of losing her eyesight, and still manages to run a successful company. She says that failure is one of the most powerful tools to learning; she inspires those around her to break down their barriers to success by talking about what their ambitions look like and stepping out of their comfort zones, even if it means being petrified for a while. She says 'It's only the failures that teach you.'

In normal language, the term feedback is associated with receiving input or getting a response from another person. The meaning of *feedback* has been expanded in the context of this NLP presupposition, however, to include the result or outcome you may get from a particular situation.

You can discover a lot about feedback from Thomas Edison. Although he's famous for inventing the light bulb, he was a prolific inventor. His genius lay in trying out his ideas, learning from unexpected results, and recycling concepts from an experiment that didn't work in other inventions. Where other people saw Edison's thousands of attempts at inventing the light bulb as failures, Edison simply saw each trial as yet another way of discovering how not to make a light bulb.

Worrying about so-called failure keeps you focused on the past and the problems. If you examine the results that you've already obtained, even if they're unwanted, you can shift your focus onto new possibilities and move forward.

When you're faced with 'failure', you can use this NLP presupposition to find the opportunities for growth by asking yourself some questions.

Think of something you 'failed' at and ask yourself:

- ✔ What am I aiming to achieve?
- ✔ What have I achieved so far?
- ✔ What feedback have I had?
- ✔ What lessons have I learned?
- ✔ How can I put the lessons to positive use?
- ✔ How am I going to measure my success?

Then pick yourself up and have another go!

Can you imagine a world in which you gave up learning to walk simply because you fell over the first time you stood up? What do you think Waterloo Station in London would look like during the rush hour if only a few people mastered the art of walking?

The meaning of the communication is the response it elicits

No matter how honourable the intentions of your communications, the success of the interaction depends on how the listener receives the message, and not on what you intend. In other words, the response that your words elicit is the meaning of your communication.

This presupposition is another very powerful assumption about communication: it places the onus of responsibility of getting your message across squarely at your door, as the communicator. When you adopt this presupposition, you can no longer blame the other person for any misunderstandings. If the response you get isn't what you expected then, as a student of NLP, you have the tools to use your senses to realise that the other person is missing the point. You also have the flexibility to do things differently, through your behaviour and your words.

Start with the required end in mind and think of what outcome you want from your communication. What would happen if a builder started by slapping bricks on one another without a plan? You certainly wouldn't get your cathedral! In order to build something with strong foundations you need to start with an architect's vision of the end product. This presupposition is also useful in keeping your emotions out of the way when you're involved in a situation that may get tough.

In Chapter 5, we discuss more ways of practising flexibility of behaviour and give a few more tips on dealing with emotions when the going gets tough. If you want to find out more about sensory awareness, please have a look at Chapter 7.

If what you're doing isn't working, do something different

This presupposition is so simple, and yet you don't always modify your behaviour when things don't go as you want. After all, wandering through life wishing change on other people is easier, and you get to enjoy all the angst from thinking those horrible thoughts about someone else!

Remember that not everyone has your internal resources; the very fact that you're reading this book means that you're showing initiative in making changes in your life. We suggest that you're going to expend a lot less energy in changing yourself than struggling to have other people conform to your ideals.

If you accept this NLP presupposition, you recognise that changing tactics is better than continuing to beat your head against a wall or spending your time lamenting your misfortune. Still, before you can actually change your tactics or do something different, you need to understand more about your present situation.

So why is what you're doing not working? Didn't you communicate exactly what you want? Perhaps the other person hasn't discovered the necessary resources to help you achieve your outcome. What can you do differently to get the desired results?

For instance, if you aren't getting all the hugs you feel you want, perhaps you need to come right out and tell your partner that you like hugs. Remember that positive feedback works brilliantly, and so when your partner does make physical overtures make sure that you clearly demonstrate your appreciation of the contact.

Patricia was a student who learned best through feeling and touch. This tendency meant that she had difficulty in following standard 'chalk-and-talk' lessons, which are more suited to people who like to see a screen and hear a teacher talk. As a result, Patricia was having difficulty staying on top of her classwork and wasn't reaching her potential.

A less talented teacher may have placed the blame on Patricia and branded her as stupid or having a bad attitude to her studies. Fortunately her teacher recognised that Patricia needed to be shown how to study and how to apply the lessons in a more practical way. Patricia was lucky that her teacher understood the reason for her problems and took the responsibility to do something different by adjusting her teaching methods to help Patricia do well. Patricia's teacher was a good one: she was flexible and took responsibility for the effectiveness of her teaching. Instead of blaming Patricia for her inability to learn, Patricia's teacher found another way to reach her.

Your lead or primary representation system

You experience your world through your five senses – visual (eyes), auditory (ears), kinaesthetic (feelings and touch), olfactory (smell), and gustatory (taste). At times, particularly when you're stressed, you may use one sense in preference to the others to collect data about your world. This system is called your *lead* or *primary representational system*, and it influences how you learn and the way you represent your external world inside your head. We talk more about using the five senses in Chapter 6.

You can't not communicate

Have you ever smiled at someone and said something really polite, but been thinking, 'just drop dead'? No? Just as well, because we bet that the way you held your body or gritted your teeth didn't fool anyone. We're sure that if the person on the receiving end of the message had studied NLP, or even had some sensory acuity, they would detect the lack of warmth in your eyes, the grimace in your smile, or the snarl in your voice. So even though you didn't say 'drop dead', you're still communicating that message.

This fact is shown in a fascinating study, pioneered by Professor Albert Mehrabian. This research established that, when talking about feelings and attitudes – particularly when a discrepancy exists between body language and the words being used – what you say has a very small impact compared with the tone you use and how you hold your body. Other studies have subsequently suggested that the influences, in percentage terms, are as follows:

- Verbal (the words you say): 7 per cent
- Tonality (how you speak): 38 per cent
- Physiology (your body language): 55 per cent

Individuals have all the resources they need to achieve their desired outcomes

We love this presupposition because it's so positive! This phrase means that everyone has the potential to develop and grow. The important point to make here is that you may not have all the internal resources you need, but you do have the necessary internal resources to acquire new internal and external resources.

Tom, a little eight-year-old boy, was being bullied at school. He was resource-ful enough to ask his father for help in dealing with the bullies. His father told him to behave more assertively and with more confidence. Tom had no idea how to do so.

Tom's hero, however, was Arnold Schwarzenegger, and so his father taught him the *circle of excellence* exercise (which we describe in Chapter 9) and asked Tom to imagine that he was Arnie as he stepped into the circle. Tom's new-found confidence affected his behaviour, his body language, and his attitude. As a result Tom's tormentors faded away and his street cred went through the roof with other little victims begging to discover his technique. The circle of excellence is a brilliant NLP anchoring technique for psyching yourself up by building a powerful resource state.

Every behaviour has a positive intent

Unfortunately this presupposition also applies in reverse, to bad or non-productive behaviour. With bad behaviour, the positive intention behind it, called secondary gain, is obscured.

Secondary gain is the benefit someone gets unconsciously from a particular behaviour that's normally considered to be disempowering or bad. For exam-ple, a child may play the clown in class in order to gain acceptance by their peers, even though their teachers and parents find this clowning around quite destructive when they want them to be well behaved.

The youngest of five children, Janet, had suffered from a bad back for as long as she was able to remember, and doctors found no reason for the pain. Janet's mother was a flighty, self-centred woman who was more interested in partying than her family. As a child, Janet's siblings helped her by carrying her books and making sure that Janet was taken care of.

The back pain became really bad after Janet's daughter was born, and so her husband did all the shopping and carrying of, and looking after, the baby. The little girl grew up to become 'mummy's little helper' and was always at her mother's beck and call. When Janet finally agreed to see a therapist, she was able to acknowledge that her bad back pain was psychosomatic. She realised that it was her way of getting the love and attention she had craved from her mother but never received.

Janet's behaviour is a brilliant demonstration of this presupposition, because the secondary gain for her was to have her family run around after her, and what she really wanted was to have her craving for love and attention satis-fied. When Janet realised her need, she was also able to recognise that she was already getting massive amounts of love and attention from her husband and daughter. One of the side-effects of the therapy was that Janet was able to understand that her own mother's behaviour was based on her mother's problems and weren't Janet's fault.

When you identify the concealed positive intention that's causing a person to behave in a particular unresourceful way, you can increase your flexibility and thereby your ability to communicate effectively with that person. You can then help to change the unwanted behaviour by satisfying the intention of the behaviour in a more positive way.

When one of the authors worked for a multinational company, a sales manager, Patrick, occupied one of the free desks in her corner of the building when he visited. Some of the kinder terms people used for Patrick were obnoxious and inconsiderate. He would spread himself out. He sprawled in his chair, which meant it was pushed out away from his desk and people in the corner had to squeeze past. He was loud, made demands on everyone around him, and was extremely unpleasant to his secretary.

An office gossip revealed that poor Patrick's behaviour was the product of a domineering mother and even more masterful wife. Unfortunately, his need for acceptance, and especially respect, made him behave in ways that gave him results that were exactly the opposite to what he craved. One of the benefits of finding out about Patrick's background was that the staff were able to think a little more kindly about him and his presence no longer sent blood pressures soaring. By showing him a degree of acceptance, they were able to satisfy his needs a little and mellow his behaviour.

People are much more than their behaviour

Romilla was watching a television programme on speeches given by important historical figures. She was intrigued by Martin Luther King's response to a journalist on how to deal with racists. King could have been quoting the presupposition that people are more than their behaviour when he said: 'I'm talking about a type of love that will cause you to love the person who does the evil deed while hating the deed that the person does.'

The point is that behaving badly doesn't make someone a bad person. Separating the behaviour from the person is really important. People can behave badly when they don't have the inner resources or ability to behave differently in that instance. Perhaps they find themselves in an environment that stops them from being the best they can be. Helping people to develop capabilities and skills, or move to a more conducive environment, can often change their behaviour dramatically and propel them to new levels of excellence.

Bob, a very sweet, kind, young man, was diagnosed as being dyslexic. Bob adores animals and is extremely good with any that have been injured or hurt. Unfortunately, due to circumstances, Bob was branded as a trouble-maker and had been in trouble with the police over drugs. People in Bob's neighbour-hood saw him as a 'bad' person. When Bob was helped to change his beliefs about his capabilities, however, he became a very valuable contributor to society by working for an animal charity.

People behave very differently in different areas of their lives. You can read about logical levels in Chapter 11, where you discover that people have several levels at which they function:

- ✔ Identity
- ✔ Values and beliefs
- ✔ Capabilities and skills
- ✔ Behaviour
- ✔ Environment

As Bob (from the earlier anecdote) increased his capabilities, his beliefs about himself began to change. This change allowed him to move into an environ-ment where he felt valuable. The result was that Bob experienced an identity shift from 'I'm a failure' to 'I can actually make a contribution'. Bob's change of identity affected his behaviour, and feedback from the animals and the people with whom Bob worked made him feel valuable, which reinforced his identity. So although Bob's behaviour had been bad, it didn't make him a bad person; he's much more than his bad behaviour, and is in fact loving and kind.

The mind and body are interlinked and affect each other

Holistic medicine works on the premise that the mind affects the body and the body affects the mind. In order to maintain a healthy human being, a medical practitioner needs to do more than just suppress the symptoms. They have to examine the mind and body and treat both together.

Recent research on emotion at the cellular level in the body shows just how integrated the mind–body connection is. Neurotransmitters are chemicals that transmit impulses along your nerves. They are the means by which your brain communicates with the rest of your body. Each thought you think reaches out to the farthest, miniscule cell in your body via neurotransmitters.

In addition, further research discovered that the same neurotransmitters that are found in the brain can also be produced by your internal organs. So the idea that messages are initiated and transmitted in straight lines along the neurons is no longer true; these messages can be initiated and transmitted by your organs as well. Dr Candace Pert, of the National Institute of Mental Health, refers to the 'bodymind' – the mind and body working as an integrated whole, because at the level of the neurotransmitter no separation exists between the mind and the body.

To get a better understanding of this connection and see it in action, follow these steps:

1. **Make a circle with the left finger and thumb.**

2. **Now link your right finger and thumb through the first circle.**

    The circles are interlinked and come apart only by you pulling on one or other of your hands.

3. **Think of someone you really like and pull hard to break the circles.**

    Pretty tough, huh?

4. **Think of someone you really dislike and pull hard to break the circles.**

    Was it a bit easier?

Many people find that they require less effort to separate the circles when thinking of someone they don't like. If a simple thought can affect the pressure that your muscles can exert, what do you think happens to your body when you subject it to constant stress?

Having choice is better than not having choice

NLP promotes choice for an individual as a healthy way of life. Sometimes you may feel that you don't have the choice to change jobs, shift to another country, or get out of an unhappy relationship. You may find yourself saying, 'I have no choice' or 'I must do this'.

You can be held back from making much needed change through fear of change, lack of confidence in your abilities, or even unawareness of what your strengths are. To combat this problem, NLP says 'what if things were different?', and aims to open up your horizons by making you conscious of all the resources you already have and can acquire.

NLP helps you to explore your reasons for wanting change, even if that reason is just a little niggle of discontent. Change can be choppy, like riding the rapids, but the people we know who have made it through – having decided on choices that they made for themselves – are much more content and in control of their lives.

You can find help with deciding what you want from your life and how to begin to implement it in Chapter 4.

A multinational company was shedding a lot of people. Many of the employees waited, hoping they wouldn't be forced to go. The IT industry was in the doldrums and jobs were thin on the ground; the general belief was that people had no choice other than to hang on to the job they were in, no matter how far the company pushed them. They believed that they had no choice.

The employees who were relieved to get away from the stress were the ones who knew what they wanted from their jobs and had made provisions to move into alternative careers; or those who were willing to look at all the available options, no matter how far-fetched they seemed.

Modelling successful performance leads to excellence

If you aspire to be a long-distance runner like Paula Radcliffe and you're able-bodied, display her single-minded determination, and have a support network, you can develop your beliefs and values to align your environment, capabilities, and behaviour to achieve your aspirations (read more about these categories in the earlier section 'People are much more than their behaviour').

NLP provides the tools for you to model someone, take what that person does well, and replicate it. You don't, however, need to have such a big ambition: you may have a very simple desire, such as modelling the skills of a co-worker who always brings projects in on time, or a friend who always knows the right thing to say at the right time. You can question people that you want to emulate to find out what inspires them, how they know the time is right to do what they do, and how they keep focused on their goal.

In the case of the co-worker, they may have a string of strategies to meet their project targets, which you can reproduce. Modelling people's successes is a great way to turn potential negative feelings of envy into a constructive process for experiencing their success for yourself. We dip into this subject more in Chapter 19.

Final Words on Presuppositions: Suck Them and See

Test the presuppositions presented in this chapter for yourself by behaving as if the generalisations are true. Practise those that you find particularly useful until they become second nature. While trying out the NLP presuppositions, make a list and pick one each day, and live by it for one day. Then pick another one for the next day. You can then find, suddenly, that you're living the presuppositions and 'the living is easier'!

One great way to increase your understanding of NLP is to explore your basic assumptions, or presuppositions, about life. Whatever you currently think about different people and problems, how you communicate, and what's important, sometimes taking a new perspective can help by triggering new action or behaviour.

No correct response exists to any of these presuppositions. As you get a flavour for each one in turn, consider it carefully. You don't have to agree with them all. You can simply try them on for size and see, hear, and feel what happens.

Chapter 3

Discovering Who's Directing Your Life

*B*reathing is something you do unconsciously. Until we ask you to become aware of your breathing you don't notice each breath, the air going in through your nose, or the movement of your chest and diaphragm with each inhalation and exhalation. By paying attention to your breathing, you bring your breathing into your conscious awareness. As you continue to read these words, you then stop noticing your breathing again; it slips back out of your awareness along with the other processes that run your body.

Do you consciously know when the time comes for you to feel thirsty or indeed, how to consciously pick up a glass of water when you're thirsty? We challenge you to activate consciously each isolated muscle in your arm, in the right order, to pick up a glass of water and get it to your mouth. Impossible? Do you need a degree in anatomy and physiology before you can attempt to raise your arm consciously? This example goes to show the huge influence that your unconscious mind has on the running of your body, out-side of your conscious awareness.

If you still have any doubts about the power of your unconscious mind on your body, consider an experiment conducted by researcher Paul Thorsen, who hypnotised a man and told him that the pen that Paul was holding was a hot skewer. Paul then touched the arm of the subject with the pen and . . . a blister formed on the subject's arm where he had been touched by the pen.

In this chapter you get to meet your unconscious mind and discover how to use your brain to focus on and help you achieve your goals more easily and quickly. You find out about the psychology of post-traumatic stress disorder (PTSD) and phobias, and discover how you can overcome them. Most importantly, you learn about your values – the buttons that motivate you. When you find out that your beliefs have a structure and that you can change that structure, you're well on your way to taking charge of your emotions, your memories, and the way you choose to respond to people and events in your life, without the baggage of the past weighing you down.

Grasping How Your Fears Can Drive You in the Wrong Direction

Your unconscious mind not only controls the running of your body, but also has a tremendous impact on the results you get in your life. Have you ever wanted to do something consciously but ended up doing something totally different?

You can decide consciously that you want to achieve a goal, but if your unconscious mind isn't on-board it may 'assist' you by fulfilling its own agenda – which may be contrary to what you consciously think you want. Imagine what you can achieve when you're in rapport with your unconscious mind and able to go in the direction that gets you to your goals quickly.

Roger started his own company. Despite setting goals and having exceptional ability in his chosen field, he wasn't getting his business off the ground and was in a complete panic as he watched his savings dwindling away. Romilla helped him identify a very closely held belief that 'I can't sing the blues in an air-conditioned room'. The writer of this song discovered that he was able to sing the blues only in poverty and that success and wealth cramped his musical style. Similarly, Roger was afraid that success would stop him experiencing life and extinguish his creativity. When he realised that he was able to choose to experience life as a millionaire or a tramp, his behaviour changed and his business improved dramatically.

The key to bringing your unconscious mind into alignment with your conscious desires and goals is understanding the strengths of each part and how they work. The following sections tell you what you need to know.

Distinguishing between conscious and unconscious

In NLP terms, your conscious mind is that part of your mind that has awareness of things around and within you at any given moment in time, which, according to research conducted by George Miller in 1956, is a meagre seven (plus or minus two) bits of information. (For more information on Miller's findings, head to Chapter 5). The conscious mind can be compared with the tip of an iceberg and the unconscious mind with the nine-tenths of the iceberg that's submerged underwater.

Your conscious and unconscious minds excel at different things (as Table 3-1 shows). A useful extension to the conscious/unconscious mind metaphor might be to think of your conscious mind as relating more to your left brain and the unconscious mind relating to your right brain. Knowing what each is best suited for can help you to recognise whether you're better at using your logical left brain or your creative right brain. You may then decide to focus on aspects of your mental development, for instance, learning to draw if you're more left-brained, or learning applied mathematics if you're more right-brained. Certainly, discovering how to meditate develops the traits of both parts and gets them communicating better.

Table 3-1   Comparing the Conscious and Unconscious Minds

The Conscious Mind Excels at	*The Unconscious Mind is Better at*
Working linearly	Working holistically
Processing sequentially	Intuition
Logic	Creativity
Verbal language	Running your body
Mathematics	Taking care of your emotions
Analysis	Storing memories

Understanding your quirky unconscious mind

As with your friends and their little foibles, your unconscious mind has some interesting quirks with which you need to become acquainted so that you can get on with it better. The ideal situation is to have your conscious and unconscious minds working as one, pulling in the same direction.

By getting your unconscious mind on-board – working with you rather than against you – you can achieve much more in life, such as setting and achieving compelling goals with much less effort.

Your unconscious mind can't process negatives

If we say to you, 'don't think about watching a film,' you may get a sense of yourself in front of your TV or in a cinema with a film playing on the big screen, before you shift your thoughts to something else in order to comply with the instruction.

This exercise shows that before you can stop yourself thinking about something, you have to deal with the thought that automatically pops into your head.

Your unconscious can't process negatives: it interprets everything you think as a positive thought. So if you think, 'I don't want to be poor,' your unconscious mind focuses on the 'poor' and, because it doesn't do negatives, the focus becomes 'poor' and everything you associate with poor. Being poor then becomes the goal in your unconscious mind and like a young child, desperate to please, it helps you behave in a way that keeps you poor; which is obviously not what you wanted!

That's why stating your goals in the positive is so important. In this instance, instead of thinking 'I don't want to be poor,' you need to think 'I want to be wealthy,' because this creates the representations in your mind of what being wealthy means to you and helps you keep your focus on what you want. For more information on the importance of stating goals in a positive way, head to Chapter 4.

Your unconscious mind needs direction

Yogis liken the unconscious mind to a mischievous monkey, always leaping from tree to tree. The way to keep the monkey occupied and out of mischief is to stick a pole in the ground and direct the monkey to climb up and down the pole. If your conscious mind doesn't provide a direction for your unconscious mind, the latter looks to find direction wherever it can. A young, directionless child, for example, may find that joining a street gang provides a structure to their life and they then find that they get their direction from the leader of the gang and the gang laws. Your unconscious mind does the same thing, and needs direction and focus or it may create destructive behaviours in you.

In order to direct the unconscious mind, you need to open up communication channels between your conscious and your unconscious minds. This rapport is developed by finding a quiet time for meditation or relaxation and examining the memories presented to you by your unconscious mind.

Your unconscious mind – the preserver of memories

In 1957, the Penfield study indicated that all your experiences are recorded faithfully in memory. While awake, a woman's brain was stimulated with an electrode and Penfield discovered that the woman was able to recall vividly the details of a childhood party, in minute detail. The storage and organisation of these memories is the responsibility of the unconscious mind.

Part of the function of the unconscious mind is to repress memories with unresolved negative emotions.

Diane's relationship with Tom broke up and she started having severe stomach cramps for which the doctors could find no physical cause. In therapy, Diane remembered the day her mother left the family for another man. She got a picture of her mother driving away and Diane sobbing 'Come back mummy, my tummy hurts.' Diane realised that the stomach ache she used as a child as a ploy to get her mother to come back had been recreated by her unconscious mind as a ploy to get Tom back. The memory had lain dormant all those years.

Another function of the unconscious mind is to present repressed memories for examination in order to release trapped emotions. Unfortunately, like very young children embarrassing their parents in public, the unconscious mind doesn't always pick the most appropriate time to present a memory that needs to be examined. So you can be at a family gathering, basking in feelings of love and contentment, when your unconscious mind says to you, 'deal with the memory when dad smacked you on your birthday . . . *now*!' and suddenly you're blubbing into your trifle in front of your highly embarrassed relatives.

Your unconscious mind is a lean, mean learning machine

Your unconscious thrives on new experiences. It needs to be fed with new possibilities and gets you into trouble when you don't keep it from getting bored.

We know of a very kind, generous, extremely clever person who got very bored at work. Instead of finding constructive ways to alleviate his boredom, he became hooked on playing computer games. This addiction had some very severe repercussions in his life. Luckily, a new job brought new challenges and he's now very successful in his chosen profession.

You can find constructive ways of keeping your mind occupied, such as reading, doing puzzles, or taking up a hobby. Activities like these make your brain cells grow more physical dendrites (the branches of a brain cell) and keep you mentally fitter. And for calming your mind, keeping stress levels at bay, and increasing your creativity, nothing works better than meditation.

Your unconscious mind behaves like a highly moral being

The unconscious mind keeps you on the straight and narrow path of whatever morality it learns, by enforcing its morality on you, even if society judges that morality to be wrong.

A terrorist can kill and destroy without qualms because his moral code teaches him that he's a freedom fighter. He therefore believes that he's in fact being a moral person in fighting against a criminal society. A gang member may kill to protect the honour of his gang, without feeling any guilt because he's learned that gang honour is more important than the Christian commandment 'thou shall not kill' or the law of the land that makes murder illegal.

If, however, your unconscious mind decides that you deserve to be punished, you can be wracked with guilt and exhibit behaviours designed to punish yourself, even though no law says that what your unconscious mind sees as bad is actually so.

In a different vein, your unconscious mind can support behaviours that can create positive results in your life, which then ripple out into other people's lives. Men like Gandhi and Nelson Mandela changed history as a result of their strongly held morals about freedom and fairness. Sadly, even grand ideals, stemming from a desire for unity and prosperity, can become grossly distorted, as happened in the case of Hitler.

Jane, had had several unsatisfactory relationships and was in one at the time she came to see Romilla. During a series of breakthrough sessions, Jane admitted to feeling that she manipulated men and discarded them when she felt they were looking for commitment. Investigations revealed a memory of when she was five years old and had 'manipulated' her father, who was verbally violent, into apologising to her. When Romilla suggested that Jane's father really loved her even though he was unable to show it, and that he had found the resources within himself to express his love by apologising to her, Jane was really shocked.

One of the consequences of identifying the negative feelings of guilt that Jane had felt all her life was to allow her to move on and leave a relationship that wasn't fulfilling her needs, and modify the behaviours that drew her into unrewarding relationships.

Tracking Information: Your Reticular Activating System

With billions of pieces of data coming in through your five senses every second, you need a way to maintain your sanity. Therefore, you filter this deluge of information through a network of cells in your brain so that only a minute proportion gets through to the rest of the brain. This filtering network is called the Reticular Activating System, or RAS for short, and it works like an antenna, noticing stimuli and alerting your brain to pay attention. The RAS lets in only data that meet at least one of the following criteria:

- ✔ **The information is important to your *survival*.** For example, when you're in a deep sleep but wake up because you hear a strange noise in the house, or when you're jaywalking in a daydream and you're alerted to traffic bearing down on you.

- ✔ **The information has *novelty* value.** Remember the last time you decorated a room? Initially you had this feeling of real pleasure each time you walked into the room as you saw the wallpaper with fresh eyes. Then, after a few weeks, you notice that a painting is askew or an ornament not quite central but don't necessarily notice the pattern on the wallpaper or the colour of the paint. This reaction is because the novelty has worn off.

- ✔ **The information has a high *emotional* content.** The survival aspect also applies to other people; you're alert instantly if your baby's breathing changes but sleep through your husband's snoring or mumbling in his sleep.

Can you remember the last time you misplaced a loved one in a shopping centre and you searched high and low, promising to do all kinds of horrible things to them for getting lost? And then, as if the crowd fades into obscurity, you catch a glimpse of your loved one in the distance and you zero in on them with nothing but relief. If you had no emotional connection with the misplaced person, they'd just be another body in the crush. But because they're a loved one, they stand out like a beacon.

Effectively the RAS operates on stimuli that are above its threshold of observation. Mundane and daily routines slip below this threshold helping you to notice things that are relevant to your current goals.

Can you remember making a list and sticking it on the wall? You may have noticed it for a while and then no longer seen it even though you walk past it several times a day. This change is because the list no longer has novelty value and has been allowed to slip below the threshold for observation.

We're sure you know of chronically unlucky people, those who say things like, 'I never win anything' or 'lucky breaks don't come my way'. These people's belief systems stop them from seeing opportunities. If an opportunity was to jump up and slap them in the face, they'd say 'that's too good to be true' as they skirt the opportunity. Then some people always land on their feet, the lucky people, ones who are open to possibilities. Their way of thinking has them seeking success out of failure because their belief systems dictate that they deserve to win.

Your beliefs affect the threshold level of the RAS. Someone who believes that they're a poor speller may not 'see' an advertisement for a reporter's job, even though this shortcoming can be helped with spelling technology and they may be much better at investigating stories than people who don't have a hang-up over their spelling ability and who apply for the job.

By being aware of your beliefs, which are essentially assumptions that you hold to be true, you can identify how these beliefs may be stopping you from achieving your goals.

 Think of a time when you really wanted to do something but, for whatever reason, were unable to find the opportunity to achieve your goal. Now examine your beliefs. You may discover that these beliefs were stopping you from noticing openings to help you achieve your goal.

Examining How Memories Are Created

Understanding how your brain works and how memories are created is important because this understanding increases your choice of behaviour. A lot of the memories, emotions, and resulting behaviours are unconscious and you're held in a trap, powerless to help yourself until you can understand how your memories were created and you can choose which memories affect your present.

Memories are normally created when information from the RAS is sent to the part of the brain called the amygdala, where the data are given an emotional weighting before being passed on to the hippocampus. The hippocampus evaluates the data against those held in long-term memory and presents them to the cortex for analysis and re-filing back into long-term memory. Figure 3-1 shows you where these strangely named brain parts are located.

Encountering post-traumatic stress disorder (PTSD)

The general public first became aware of PTSD when films about veterans from the Vietnam War started to be made. Today, the news coverage has made people much more aware that PTSD is common among those working in the emergency services as well as the unfortunate victims of war, abuse, and crime.

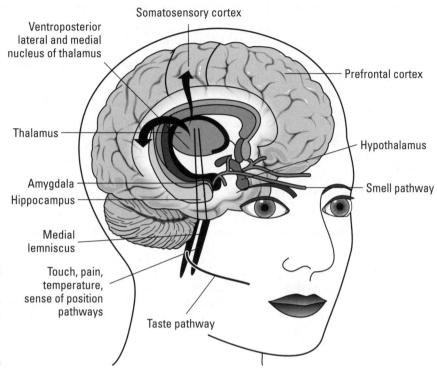

Somatosensory cortex

Ventroposterior
lateral and medial
nucleus of thalamus

Prefrontal cortex

Thalamus

Hypothalamus

Amygdala
Hippocampus

Smell pathway

Medial
lemniscus

Touch, pain,
temperature,
sense of position
pathways

Taste pathway

Figure 3-1:
Finding your
way around
the human
brain.

PTSD occurs when the amygdala receives input with a very high emotional
value, gets in a panic, and can't send the information to the hippocampus.
Because of this, the traumatic event gets trapped within the amygdala and
the hippocampus is unable to present the memory to the neocortex for evalu-
ation, which means the brain can't make sense of the event. Because the
amygdala is the organ primarily involved with your survival, in PTSD suffer-
ers it stays in a constant state of arousal, causing flashbacks and high levels
of anxiety.

Virginia Woolf wrote the novel *Mrs Dalloway* in the early 1920s and her
portrayal of Septimus Smith clearly identifies him as suffering from post-
traumatic stress after the horrors of World War I. Unfortunately, at the time,
conventional medicine was relatively inexperienced at dealing with psychological problems. Patients like Septimus Smith were advised to have plenty of
rest in order to recuperate and were given useless advice such as 'pull yourself together, man'.

Fun with phobias

Below are some words to have fun with at the dining table. A word of caution . . . please don't accuse members of the opposite sex of having phronemophobia (fear of thinking), and you may want to sit someone suffering from ablutophobia (fear of bathing) near your mother-in-law if you suffer from pentheraphobia (fear of mother-in-law):

✔ Chaetophobia – fear of facial hair.

✔ Peladophobia – fear of bald people.

✔ Philophobia – fear of falling in love or being in love.

✔ Phobophobia – fear of phobias.

✔ Xyrophobia – fear of razors.

✔ Galeophobia – fear of cats.

✔ Triskadekaphobia – fear of the number 13.

✔ Otophobia – fear of the number 8.

Phobias and PTSD are part of a group of *anxiety disorders*. Both have a similar structure, in that a memory stays trapped in the amygdala. Fortunately, these days you have the NLP Fast Phobia Cure, which can be very useful in helping people recover from both anxieties. Head to the section 'Employing the NLP Fast Phobia Cure' later in this chapter for details.

Handling phobias

Experts have differing opinions about the origins of phobias. Some psychologists say phobias are the result of a trauma, such as having a frog dropped down your back as a child, whereas others believe that phobias are a learned response: such as when a two-year-old child is confronted by a cobra and becomes phobic as a result of the reactions of the adults around her. Flip to the later 'Employing the NLP Fast Phobia Cure' section for help in overcoming phobias.

Romilla used to have a very strong phobia of snakes. The phobia was so severe that when she dreamt of snakes, which was fairly frequently, she woke up with her limbs locked in a cramp and had consciously to relax each part of her body. In fact, she let herself down rather badly when she walked into a friend's living room and freaked out in front of a group of complete strangers. The cause of her out-of-character behaviour was a stuffed cobra on display.

She overcame her phobia dramatically in a small zoo in Mombasa, Kenya. By the time she was persuaded to drape a python around her neck she had an audience of very amused locals, and was laughing. (By the way, snakes don't feel slimy!)

Had she known NLP at the time, the process of overcoming her phobia would have been much less traumatic, using the NLP Fast Phobia Cure.

Employing the NLP Fast Phobia Cure

The NLP Fast Phobia Cure allows you to re-experience a trauma or phobia without experiencing the emotional content of the event or having to face the trigger that normally sets off the phobic response. You need to ensure that you work on this process in an environment where you know yourself to be completely safe, in the presence of another person who can help to keep you grounded if you begin to panic.

This process ensures that you examine an experience while you're doubly dissociated from the memory, creating a separation between you (in the now) and the emotions of a trauma or a phobic response. In the following list, the double dissociation is done through having you watch yourself in a cinema (dissociation), while watching yourself on a cinema screen (double dissociation) (you can find more on dissociation in Chapter 10):

1. **Identify when you have a phobic response to a stimulus or a traumatic or unpleasant memory that you want to overcome.**

2. **Remember that you were safe before and are safe after the unpleasant experience.**

3. **Imagine yourself sitting in the cinema, watching yourself on a small, black-and-white screen.**

4. **Now imagine floating out of the 'you' that's sitting in the cinema seat and into the projection booth.**

5. **You can now see yourself in the projection booth, watching yourself in the seat, watching the film of you on the screen.**

6. **Run the film in black and white, on the very tiny screen, starting before you experienced the memory you want to overcome and running it through until after the experience when you were safe.**

7. **Now freeze the film or turn the screen completely white.**

8. **Float out of the projection booth, out of the seat, and into the end of the film.**

9. **Run the film backwards very quickly, in a matter of a second or two, in full colour, as if you're experiencing the film, right back to the beginning, when you were safe.**

10. **You can repeat steps 8 and 9 until you're comfortable with the experience.**

11. **Now go into the future and test an imaginary time when you may have experienced the phobic response.**

In Chapter 9 you discover all about setting anchors. You can use anchoring to put yourself or a client into a resourceful emotional state before doing the Fast Phobia Cure.

Accepting That Beliefs and Values Make a Difference

You may have heard someone say, 'teenagers today, they have no values'. Well, everyone has values; they're just different for different people and different groups of people. Your values and beliefs are unconscious filters that you use to decide what bits of data coming in through your senses you pay attention to and what bits of data you ignore. You know what that means, don't you? The unconscious nine-tenths of your brain has been sitting there on the quiet, building up all sorts of beliefs and making all sorts of decisions about you and your environment, and you're not even aware of them.

Getting to grips with the power of beliefs

Your beliefs can, when allowed to go to the extreme, have the power of life and death over you. Your beliefs can help you to health, wealth, and happiness or keep you unwell, poor, and miserable.

The beliefs we're talking about here are distinct from religious beliefs – these beliefs are the generalisations you make about your life experiences. These generalisations go on to form the basis of your reality that then directs your behaviour. You can use one empowering belief, for example, to help you to develop another belief to the next level of achievement. So 'I'm a really good speller' helps you develop the belief that you enjoy words and are quite articulate. This belief may lead you to believe that you can tell stories and suddenly you find that you have the courage to submit a short story to a magazine; and suddenly you're a published author.

Just as you have positive, empowering beliefs, you can also have negative, disempowering beliefs. If you had the misfortune of being bullied at school, you may have developed a belief that people, in general, aren't pleasant. This belief may make you behave quite aggressively towards people when you first meet them. If some people then respond in a similarly aggressive way, their behaviour may well reinforce your belief that 'people aren't pleasant'. You may not even notice when someone responds in a friendly manner because your belief filters aren't geared to noticing pleasant people.

Be aware that a limiting belief may be lurking if you find yourself using words or hearing words such can't, should, shouldn't, could, couldn't, would, ought, and ought not, as in 'I couldn't possibly do your job'. As Henry Ford said: 'He can who thinks he can, and he can't who thinks he can't. This is an inexorable, indisputable law.'

Being impacted by the beliefs of others

The really scary thought is that other people's preconceptions can place false limitations on you, especially if the other people are teachers, bosses, family, or friends.

A very interesting study conducted with a group of children who had been tested and found to be of average intelligence illustrates how a teacher's belief can enhance or hinder a child's learning ability.

The students were split into two groups at random. The teacher for one group was told that the students in the group were gifted, whereas the teacher for the other group was told that these students were slow learners. Both groups of children were retested for intelligence a year later. The intelligence score for the group in which the teacher thought the students were gifted was higher than when previously tested; whereas the group in which the teacher had been told the students were slow learners scored lower on the intelligence test than they had done before.

Sadly these limitations aren't just the domain of overcrowded schools but exist in homes where parents shoehorn their children into an 'acceptable' position. Other examples include when your friends remind you to be careful of changing a secure job to pursue a dream, or when a boss whose communication style is different from yours has a detrimental effect on your career progression. We hear of many cases in which doctors declare to patients that they are never going to recover, and how this statement negatively impacts the life span of the patients. Not only are some of these professionals perceived always to know more than you, but also you may even place them on a pedestal.

A child can have difficulties overcoming the shortcomings of a teacher without parental assistance and even more so the restrictions of a parent or family environment. As an adult, however, you can weigh up the pros and cons of the advice you're being given by seeing it from the other person's point of view. (We cover this situation in Chapter 7, where we write about exploring perceptual positions.) When you understand the reasons for the other person's opinion, you can choose to follow the given advice or not. Also, with this knowledge behind you, you can always start to use your boss's communication style in order to get your message across and so progress in your chosen career.

Changing beliefs

Some of your beliefs can empower you, while others can limit the way you think and hold you back. The good news is that beliefs can and do change. Take the example of the four-minute mile. For years athletes didn't believe someone could run a mile in less than four minutes. Roger Bannister achieved this aim in May 1954. Soon after, even this record was broken several times over.

Are you thinking, 'But why would I want to change something that glues my world together?' Yes, beliefs do hold your world together, but ask yourself whether it's for better or for worse. If a belief is holding you back, change it. If you find you need the security blanket of the old belief, you can always change it back.

When you think of a belief you have, you may make a picture, have a feeling, hear something, or experience some combination or all three of these sensations. These qualities of your beliefs – visual (pictures), auditory (sound), and kinaesthetic (feelings) – are called *modalities*, which can be fine tuned using *submodalities*: qualities such as brightness, size, and distance for pictures; loudness and tone for sounds; and pressure, heat, and location for feelings. Check out Chapter 6 for much more on senses and modalities.

One way of changing a belief is to adjust its submodalities. This process is useful because it helps you to loosen the grip that a limiting belief has on you and reinforce the effects of a positive belief, in order to develop a more empowering belief. Suppose that you can't help but be drawn to people and have long been told that being subjective is bad – changing your belief to 'I'm good with people' can make a huge difference to your confidence when dealing with others. Similarly, if you know that you're good at art, this belief can help you branch into a more art-based career. You can find out how to go about changing a belief in Chapter 10.

As a member of the human race, what beliefs are holding your 'isms' (sexism, ageism, racism) in place and whose 'isms' are you allowing to box you in? A cluster of beliefs is called a belief system. A belief or belief system can support a particular value. Values are the *why* you do something. Beliefs direct your behaviour, which then helps you to fulfil a value – provided of course your unconscious mind creates no conflicts.

Working with your values

Values are the 'hot buttons' that drive all your behaviours and are your unconscious motivators and demotivators: you act because of your values.

After you've acted, you use these values to judge whether the deed was good or bad. For instance, if you value honesty you may decide to pick up a wallet you find in the street for safe-keeping and feel good about handing it over to the police.

When considering your values, ask yourself the question 'what's important to me?' Your answers reflect your values.

Values affect the choice of your friends and partners, the types of goods you purchase, the interests you pursue, and how you spend your free time. Your life has many facets. You're probably a member of a family, a team at work, and maybe you belong to a club in your pursuit of a hobby, just to name a few. Each of these areas of your life, family, work, leisure, and so on has its own values hierarchy, with the most important value at the top. The values at the top of the hierarchy are usually more abstract than those further down and exert the most influence in your life. For example, in Figure 3-2, family and friends is fairly concrete, whereas happiness is more intangible.

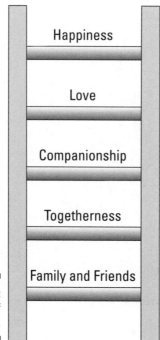

Figure 3-2:
A ladder of
values.

Distinguishing means-to-an-end values

Values can be *ends* values or *means* values, with means values occurring further down the hierarchy, acting as the rungs in a ladder that enable you to reach your ends values. Freedom is an ends value and all the other values in Figure 3-3 are means values. Means values are those that need to be fulfilled in order to get you to your final, ends value. Freedom is harder to quantify than, say, money. In the example, you can have money without having freedom, but to have freedom you need money. So freedom – which is an ends value – is dependent on money – a means value.

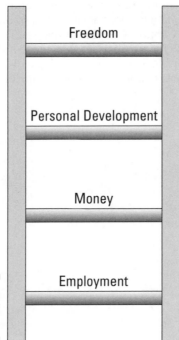

Figure 3-3:
A ladder of happiness.

Your values can drive you towards pleasure or away from pain:

'Towards' values	*'Away-from' values*
Love	Guilt
Freedom	Sadness
Health	Loneliness
Happiness	Anger
Wealth	Poverty

Values with *away from* tendencies are indicative of negative emotions, negative decisions, or emotional traumas that may be exerting an influence on your life. These tendencies can be released using techniques such as *time-line therapy* (which we discuss in detail in Chapter 13. The main purpose of any such technique is to learn the lessons that may be of value from negative events in order for the unconscious mind to release the trapped emotions. Essentially, time-line therapy works on the principle that your memories are arranged along a time line, and by changing a memory along this time line you can release the hold of some memories, which in turn helps you to gain more control over your reactions to events and create more options in your life.

Creating values

Your values are essentially formed over three periods in your life:

- ✔ The *imprint* period occurs from the time of your birth to when you're approximately seven years old. During this time you learn largely unconsciously from your parents.

- ✔ The *modelling* period occurs between the ages of 8 and 13 when you learn by consciously and unconsciously copying friends. Some of your most important values – core values – are formed when you're around 10 years old.

- ✔ The *socialisation* period occurs between the ages of 14 and 21 years. During this time you acquire values that affect your relationships.

Eliciting your values

If you recognise areas in your life that you think can be improved, you can then examine your values to get a clue to help make positive change. By following the suggestions in the following steps, you can discover what's holding you back from getting what you want:

1. **Pick an area (or context) in your life that you're not happy with or want to improve.**

   For instance, are you living or working in an environment that you don't like and want to make more enriching?

2. **Make a list of what's important to you in this context.**

   Notice that the first few values come to mind very quickly. Stay with it and another batch of values are sure to surface.

3. **Put these values in order of importance to you, with the most important appearing at the top.**

   If you have trouble rearranging the list, just ask yourself, 'If I could have A but not B, would this be okay?' If the answer is yes, A is of greater importance than B; if the answer is no, B needs to be moved above A. For example, in the list of values below, which relate to your job, you may decide that security is much more important to you than adventure:

Success

Power

Achievement

Adventure

Security

When you put these values into an order of importance, you may well find the ones that surfaced later have greater significance for you.

4. **After you arrange your values, ask yourself if one value would be useful for you to have in this area of your life, but which is currently missing. Where would you slot it in the list of existing values?**

For instance, if you value your job but can't get the level of success you want, perhaps you need the element 'fulfilment' in your hierarchy. In fact, by going through the above process you may decide that your new hierarchy looks as follows:

Success

Fulfilment

Achievement

Adventure

Security

You may find step 3 easier to do if you write your values down on pieces of paper; you can then move them around rather than crossing out and adding values.

Conflicting values

When your means values are aligned (see the preceding section), achieving your ends value becomes much easier. Unfortunately your values can end up in conflict. You think you want to move towards an outcome but your unconscious mind has other ideas that actually move you away from your objective.

You may have had a very financially poor childhood and have a strong *away from poverty* value, which is in direct conflict with a *towards wealth* value. So you want to be wealthy but keep thinking 'I don't want to be poor', which is what your unconscious mind helps you create in your life.

Another conflict can occur when you want to move towards two outcomes simultaneously and you think you can only have one or the other: for example, you want to be thinner but also want to be able to enjoy your food.

Is an overriding value in your life stopping you from getting satisfaction in other areas of your life? For instance, having money as your number one value may make you incredibly rich, but it may detract from your having a fulfilling relationship.

Make sure that you don't spend so long fulfilling your means values that you miss achieving your ends value!

Changing values

When you think of your values you may experience them as pictures, sounds, or feelings. In this section, we encourage you to change the hierarchy of your values by changing the characteristics of the image that the value creates. Say, for example, that your values for living are in the following order of importance:

1. **Freedom**

2. **Achievement**

3. **Financial security**

4. **Fun**

5. **Family**

6. **Health**

However, you find yourself let down by poor health. You may decide that having good health is more important for you than fun and decide to make a swap in your hierarchy. You can do so by using the following technique:

1. **When you think of fun, notice the picture you make in terms of the following:**

    Size

    Colour/black and white

    Position

    Still or movie

    Focused or hazy

2. **Notice the picture you make when you think of health.**

3. **Swap the qualities of the images.**

   As with changing the picture qualities of a belief (check out Chapter 10), altering the qualities of the picture you have for health to make it the same as the one you have for fun moves health up and places it at the same level as fun. Now change the picture for fun so that it has the same qualities as the one you had for health. This process moves fun down to the previous level of health.

Now that you've experienced working with pictures, try changing the hierarchy of your values by altering the sounds and feelings you may experience.

Daydreaming Your Future Reality

Contrary to what your school teachers may have told you when they saw you gazing out of the classroom window, allowing your mind to wander can be a powerful first step in achieving your goals. By using the techniques described in earlier sections of this chapter, you can discover your heart's desire and take the first steps towards achieving it – all by daydreaming.

Give yourself permission to dream and play. What would you want to succeed at if a fairy godmother came and gave you one wish? Imagine that you have all the influence, contacts, and resources that you need to fulfil your deepest desire. Got your goal? Now follow these steps:

1. **Make a list of what's important to you about your goal, all the reasons why you want it, and put them in order of importance.**

   Are you surprised by your values? Did you realise something you thought important wasn't that important after all, and did you think of a value that may have been missing in the beginning?

   If you're not sure how to do this exercise, refer to the section 'Eliciting your values' earlier in this chapter.

2. **Now, while still daydreaming, imagine floating out of your body and into the future, to a time when you may have achieved this goal.**

3. **Notice the pictures, sounds, and feelings, and manipulate them.**

   Can you make these stronger, more vibrant, and then even more so?

4. **From the place in the future, turn and look back to now and let your unconscious mind notice what it needs to know about and help you do in order for you to achieve your goal.**

   Remember to notice what the first step would be!

5. **When you've savoured the dream fully, come back and *take that first step*!**

You may surprise yourself!

Chapter 4

Taking Charge of Your Life

· ·

In This Chapter

▶ Understanding that you can choose to feel good or bad

▶ Influencing how the world treats you

▶ Placing yourself firmly in the driving seat of your life

▶ Working with your brain to achieve your goals

▶ Discovering the formula for success

· ·

Memories can be a wonderful gift or a terrible scourge. They can cradle you softly or bind you in coils of barbed wire; they can propel you towards your dreams or trap you in the past. With the help of NLP, and by understanding how you can program your mind, your past doesn't need to affect your future negatively.

This chapter is about making you the driver of, and not a passenger in, your life. So put on your seat belts and prepare to go for a drive!

Taking Control of Your Memory

Your memories are recorded as pictures, sounds, and feelings, and by adjusting the quality of how you see, hear, and experience them, you can enhance positive memories and take the sting out of negative ones. (Read more about adjusting the quality of your memories in Chapter 10). You can start off by flexing your 'taking-control-of-your-memory' muscles with the following simple exercises.

In the first exercise, you find out how to recall and manipulate a positive memory so that you can feel good, or even better, at will:

1. **Recall a day when you felt really happy.**

2. **Notice what you see, hear, and feel when you bring back the memory.**

3. **If the memory is a picture, adjust its quality by making it bigger, brighter, and bringing it closer.**

   If you're observing yourself, try stepping into the picture to see whether this makes you feel even better.

   You can find out about 'stepping into the picture' in Chapter 10. Adjusting the qualities of the picture helps you to heighten the positive emotions.

4. **Take note of any sounds in the memory.**

   Does making them louder, or imagining that you can hear the sounds either inside or outside your head, increase the positive feelings?

5. **Examine any feelings you have.**

   Where in your body are you experiencing them? Do they have a colour, texture, or weight? Does moving the location of the feelings or changing their colour, texture, and weight alter these feelings? Adjust these parameters to enhance the feelings.

This exercise allows you to manipulate the qualities of past experiences. More importantly, you see that you can change the structure of your memories in order to re-experience and heighten joyful ones, which means that you can also diminish the effect of negative experiences.

Of course, not all memories are good ones. This second exercise shows you how to change the qualities of an unpleasant memory and distance yourself from it. By altering the attributes of a negative memory, you're able to release negative emotions that may still be holding you in their grasp. Follow these steps:

1. **Recall a memory that's only marginally unpleasant.**

   For this exercise, and until you become more practised at NLP techniques, use a memory that isn't too unpleasant. Please leave heavy-duty memories such as traumas to when you're with an experienced NLP practitioner or therapist.

2. **Notice the pictures, sounds, and any feelings that the memory brings up.**

3. **If you're in the picture, step out of it to become an observer.**

   We discuss stepping in and out of a picture in Chapter 10. For now, imagine that you're behind a video camera, filming yourself acting out the memory.

4. **Change any sounds so that they're softer, or perhaps make people in the picture speak in ridiculous voices.**

If you hear sounds such as sirens or crying, reduce their volume and harshness. If you hear people saying something unpleasant, have them talk to you in a cartoon voice to mitigate their painful words.

5. **Adjust the quality of the picture.**

   Make it smaller, darker, and in black and white; move it far away from you until it's a dot and almost invisible. You may want to imagine sending the image up into the sun and watch it disappear in a solar flare. In this way, you experience yourself destroying the hold the memory previously had on you.

Changing the memory doesn't mean that the event didn't occur. It does, however, prove that you have a choice over how the memory affects you now and the impact it has on your future.

You See It Because You Believe It

Imagine that you're among a group of people who witness a robbery. The chances are that everyone gives the police a different account of the robbery.

This situation arises because people receive the data that create their reality through their five senses (visual – eyes, auditory – ears, kinaesthetic – touch, gustatory – taste, and olfactory – smell). Your senses, however, bombard your brain with so much data at any one time that, in order to maintain your sanity, you process only a very small fraction of the incoming data. Filters – combinations of who you believe you are, your values and beliefs, and your memories – dictate what your brain accesses. You can pick up more about these filters in Chapter 5.

Just as your filters direct what you perceive, they also affect what you project out into the world. Maybe you find yourself surrounded by angry, selfish, or jealous people. If so, perhaps you're harbouring unresolved anger, believing in a win–lose scenario because there isn't enough in the world to go around, that somebody else can only do well if you don't, or feeling jealous of someone else's success.

One of Romilla's clients, Mary, was extremely unhappy at work because she was being bullied. Her supervisor, along with the departmental secretary, ganged up on Mary, being very unpleasant and extremely petty.

Romilla helped Mary to recognise that the supervisor was a very lonely woman who had no friends and was very unpopular at work. Whenever Mary looked at the supervisor she imagined that the supervisor was holding a placard saying: 'I feel I'm worthless and unlovable.' Mary started to replace fear with compassion. She realised that her own self-esteem needed a prop and began standing her ground – she discovered how to challenge her colleagues whenever they were unpleasant to her.

Although the process was difficult in the beginning, Mary not only raised her own sense of self-worth, but also became less troubled by the supervisor's behaviour. Changing her thoughts about her own positive qualities increased her own confidence, which in turn led to a change in the behaviour of people around her.

One way in which you can change things around you is by examining and changing yourself, and you can achieve this aim by taking responsibility for your thoughts and actions, and overcoming obstacles such as blaming others.

Focusing on blaming others

Blaming others for your misfortunes is a lot easier than taking responsibility for putting things right yourself. You can have difficulty recognising that by blaming someone else you're handing over your power to that person: you're adopting the role of victim and perpetuating the problem.

Mary complained that her boss refused to give her a pay rise, which was true. However, Mary was overly modest about her achievements at work, and because her boss wasn't the brightest penny in the purse she was unaware of Mary's good work. Romilla made sure that Mary prepared well for her next appraisal, and Mary confidently presented a list of her successes since her previous appraisal as well as areas for improvement. She talked about her goals for her job and suggested ways in which she planned to work with her manager to achieve these aims.

In NLP terms, when you focus on something you give it a 'frame'. For example, by focusing on the problem, 'I can't get my leaking roof fixed because I don't have the money,' you put yourself in a *problem frame*. Blaming someone else for your problem – for example, 'I don't have the money because my louse of an ex hasn't paid me my settlement' – is putting yourself in a *blame frame*. The problem frame and blame frame are closely linked because of the tendency in both to blame someone or circumstances for a problem, and putting frames around experiences like this limits you to thinking within a box. By reframing the experience, however, you think differently and can break out of constraining thought patterns.

Mary switched away from the *blame frame* – in which she blamed her lack of a rise on her boss – and moved to taking action herself. When she realised her boss's inability to recognise her strengths, Mary showed the flexibility of a master communicator by changing her behaviour to get the response from her boss that she wanted . . . and yes, she did get a pay rise and a promotion!

In order to bring about positive change for yourself, you need to step away from the problem frame and take actions to secure what you want.

Getting stuck in a problem frame

As a gross generalisation, because our culture is focused on solving problems, you tend to look backwards when something goes wrong in order to analyse what didn't work. One of the nasty side-effects of this tendency is to lay blame. The difficulty with the problem frame is it keeps you trapped and stops you from taking the following positive actions:

- ✔ Moving forward
- ✔ Thinking about the real results you want
- ✔ Examining previous successes and modelling them for future use
- ✔ Learning from what worked for other people and emulating their strategies
- ✔ Resolving an issue

Instead, when you keep returning to analyse why things didn't work as you wanted them to, you tend to focus on the following negative aspects:

- ✔ What's wrong?
- ✔ How long have you had this problem?
- ✔ Who's to blame for you having this problem?
- ✔ Why did this problem occur?
- ✔ Why haven't you done something about the problem?

Constantly asking 'why' is a negative approach and forces you to go even deeper into the problem, become defensive, and move farther away from finding a positive solution. A more constructive approach is to ask what you hoped to achieve by doing something, or what your purpose was behind doing something.

Think of a time when you were so stuck in a problem that you were unable to see any solution. Maybe you're having such a problem right now. Ask yourself whether you're positively focusing on the result you want or getting too tied up negatively in the emotion of the moment to have clarity.

Help is at hand in the form of the outcome-frame process, which we introduce in the following section, and the well-formed outcome process (described in the later section 'Becoming smarter than SMART: Creating well-formed outcomes').

Shifting into the outcome frame

The outcome-frame approach is a smart, constructive process that suggests a different way of thinking about your problems and issues, a process that helps you to identify and then focus your mind on what you positively want. When you add in an efficient goal-setting process and monitor each step along the way, you can correct any deviation from your plan to attain the desired results easily and promptly.

Often, you can find yourself experiencing the same sorts of problems time and again. In our experience, this cycle usually indicates that you have something to take on-board.

Keep asking yourself, 'What's the lesson that I need to learn so that this problem is no longer an issue?'

One day, after asking this question for a while – or perhaps even instantly – the answer comes to you. Strangely, after you fully experience that 'Aha' moment of realisation, you can find that you no longer notice the problem recurring.

Perhaps the change comes about because you stop investing emotional energy in the problem or because you move on to tackling another set of lessons. Whatever the reason, the process worked!

The Path to Excellence

Your brain is a learning machine that needs to be kept occupied. If it isn't, it can start to dwell on the negative and get you into all kinds of trouble. As a human being, you need to use all your ingenuity to direct your brain towards helping you to achieve your goals. If you can create a compelling, irresistible future, your brain helps to align your behaviour in a way that moves you towards your desired outcome quickly and easily. The first step is working out what you want.

Knowing what you want

Alice (in *Alice's Adventures in Wonderland* by Lewis Carroll) asks the Cheshire Cat, 'Would you tell me, please, which way I ought to walk from here?', without having any clear idea of where she wants to go, she just wants to go somewhere. The Cheshire Cat responds that Alice is sure to get somewhere if she just walks long enough. Like Alice, imagine what would happen next time you go to a train station and ask for 'a ticket to somewhere'.

When you're trying to move forward and achieve your goals, life is so much easier if you become very clear about what you really want. So often in life, you get caught up in what you don't want and spend an awful lot of energy, both physical and emotional, in avoiding the undesirable result.

To figure out what you want and put your energies towards achieving it, sit down and write your own obituary. You can then decide on the legacy you want to leave to posterity and the actions you need to take to fulfil that legacy. For more information on this technique, head to Chapter 3, where you can discover that your unconscious mind is a wonderful ally in assisting you to achieve the goals you want.

A client, Denise, was trying to 'escape' from her second marriage. One of her first statements was, 'I'm bad with relationships.' On working through her issues, we discovered that she had lost her much loved grandfather as a very young child. The trauma of this particular event had gone very deep into Denise's psyche, and her fear of loss had been driving her to end her relationships before she had to experience the pain of loss again. Because Denise was focusing, at a subconscious level, on what she didn't want – the pain of loss – her unconscious mind was assisting her in maintaining behaviours that made her avoid the pain. Unfortunately, this approach created other problems. For her to get the relationship she craved, she had to think about and design exactly what she wanted in a relationship, and then focus on creating that in her life.

One way to discover what you really want is to go way into your future. Imagine that you're a grey-haired grandparent. You're sitting on a rock, under the stars, with a roaring campfire in front of you, and your grandchildren are at your feet demanding another story about your life. Would you want to tell them of the time you missed the chance to fulfil a dream because you were too scared or too influenced by someone else's 'you can't'? Or would you want to tell them that, despite all the odds and in keeping with your values, you did something spectacular?

Fast-forward through the years and look back at your life as it is now. Make a list of the dreams you'd dare to aim for if you had all the money and influence in the world and knew you wouldn't fail.

You may decide that you want material things like a huge nest-egg, a big house, and nice cars, you may want a home and family of your own, or you may decide you want to be influential in the political arena. Your life is your choice. Working through the following section, and flicking to Chapter 5 to read about values, helps you to discover the reasons why you want the goals you do and find the hot buttons that drive you.

Becoming smarter than SMART: Creating well-formed outcomes

SMART goals were all the rage a few years ago in the corporate world. According to the SMART model, goals need to be Specific, Measurable, Achievable, Realistic, and Timed (hence the acronym). This approach is a great discipline so far as it goes. NLP, however, allows a better way forward by adding sensory-specific information, which can help you modify your behaviour or seek help in the form of extra resources, including guides and mentors.

NLP makes SMART goals even smarter by helping you work out what you want using the *well-formed outcome process*. NLP builds on the SMART approach by making you use all your senses to design a goal, and to fine tune it to be more than just Specific, Measurable, Achievable, Realistic, and Timed.

This process requires you to answer a series of questions that really help you explore the hows, whys, and wherefores of your desired outcome. By following this process you begin to understand your true motives for wanting your goals, and you can weigh up the pros and cons of success versus failure! A fairly common example of a well-formed outcome may be to want a better paid job.

When your desired outcome meets the following criteria, NLP says that it satisfies the *well-formed conditions*. For every result you want to achieve, ask yourself the following seven questions:

1. **Is the goal stated in the positive?**

2. **Is the goal self-initiated, maintained, and within my control?**

3. **Does the goal describe the evidence procedure?**

4. **Is the context of the goal clearly defined?**

5. **Does the goal identify the necessary resources?**

6. **Have I evaluated whether the goal is ecological?**

7. **Does the goal identify the first step I need to take?**

The following sections we explain these points in more detail.

Is the goal stated in the positive?

What do you want? Or, to put it another way, what would you rather have?

These questions help clarify your desired outcome, because you must know very clearly what you want in order to maintain focus and direction. Vague goals like 'I want to be thinner' or 'I want more money' are insufficient because you're then satisfied by being a pound lighter or finding a £5 note on the pavement.

Better goals are 'I want to weigh 12 stone' or 'I want £1,000 in my bank account' or 'I want a gross salary of £50,000 per annum'. Also, having negative goals like 'I don't want to stay in this job' can adversely affect your desires (see the later sidebar 'Dwelling on the negative can damage your health'). Therefore, when you find yourself saying 'I don't want. . .', ask yourself instead 'What do I want?'

Is the goal self-initiated, maintained, and within my control?

So often we hear of a person wanting to give up smoking who, when questioned, replies: 'My wife wants me to stop.' A person has a far better chance of succeeding if the drive to attain a particular outcome comes from within, for example: 'I want to enjoy a long and healthy life – for me.' In contrast, if your goal is 'I want my partner to take me away for two weeks in the sun during March,' you need to recognise that your partner may have a different agenda and this goal is therefore not under your control.

Ask yourself these questions:

✔ Am I doing this for myself or someone else?

✔ Does the outcome rely solely on me?

When Kate ran a marketing consultancy, she realised that several projects involved working closely with corporate business clients who were extremely stressed, very busy, and disorganised. She was spending long meetings sitting with clients at their chaotic desks while they made phone calls or gathered together the project information while she waited.

Dwelling on the negative can damage your health

Romilla knows at least two people who managed to get themselves sacked from jobs by unconsciously adopting damaging behaviours that were out of character. When examining the situation later, the people realised that they would have behaved differently if they had focused their energy on defining the jobs they wanted and finding better employment. Instead, they sapped their energy by just not wanting to be there and fell into destructive, aberrant behaviours.

Therefore, her well-formed outcome for future client assignments was 'to work in a calm, efficient, and commercial way'. Looking at her goal, it may not initially be apparent that she had control of the outcome because she was dependent on the clients playing their part. However, in applying the principles of the NLP well-formed outcome, she set clearer expectations with disorganised clients. Her strategies included arranging meetings in quiet offices with no distractions, or holding a videoconference rather than visiting the client site. Her goal involved setting specific boundaries such as defining the start and end times of meetings and distributing the objectives, agenda, and actions and information required in writing. Also, by fully itemising the time spent and billing for every hour wasted – like the legal profession – she also had a direct impact on making others more efficient.

Initially, Kate's goal didn't appear to depend solely on her and therefore, on the face of it, she may not have been able to satisfy it. By showing flexibility of behaviour, however, she took responsibility for achieving her goal and influencing her clients with complete integrity.

Does the goal describe the evidence procedure?

Evidence procedure is another way of asking 'When do I know that I've achieved my goal?' Here are some extremely important questions that can help to identify goals that are too vague, or when you're unclear on the outcome:

- How do I know that I'm getting the desired outcome?
- What will I be doing when I get it?
- What will I see, hear, and feel when I have it?

On one of Romilla's workshops, David, an accountant, wanted to become self-employed. His only stated desire was to earn enough income within three months. By answering the above questions he discovered that he hadn't really worked out what he truly wanted from working for himself. His initial goal, although stated in the positive, was too vague to help him get anywhere: it was as bad as saying, 'I know I don't want to work for someone else' (a negative). Instead, he followed the well-formed outcome process and worked out that what he really wanted to do was to teach other self-employed accountants how to win business by training them in NLP-based sales techniques.

Is the context of the goal clearly defined?

Ask yourself, 'Where, when, how, and with whom do I want to achieve my goal?' This question is very good in helping you fine-tune what you want by eliminating what you don't want. For instance, if you know you really didn't enjoy that holiday on the moon, your goal of 'I want my own holiday home' immediately excludes the lunar colony, or if Martians aren't your favourite people, you know that you don't want to settle on Mars.

By defining when you want something, you may in the process identify steps that need to be taken before you can have it. For instance, 'I want my holiday home when I can afford to have someone else maintain it,' may make you realise that you need an income of £50,000 per annum before you can buy your holiday retreat.

When Kate coached Simon, a small-company owner who wanted to expand his technology enterprise, his first desired outcome was to build a separate outbuilding for the business in the grounds of his house. As a result of questioning him about the context, his outcome changed to finding office premises away from the home. He realised just how much the business was intruding on family life. The happy result was that his six-person team moved into luxury, purpose-built offices close to a university campus, at a low rent, which provided the space to grow the business. He and his wife regained the use of the two main rooms in their house with the bonus of quality leisure time without the hassle of 'living above the shop'.

Does the goal identify the necessary resources?

The questions below help to identify what you need, by way of people, knowledge, and so on, to satisfy your outcome. They enable you to draw on possible past experiences when you previously made use of resources that may prove useful in the current exercise. To give you an idea of the sort of answers that can be helpful, we also list those that Peter (who wants to take up hang-gliding but is afraid of heights) would give to these questions.

✔ **What resources do I have now?**

Peter: 'I have the desire to learn and friends who are hang-gliders to guide me. I'm athletic and easily pick up new sports. It can't be that different to water skiing!'

✔ **What resources do I need to acquire?**

Peter: 'I need to get over my fear of heights, and so I'm going to find a therapist or hypnotherapist who can help me get over my fear. I also need to find a club where I can hire an instructor and a hang-glider. I need to adjust my availability to make time for my new hobby.'

✔ **Have I evidence of achieving this type of goal before?**

Peter: 'Well, I learnt to drive, and boy was that scary, the first time that police car seemed to drive at me sirens blaring and lights flashing, but I persevered and am a good driver now.'

✔ **What happens if I act as if I have the resources?**

Peter: 'Oh, I can feel myself soaring and I don't have those butterflies in my stomach when I look down. I never thought I could leave terra firma without metal below me. Can't wait to get soaring!'

Acting as if you have the resources now helps you to recognise and shift any beliefs that may be holding you back. It also enables you to try the outcome on for size – you may change your mind at this point. This approach is a great help because it can save you spending money on equipment that ends up taking up space in the garage, if you later find that the new hobby isn't right for you.

Have I evaluated whether the goal is ecological?

The dictionary defines *ecology* as a 'branch of biology dealing with living organisms' habits, modes of life, and relations to their surroundings'. In NLP, when we talk about *ecology checks*, we're simply asking questions to make sure that the outcome fits within all aspects of your life. Ecology checks shine a strong beam of light on any hidden agenda or secondary gain of which you may be unaware when setting your outcomes. A *secondary gain* or *positive by-product* is defined as a behaviour that appears to be negative or problem-causing, when in fact it serves a positive function at some level.

The following questions are the laser-guided system that helps you lock on to the nub of your desires. As you ask yourself these questions, be aware of any pictures, sounds, and particularly feelings that your unconscious mind raises. Be sympathetic to the response you get and adjust your goal accordingly.

✔ What is the *real* purpose why I want this?

✔ What will I lose or gain if I get it?

✔ What will happen if I get it?

✔ What won't happen if I get it?

✔ What will happen if I don't get it?

✔ What won't happen if I don't get it?

One of Kate's career-coaching clients, Raz, was in a quandary. He was an average student and achieved good enough grades to go to university to study art. His real passion, however, was working with wood. Kate encouraged him to use the well-formed outcome process to clarify what to do with his future. He saw that he wanted to do something creative, and so an art degree was fine. He imagined himself at exhibitions, talking to people about his work. He knew he was creative and quite capable of reading around his subject and so he had all the resources he needed. However, when it came to checking the ecology of going to university, he realised that he didn't want to spend years studying theory. He discovered that he really wanted to work alongside a furniture-maker and learn in a very practical way.

Does the goal identify the first step I need to take?

Lao-Tzu, the ancient Taoist philosopher, is credited with saying that a journey of a thousand miles must begin with a single step, which is well worth remembering. Often, change isn't of the dramatic breakthrough kind, but a drip, drip, drip effect – slowly getting what you want. You must create a breakdown of an action plan, showing the steps to get you to your goal.

If you decide that in order to be an Oscar-winning scriptwriter, you have to join a class and start writing, and yet every time you plan on sitting down to write, you allow yourself to be sidetracked, your goal is going to remain a dream. For you to turn your dream into a concrete reality you have to take that first vital step, because without it you may not build up sufficient momentum to take the next step . . . and then the next step.

The Four-Point Formula for Success

The four-point formula consolidates the information on creating your well-formed outcome (which we describe in the earlier section 'Becoming smarter than SMART: Creating well-formed outcomes'). This formula can be equally effectively applied to long-term, lifetime goals and short-term ones.

Hitting a target is much easier when it's clearly defined and visible. Robin Hood would never have won Maid Marion if he hadn't aimed for the bull's eye!

To hit the target, follow these steps:

1. **Know your outcome.**

   Specifying precisely what you want is vital. You can use the outcome frame to fine-tune your desired outcome (check out the earlier 'Shifting into the outcome frame' section) and satisfy the well-formed outcome conditions in the earlier section 'Becoming smarter than SMART: Creating well-formed outcomes'.

2. **Take action.**

   Unless you take that first step, and then the following ones, nothing's going to happen to help you move towards your outcome, no matter how clearly you define it.

3. **Develop sensory awareness.**

   If you have the awareness to see, hear, and feel what isn't working, you can modify your behaviour to steer you towards the desired outcome. Chapter 6 shows you how to develop sensory awareness.

4. **Maintain behavioural flexibility.**

   This step ties in beautifully with the following NLP presupposition: 'In interactions between people, the person with the most flexibility of behaviour can control the interaction.' Or more directly: 'If it ain't working, do something different.' Head to Chapter 2 for a detailed explanation of this powerful presupposition.

If you always do what you've always done, you always get what you always got.

Spinning the Wheel of Life

This section helps you to identify whether you're satisfied with your life, and if scope for improvement does exist, which areas need to be worked on in order to get your life back on track, simply and effectively.

Take a look at the diagram of the wheel in Figure 4-1. If you were to label the wedges of the wheel with words that indicate the most important areas of your life, what areas would you choose? Do they tie up with those we entered in the figure? Typically people select labels such as work and career (including working within the home), finances and money, friends and family, relationships, personal growth and learning, fun and recreation, spirituality, and physical environment.

Taking the centre of the wheel as 0 and the outer edge as 10, rank your level of satisfaction with each life area by drawing a straight or curved line to join each number and create a new outer edge. This new perimeter of the circle represents your personal wheel of life. The ideal situation is obviously to have all the sections at 10, giving you a beautifully round wheel, like the one in Figure 4-1.

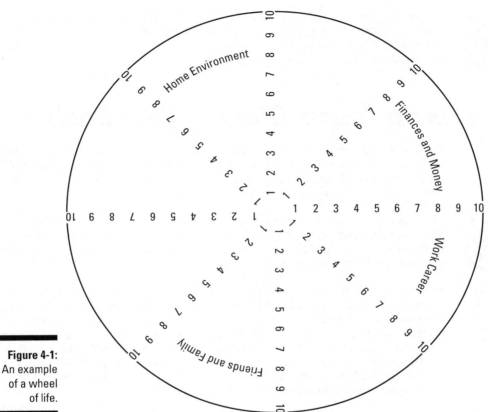

Figure 4-1:
An example
of a wheel
of life.

In a normal life, however, expecting to score perfect 10s for everything, all the time, is unrealistic. Life just isn't like that. When you're working hard, another aspect of your life may slip down the agenda. If you've been spending lots of time doing up your home, for example, you're unlikely to have had time to socialise with friends. Or if you've been studying for exams, your exercise routine may well have flown out the window.

By noticing those areas of your life where you're not happy with the scores, you have an opportunity to set yourself a well-formed outcome to address that area. Do you, for example, want to pay off your credit cards and get your finances in good shape, or join an online dating agency to get more romance back into your life? As you focus on what you want, you take charge of your life rather than simply reacting to what comes at you.

The end of a year is always a good time to gather yourself together, review your whole life, and set yourself new outcomes for the coming year. You can become even more focused by carrying out this activity in conjunction with a dream diary, as we describe in the next section.

Keeping a Dream Diary of Your Goals

Have you ever agreed to an appointment and forgotten to write it down? Did you make the appointment anyway? If you did, thank your unconscious mind for its vigilance. If you missed your appointment, did you learn your lesson and do you now always write down your appointments?

Think of a goal as an appointment with a desired outcome and write it down. The most important message to take away from this book is the following: make sure that you write down your goals, commit to actions to achieve them, and work on your plans every single day.

In Chapter 3, we tell you all about your *Reticular Activation System*, or RAS for short. The RAS is a network of nerve cells that operates like a radar, directing your attention to what's important to you. For instance, for survival your RAS draws your attention to the car speeding towards you when you're out driving and your mind wanders. Your RAS works like an antenna, honing in on opportunities, people, and resources that you need to meet your goals. Your RAS also keeps you alert to opportunities connected to your goals. Crucially, the act of writing down your goal switches on your RAS.

For this reason, in her goal-setting workshops, 'Going for Goal™', Romilla recommends that delegates buy or create a 'dream diary'. The idea is to have a journal that's attractive to look at and touch so that the delegates find themselves drawn to handling the diary regularly. They are then more inclined to record their dreams and aspirations, and so better positioned to realise them.

Create your dream diary simply by buying a diary that appeals to you, perhaps one of those discreet black leather bound ones or a gorgeous, vibrantly coloured one with magnetic clasps.

If you're feeling really creative, cover an ordinary ring binder with material that entices you. You can even put some light padding between the covering material and the binder to make your dreams a really sensory experience.

Pick some areas in your life in which you'd like to have goals. This process may be a little involved and so take your time and savour each stage, because what you're really doing is *designing the future you want to live*. Basically, you're going to create your own dream diary and fill it with your own dreams and goals. Follow these steps:

1. **Buy or create your dream diary. Just make sure that you're going to enjoy working with it every day; get some colourful dividers, and pens too.**

2. **Draw and fill in a wheel of life (as we illustrate in Figure 4-1).**

3. **Pick the areas in your life that you want to address and label each divider with one such area.**

   You may decide to work on only one or two areas to start with.

4. **Think of some goals for each area.**

   Consider both long-term (lifetime, five years, a year or more) and short-term (six months to a year) goals.

5. **Apply the well-formed outcome process to your goals.**

   Refer to the earlier section 'Becoming smarter than SMART: Creating well-formed outcomes'.

6. **Write down your goals and include the date by which you want to achieve them.**

7. **Break the goals down into monthly, weekly, and daily goals, and write them in your diary along with their dates.**

8. **Each night before you go to sleep (and this takes only a few minutes) look at your dreams and make a list of what you're going to do the next day in order to meet your goals.**

Savour the sense of achievement when you come to tick off the goals you have achieved and do this with a sense of gratitude, both for the opportunities you've had and the people you've met along the way who've enabled you to get to where you are.

After all that activity, put your feet up for some well-earned rest and recuperation, watch the movie *UP*, and see how Ellie creates her journal (turn to Chapter 24 for more on *UP* and Ellie's diary.)

Just Go for It

In her 'Passion to Publication' writing workshops, Kate coaches many budding authors at various stages of their projects, authors such as Janice.

Janice was putting all her spare time and passion into researching and writing a travel guide. At one point, she started to lose motivation and talked about a relative who belittled her efforts by saying things such as: 'Don't expect any people to buy the book.'

Janice was hurt and stunned and wondered why she was unable to move through her writing block. Then she realised that she was doing what the negative relative had wanted, and failed, to do. Janice was following her passion whereas the relative was deeply envious of her travel adventures.

Unfortunately, you'll encounter people in the world who operate from a position of believing that they have few or no options and project their fears and lack of confidence on to others. They hate the fact that others are free from such limitations, and so – remembering the NLP presupposition that 'there is no failure, only feedback' – you can be like Janice and have the courage to chase your dreams.

Part II
Winning Friends and Influencing People

The 5th Wave   By Rich Tennant

"How can you not feel confident? You're wearing Versace sunglasses, a Tommy Hilfiger sweater, Calvin Klein jeans, and Michael Jordan gym shoes. Now go on out there and just be yourself."

In this part . . .

Have you ever wondered what makes you tick but not known where to start? Or been confused when people behave in unexpected ways? Don't worry: this part helps many things become clearer to you so that you can connect elegantly with all kinds of characters. You see that life's all about people connecting with one another. You find out about two key subjects of NLP known as Sensory Awareness and Rapport: the first is all about noticing more of the world around you and how you can engage with it, and without the second you simply don't get listened to.

We also show you the value of hearing how people use words in different ways, and how to switch perspective so that you can see a situation from another point of view. We want you to begin to master the skills of great communicators, and if you read the chapters in this part you're well on your way.

Chapter 5

Pushing the Communication Buttons

*W*hen you're engaged in a dialogue, for what percentage of the communication do you think you're responsible? Did you say 50 per cent? After all, two people are involved in a dialogue, and so logically each of you has half the responsibility to make and elicit responses, right?

If you're familiar with the following NLP presuppositions (which we discuss in detail in Chapter 2), you'd reply that you're 100 per cent responsible:

✔ The meaning of the communication is the response it elicits.

✔ If what you're doing isn't working, do something different.

✔ The person with the most flexibility within a system influences the system.

This chapter shows you how to take total responsibility for any communication in which you're involved. We provide tools to help you become more aware of how the people with whom you're communicating are transforming what they receive through their senses: what they hear you say and what they see and feel. When you understand their thinking process, you have the means to adapt your words, deeds, and actions to get the response you want.

Do bear in mind that in this chapter we're giving you a general overview of how people's filters affect the messages they receive. We explore this aspect in more detail in other chapters: for example, Chapter 8 describes the meta programs that you run and Chapter 15 tells you more about the deletions, distortions, and generalisations that we introduce in this chapter.

What you intend to communicate isn't necessarily the message that the recipient understands.

Introducing the NLP Communication Model

The NLP communication model is based on cognitive psychology and was developed by Richard Bandler and John Grinder.

According to the NLP communication model, when people behave in a certain way (their *external behaviour*), a chain reaction is set up within you (your *internal response*), which in turn causes you to respond in some way (your *external behaviour*), which then creates a chain reaction within the other person (their *internal response*), and the cycle continues. Figure 5-1 shows this chain reaction.

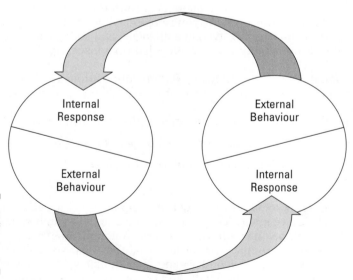

Figure 5-1:
The circle of communication.

The internal response is made up of an *internal process* (consisting of self-talk, pictures, and sounds) and an *internal state* (the feelings that are experienced).

The following sections present two scenarios, showing the NLP communication model in practice.

Scenario 1

For some people, today has been a lovely, hot summer's day. But the air-conditioning in the office wasn't working and Dan had an awful day. He gets in the car and with a sigh of relief puts on the air-conditioning to battle his weary way home. His son, Drew, had promised he would cut the grass. Dan's looking forward to sitting out on a tidy, freshly mown lawn with a glass of chilled lager. As he drives up he notices the grass is *uncut.*

Dan storms into the house, so caught up in his emotions that all he can feel is bitter resentment welling up. He starts ranting at Drew, who retreats into his sullen teenage shell muttering about the broken lawnmower, a statement that Dan doesn't hear. Finally, Drew yells 'Cut the damn grass yourself,' as he storms off. Neither person is willing to communicate any more and both slide down the spiral of shouting, slammed doors, and finally silence.

In this example, when Dan explodes, the uncut grass is the trigger for setting up an internal state of anger, resentment, and frustration in him. The internal process may be a monologue such as, 'He promised. I knew I shouldn't expect anything from him. We always give him the best and he always lets us down.' This monologue is accompanied with pictures from the past when Drew didn't live up to Dan's expectations.

Dan's external behaviour of ranting at Drew, in that particular tone of voice or with that look on his face, provokes an internal state in Drew. Drew may experience feelings of anger, resentment, and frustration very similar to those felt by Dan. He may make pictures of previous altercations with his father and know that he isn't going to be heard, just like all those other times. Drew's external behaviour of adopting his usual, sulking manner and muttering may then further inflame his father . . . and so the process continues.

Scenario 2

Now imagine scenario 2. Dan drives up and sees the uncut grass. Instead of exploding, he recognises his internal state and how that can affect his behaviour. So he takes a deep breath and asks Drew why the grass hasn't been cut. Drew, expecting recriminations, gets defensive as he explains that the mower broke down. From past experience, Dan realises that Drew is likely to retreat into his shell and so he offers to show Drew how to mend the mower. He chills out with a glass of lager before helping Drew carry out the repairs. Drew mows the lawn before the family sits down to a companionable meal.

In this scenario the father changes his internal process and makes a conscious effort to remember when he was a teenager himself, in need of guidance and a firm hand. He decides on the result he wants from his interaction with the teenager and, having disengaged his emotions, is able to proceed down the path that keeps communication channels open in order to achieve the desired outcome: to get Drew to mow the lawn.

This scenario illustrates how, by putting the NLP presuppositions into practice, Dan is able to achieve his outcome of having Drew mow the lawn. (For example, the presupposition that 'the person with the most flexibility in a system is the winner'.) The male bonding is an added bonus. The response he gets from Drew when the teenager starts to become defensive is obviously not the one Dan wants. Dan has the flexibility to recognise Drew's behaviour patterns and modify his own responses in order to get his outcome, thereby controlling the system.

Understanding the Process of Communication

John Grinder and Richard Bandler discovered that master communicators have three sets of capabilities:

- ✔ They know what they want.
- ✔ They're very good at noticing the responses they get.
- ✔ They have the flexibility to modify their behaviour until they get what they want.

Simon taught Kate some valuable lessons about dealing with people. Simon always manages to keep his cool and usually achieves his outcome even in the most difficult situations. He does so by distancing himself from his emotions and keeping his focus on the result he wants. He also attempts to understand the other person's point of view in order to arrive at a win–win result.

Everybody processes information differently and so reacts to situations differently. Wouldn't it be really useful to understand how another person's brain works? Read on for some clues.

Processing pieces of information

Professor George Miller conducted research into how many bits of data people can process at any given time. He came to the conclusion that a person can hold seven, plus or minus two, bits of information; that is, nine bits if they're feeling good or have an interest in a subject and as few as five if they're feeling a bit low or aren't particularly interested in what they're trying to remember. If you're not into multi-tasking, you may have trouble coping with more than one!

Every second you're hit by millions of bits of information. If you tried to deal with this vast array of input, you'd go mad. In order to preserve your sanity, you filter the incoming information before your brain processes it and makes internal representations from this information (we discuss internal representations more in Chapter 2).

In addition, all your different experiences and filters influence the processes by which you create these internal representations of the external events you perceive through your senses.

The way in which the external stimuli of the world are converted into internal representations in your brain involves three fundamental processes: deletions, distortions, and generalisations. The following sections give you a brief overview of these processes. For more in-depth information, head to Chapter 15.

Deletion

Deletions happen when you pay attention to some information coming in through your senses but are completely oblivious to other stimuli. Think of a nutty professor, so caught up in his work that he leaves home wearing his bedroom slippers.

Kate's story about her mother-in-law illustrates nicely how your unconscious mind makes deletions. Her mother-in-law used to travel by bus to Kennington in London to work for The Children's Society, a British charity. Normally she put her rubbish out before returning for her handbag and briefcase. One morning, however, she was running a little late and grabbed all three bags together – handbag, briefcase, and rubbish bag. Only when she found herself sitting on the bus, thinking that it was really whiffy that morning, did she realise that she'd taken her rubbish bag on to the bus with her!

Distortion

A distortion occurs when you misinterpret information coming in through your senses and create meaning from a situation that's not necessarily true: for example, when a wife complains that her husband 'didn't help me and so that means he doesn't care'. You may see what you want to see to reinforce your viewpoint instead of what's in front of your eyes. Distortion can also involve deletion of information.

A cynic may say that being in love is a form of distortion, where you go all starry-eyed behind your rose-tinted glasses (to mix metaphors), completely oblivious to the faults of your 'perfect' partner. Perhaps you're so keen to find your true love that you ignore aspects of the person's behaviour that can ruin the relationship in the long term.

Persecuted by the number seven

Here's a revealing quote by George Miller, from his article 'The magical number seven plus or minus two':

My problem is that I have been persecuted by an integer. For seven years this number has followed me around, has intruded in my most private data, and has assaulted me from the pages of our most public journals. This number assumes a variety of disguises, being sometimes a little larger and sometimes a little smaller than usual, but never changing so much as to be unrecognisable. The persistence with which this number plagues me is far more than a random accident. There is, to quote a famous senator, a design behind it, some pattern governing its appearances. Either there really is something unusual about the number or else I am suffering from delusions of persecution.

Romilla was driving down a dual carriageway late one night, when it started to rain: a very fine, misty drizzle. She could see a white, ethereal figure in the distance, by the side of the road. With a pounding heart, the conversation with herself went something as follows:

'Oh my goodness, it's a ghost.'

'Don't be stupid, there's no such thing as ghosts.'

'You know you're being idiotic. It isn't a ghost.'

'Yes it is. What if it's a ghost?'

'But it isn't.'

'Yes it is.'

And so on. To her extreme relief, but also in another sense bitter disappointment, the figure turned out to be a tramp in white plastic sheeting looking really spooky in the misty rain.

This anecdote involves distorting an image, but you can also distort the meaning of another person's actions.

Jacqui had a male boss, Tom, who because of his cultural background, found dealing with women at work very difficult, and was very abrupt in his interactions with female employees. Jacqui misunderstood Tom's behaviour and decided Tom didn't like her; she distorted the facts. The situation may have spiralled out of control if Jacqui hadn't confided her misgivings to another colleague. When Jacqui understood that Tom's upbringing was responsible for his behaviour, she no longer reacted emotionally. As a result her behaviour changed to reflect her confidence in herself, which resulted in an improvement in the way Tom treated her.

Generalisation

You make a generalisation when you transfer the conclusions you came to from one experience to other similar situations or occurrences. Imagine that you gave a very good speech that was well received. Afterwards, you may form a generalisation that you're good at public speaking.

Generalisations can be useful; they help you to build a cognitive map of the world. If you didn't generalise, for example, you'd need to relearn the alphabet and how to put together individual letters every time you read a book. Generalisations allow you to build on what you already know, without reinventing the wheel.

They can be limiting, though. The beliefs you hold about your world are generalisations and you delete and distort to the best of your ability to hold them in place. So, in other words, your generalisations can become restrictive because they can make you less likely to accept or trust actions and events that don't fit with your preconceived notions.

This tendency can in turn lead to self-fulfilling prophecies. Confidence and self-doubt are two sides of a coin. When you feel confident about doing something, the chances are that you're usually successful because you expect a positive result. Even on the odd occasion when things don't work out quite as you'd wanted, you move on. If you're riddled with self doubt, however, and convinced something isn't going to work out or no one's going to talk to you when you go to an event, a very high chance exists that your experience goes on to reflect your beliefs. Do you experience a slight disappointment when someone or a situation fails to meet your worst expectations? And do you feel a little triumphant when you're duly disappointed? Sometimes, having your negative generalisation confirmed is more satisfying than a situation going better than expected. How self-defeating is that!

Getting to grips with individual responses

When different people are exposed to the same external stimuli, they don't remember the event, and react to it, in the same way. The difference is because all people delete, distort, and generalise differently based on their own meta programs, values, beliefs, attitudes, memories, and decisions: we discuss these aspects in the next few sections.

Meta programs

Meta programs, which we describe in more detail in Chapter 8, are filters. They are the way in which you reveal your patterns of behaviour through your language. For instance, someone who's inclined to take charge and get things done (meaning that they display more proactive tendencies) may be heard to say, 'Don't give me excuses, just give me results.' Whereas someone who's likely to take their time to think things over before acting (a reactive tendency) is likely to be heard saying, 'Don't rush, think about all the factors and make sure that the results are right.'

If these leanings are abused and combined with a tendency to generalise, you may end up pigeonholing people: for example, 'you mean Tom, that geeky introvert?' (distortion) or 'yeah, typical salesman, always in your face' (generalisation). Remember, however, that people can change their behaviour patterns, depending on the environment and situation in which they find themselves.

Table 5-1 contains a little taster about introvert/extrovert tendencies and how they affect your filtration process. Both of these tendencies are basic meta programs. Although your meta programs are there in the background, you tend to have a proclivity to focus on certain aspects of particular meta programs, depending on different situations. For example, think of social interactions and how a gregarious person behaves as opposed to someone who's more solitary.

Table 5-1 Comparison of Introvert and Extrovert Meta Programs

Introverts	Extroverts
Want to be alone to recharge their batteries	Need to have people around when in need of rest and relaxation
Have a few friends with whom they have a deep connection	Have a lot of friends with whom they connect at a more superficial level
May take a real or imagined slight to heart	May not notice the slight and if they do may attribute it to the other person having a bad day
Are interested in a few topics, which they know in great detail	Know about a lot of things, but not in as much detail as an introvert
Tend to be more solitary	Tend to be more gregarious

An introvert isn't superior to an extrovert and an extrovert is as good as an introvert.

A useful way to think of how meta programs work is to imagine a sliding scale with a tendency towards one aspect or another at a certain time and in a particular setting (as illustrated in Figure 5-2).

At work, where you're confident and enjoy the environment, you may find yourself behaving like an extrovert. This tendency allows your antennae to pick up a broader band of information and has you noticing contacts and opportunities that help you in your job. When meeting your colleagues in a social setting, however, you may feel very uncomfortable and slide along the scale to display more introverted tendencies. As a result of your discomfort, you may delete subtle messages that would be very obvious to you in your familiar office environment.

Figure 5-2:
Meta pro-
grams work
along a slid-
ing scale.

Introvert ⟵⟶ Extrovert

0 1 2 3 4 5 6 7 8 9 10

Extroverts can really annoy their more introverted friends and acquaintances. So, extroverts, please take care to tone things down when you meet people who aren't as responsive as you are, and be careful not to encroach on their body space!

An extrovert NLP nerd (who plays at NLPing with everyone and everything, all the time) danced a poor introvert that they met at a party all around the room, invading the body space of the introvert who kept moving away only to have their body space encroached upon again.

Remembering that people can show different tendencies in different settings, can you think which side of the scale you favour? Can you make a guess at assessing your friends and family? Here's a tip: the answer to the question 'Do you prefer company or being alone when you need to recharge your batteries?' gives a very strong clue to a person's tendencies.

Some people with an extrovert preference may have a very strong bond with their pets and seek out the company of their four-legged friends instead of other humans when recharging!

Values

Your values are also filters that are unconscious, although less so than the meta programs that we describe in the preceding section. You learn your values, almost by osmosis, from your parents and close family up to about the age of seven, and then from your peers and friends. Values are what motivate you to do something, but they can also work as brakes, stopping you from achieving your desires. They are the factors that are important to you and let you assess whether something that you're considering doing, or have done, is good or bad. They influence how you delete, distort, or generalise data from incoming stimuli.

Values are arranged in a hierarchy, with the most important at the top of the ladder. Examples of values are health, wealth, happiness, honesty, friendships, job satisfaction, and so on. You can find out more about values in Chapter 3.

James worked for a charity helping to organise an education programme in Africa. He had a young family and loved his work. Although he was as poor as a church mouse, the charity took care of all his day-to-day living needs. His values hierarchy was satisfied by his work and looked something like the following:

1. Happiness

2. Enriching lives

3. Being with my family

4. Freedom

5. Variety

6. Support network

These values were obtained by asking James 'What's important to you about your work?'

Because James's values were being satisfied he didn't pay attention (deletion) to any job advertisements that would offer him greater monetary reward, thinking they'd detract from the other aspects of his work that he valued. He admits that he bought into the distortion that all (generalisation) Western interests in Africa were aimed at exploiting the local people. Although, later, he did realise that in some cases this view was simply an excuse by some people not to take responsibility for their own lives.

Values are very contextual, which means that some of your values apply only in certain areas of your life and that their importance in the hierarchy also changes depending on which aspect of your life you're examining. James's values were relevant only in the area of his work.

To work out what values are important to you in an area of your life, you have to stop, get off life's treadmill, and think! To do that, follow these steps:

1. **Choose an aspect of your life in which you may not be as successful as you'd like.**

   You can use work or you may want to think about relationships, education, the environment in which you live, and so on. Chapter 4 has further suggestions.

2. **Make a list of what's important to you in this context.**

3. **Look at the list and think again. Do you need to add something that may be missing that's important to you?**

4. **Arrange the list in order of importance.**

   Ask yourself, for example, whether your second value really is more important than your third value or whether your fifth value needs to move up to position two.

5. **For each value, can you identify how you may be making a deletion, a distortion, or a generalisation that's stopping you from fulfilling a desire?**

   This question's the crucial one!

6. **Also note whether any limiting decisions are lurking, which may be impacting on your values.**

   We describe limiting decisions in the later section 'Decisions'.

During a deep relaxation, James remembered, when he was about six, his parents having a discussion about their landlord increasing the rent on their house. He recalled how worried his parents sounded. He realised that he'd formed a belief then that rich people were greedy and bad.

Beliefs

Beliefs are really powerful; they can propel you to the heights of success or drag you to the depths of failure because, to paraphrase Henry Ford, 'whether you believe you can or whether you believe you can't . . . you're right'.

Your beliefs are formed in all kinds of unconscious ways. You learn that you're gifted from your parents, that you can't draw from your teacher, that you must support your friends from your peers, and so on. In some cases, as with the teacher, when you're told that you can't draw, you delete any opportunities you may have to find out how to draw. After all, one teacher told you that you can't draw.

Beliefs can start off like a 'splinter in your mind' (remember Morpheus talking to Neo in the film *The Matrix*?) and, as it irritates and niggles, you begin to find instances that validate the splinter and over a period of time you develop a concrete belief.

Choose your beliefs very carefully because they have a tendency to become self-fulfilling prophecies!

Attitudes

Your attitude is your way of thinking about a topic or perhaps a group of people: it tells others how you're feeling or your state of mind about someone or something. Your attitude is a filter of which you're very conscious and is formed by a collection of values, beliefs, and opinions around a particular subject. Changing an attitude is challenging because your conscious mind is actively involved in building and holding on to attitudes.

You can get some awareness of other people's attitudes from what they say and how they behave. At work, someone who goes the extra mile and has a positive frame of mind is considered to have a good attitude to their work, whereas a dodger or malingerer may be seen as having a bad attitude to work.

Because your attitude is based on your values and beliefs, it affects your abilities by making you behave in certain ways. Someone with a positive attitude may always expect to get a positive outcome, and by demonstrating a pleasant and helpful demeanour, that person influences others to behave in a similar vein.

Next time that you're with someone who's prone to whingeing, experiment by getting that person to catch your positive attitude virus. If you find someone who is always moaning about paying their taxes, ask them if they'd rather live out of a cardboard box and sleep in a doorway, saying that vagrants definitely don't pay taxes. If you know someone who regularly moans about Monday mornings and all the work that lies ahead of them, tell them to think of how good Friday afternoon will feel when the work is done. Or if you hear someone backbiting another person, say something positive about the victim. Tell the whiner that people who have a positive attitude to life are less stressed and live longer. You may even get to see your moaning Minnie doing something good and decide to praise them!

Memories

Your memories determine what you anticipate and how you behave and communicate with other people. Memories from your past can affect your present and your future. The problem occurs when your memories don't stay in the order in which they were recorded. When memories get jumbled up, they bring along all the emotions of when they actually happened. By this we mean that your current experience invokes old memories and you find yourself responding to memories and emotions of the past rather than to the experience you're currently having.

Tamara worked with a woman called Sheila, and their relationship was unsuccessful, to put it mildly. Sheila was a class-A bully who focused her attentions on Tamara. The situation wasn't helped by the fact that Sheila was Tamara's supervisor. When a very relieved Tamara found a new job, she found that she was working, in a similar relationship, with another person named Sheila. Because her new colleague was also called Sheila and was senior to her, Tamara took a lot of convincing that the second Sheila was in fact a lovely person and, until Tamara was able to accept this reality, she was very wary of her. If her memories had stayed in the correct order, Tamara wouldn't have re-experienced the negative memories and emotions from the past. She made generalisations and distortions about the second Shelia from her experiences with the first.

Decisions

Your decisions are closely linked to your memories and affect all areas of your life. This ability is especially important as regards decisions that limit the options you feel you have in life – what NLP calls *limiting decisions*.

Examples of limiting decisions include: 'I can't spell', 'money is the root of all evil, so to be good I mustn't be rich', and 'if I go on a diet I won't be able to enjoy my food'.

Many of your limiting decisions are made unconsciously, some when you are very young, and may be forgotten. As you grow and develop, your values may change and you need to recognise and reassess any decisions that may be hindering you.

In the earlier section 'Values', we tell you about James who worked in Africa for several years. Well, when he returned to England, he was even poorer than a church mouse, because he now had to provide for his family, without the help of the charity for whom he'd worked. On thinking about their circumstances, he drew up a new hierarchical set of values as follows:

- ✔ Happiness
- ✔ Enriching lives
- ✔ Being with my family
- ✔ Security
- ✔ Financial freedom
- ✔ Variety

When he decided that he needed financial freedom, he realised that the decision he'd made (rich people = greedy = bad) when he was little was hampering him from providing for his family. He thought about how he may be able to earn good money, help people, and stay close to his family. Today, James is extremely happy, very wealthy, and enriching lives. How? He topped up his MSc in Business Management with a PhD in Psychology. He runs workshops around the world, travelling with his wife.

Giving Effective Communication a Try

As the earlier sections in this chapter show, much of the way you think and behave is unconscious; your values, beliefs, memories, and so on, form and impact upon your responses. Fortunately, you don't have to be at the mercy of your unconscious mind.

With awareness, you can take control of how you communicate with people, which is a liberating and empowering thought in itself! Just keep these pointers in mind:

- ✔ **Engage your brain before your mouth:** Think of the result you want when you're interacting with people, and speak and behave with that desired outcome in mind.

- ✔ **Tread softly:** Having this knowledge gives you power, and of course power can corrupt. On the other hand, power can also free you from fear. Power allows you to work with generosity and kindness, so that with the knowledge of someone else's model of the world you can come to a win–win conclusion.

Chapter 6

Seeing, Hearing, and Feeling Your Way to Better Communication

• •

In This Chapter

▶ Exploring the amazing power of your senses

▶ Getting truly in touch with the world around you

▶ Noticing through their preferred language, how people think differently

▶ Spotting and deciphering people's eye movements

• •

*I*n Chapter 1, we introduce you to the four main pillars of NLP. One of these upstanding elements is what NLP labels *sensory awareness*, the ability to understand how people make meaning of the world and create their own reality through their senses.

Just for a minute, imagine a special creature with highly developed personal antennae. Well, actually that's you. You come tumbling into the world as a new human baby ready to discover all about the surrounding world. Unless you're born with difficulties in some way, you arrive as a mini learning machine with eyes and ears, and a sense of smell, taste, and touch, plus that most distinctly human quality – the ability to experience an emotional connection with others.

As you develop, you form mental maps of the world and get into habits of thinking and behaving during childhood. You discover how to learn about the world in certain ways that work best for you, by looking at, touching, tasting, and smelling things, and hearing words.

NLP encourages you to become curious about how you form these mental maps. Understanding how you use your senses to represent your experience enables you to notice how your perceptions are shaped, thus influencing your ability to communicate with other people.

Ever heard the term 'use it or lose it'? Through your life experiences, you become conditioned, which can make you a bit lazy about learning. When you find that you're good at one way of doing things, that's the method you continue to use. So, assume that as a child you draw a picture, sing, or dance, and you enjoyed doing so and received positive reinforcement from a teacher. Clearly, you're most likely to concentrate more attention on that successful area, in which you show promise, to the detriment of other endeavours.

The same thing can happen with your sensory awareness. You get very good at using one method of thinking, processing, and indeed, sharing information in a particular context, until it becomes more natural to focus consciously on that one sense to the detriment of the others. You use your other senses, of course, but aren't consciously aware of them. For example, when you watch a film in vivid 3D, you may not be as aware of the soundtrack as the visual images in front of your eyes.

Leonardo da Vinci mused that the average human 'looks without seeing, listens without hearing, touches without feeling, eats without tasting, moves without physical awareness, inhales without awareness of odour or fragrance, and talks without thinking.'

What an invitation for personal improvement!

In this chapter, we invite you to try out some new ways of engaging with the world, fine-tuning your incredible senses, and noticing what a difference doing so makes to your life. You can look forward to fun and self-discovery along the way.

Getting to Grips with the Senses

The NLP model describes the way that you experience the external world – which by the way is called real life – through your five senses, of sight, sound, touch, smell, and taste.

Notice what happens inside your head and body, for example, when we write: 'Think about a delicious meal you've enjoyed.' You may see a picture of the table spread with colourful dishes, hear the sound of knives and forks, a waiter telling you about today's specials, or a friend chatting in the kitchen. Perhaps you notice a warm and pleasant anticipation inside as the aromas of food drift your way, you hear the uncorking of a bottle of wine or feel a cool glass of water in your hand, and then you taste the first mouthful: a delicious, multi-sensory experience. And you're only thinking about it.

Until now you may not have thought about *how* you think (the process), only *what* you think about (the content). However, the quality of your thinking determines the quality of your experience. So the *how* is just as important, if not more important, than the *what*.

This section introduces you to some dimensions of your thought processes that you may never have considered before. As you open up your own awareness as to how you think and make sense of the world, some interesting things happen. You begin to notice that you can control how you think about a person or situation. You also realise that not everybody thinks like you do about even the most mundane, everyday events, which seem so clear and obvious to you. You may well decide that life can be more rewarding when you begin to think differently by paying attention to different senses.

Filtering reality

As you experience reality, you selectively filter information from your environment in three broad ways, known in NLP as visual, auditory, and kinaesthetic, or VAK for short (or VAKOG if you include the olfactory and gustatory aspects):

- **Visual dimension:** Some people see clear *pictures* of the *sights*.

- **Auditory dimension:** Other people tune in to *hear* the *sounds*.

- **Kinaesthetic dimension:** A third group grasp the *emotional* aspects or *touch* – they experience a *body awareness* (for our purposes we include in this group the sense of smell (olfactory) and taste (gustatory)).

Think for a moment about the way you experience using this *For Dummies* book. Everybody who picks it up notices the look, sound, and feel in different ways. Take three individual readers. The first one chooses the book because of the friendly layout and amusing cartoons. The second likes the sound of what's said and discussed in the text. The third enjoys the feel or smell of the paper or has a gut feeling that this book is interesting to get hold of. Perhaps you experience the book as a mix of all three senses.

Check it out for yourself. As you use this book, start to notice how you prefer to take in information. Begin to check which pages make you sit up and pay attention. What works best for you? Are you most influenced by the words, the pictures, or the feel?

In everyday life, you naturally access all your VAK senses. However, in any particular context, one sense may dominate for you. As you become more sensitive to the three broad groupings of visual, auditory, and kinaesthetic at work and play, we promise that you're going to benefit from this exercise.

Imagine, for example, that you want to change a room in your home. You may have been thinking about this task in purely visual terms – what paint colours to choose or patterns for the fabrics. If you begin to engage in the auditory dimension, you may think about the sounds of objects in the room, those squeaky floorboards, the music or conversations you want to take place, and how to cut out the noise of the external traffic or let in the birdsong. Or what happens if you consider this space in terms of textures – the kinaesthetic dimension? Perhaps then you choose a plush, velvety carpet or rush matting. You may expose some brickwork or prefer a new smooth plaster finish on the walls, depending on the feel that appeals to you.

In the context of learning, when you know about VAK you can start to experiment with different ways of taking in information. Say, in the past you've studied a language by listening to CDs in your car. Perhaps now you may make faster progress by watching foreign films or plays instead, or by playing sport, sharing a meal, or learning a dance routine with native speakers of that language. When people discover how to develop their abilities to access pictures, words, and feelings, they often discover talents of which they were previously unaware.

When Kate began to learn Italian from her friend Paola in Abruzzo, she initially wanted to see everything written down in order to remember what she'd heard spoken; and she felt she had to learn the vocabulary by rote. Paola encouraged her to relax on a comfortable sofa after each lesson, listen to what she had practised earlier, and allow the words to sink in naturally. This approach saved Kate from getting anxious about how she was going to remember everything and made the experience fun.

As a teacher who has studied NLP, Paola recognises two important things: pupils learn best when in a resourceful state; and all pupils have their own natural learning style.

A *resourceful state* is one in which you're able to be open, curious to learn, and able to access all the resources you need to solve any problem you're dealing with. The resources you access may be internal – such as your natural attributes of a desire to learn – or external – including other people or technical gadgets. In a resourceful state, you have a sense that you're behaving 'at cause' where you have choices, rather than 'at effect' where you feel powerless and that life is something being done to you.

In 'NLP-speak', the different channels through which humans represent or code information internally using their senses are known as the *representational systems,* also called the *modalities.* (In NLP, speaking about the visual modality is the equivalent of speaking of the visual representational system.) You can also hear NLPers talk about rep systems for short, VAK preferences, or preferred thinking styles. Visual, auditory, and kinaesthetic make up the main representational systems. The *submodalities* are the characteristics of each representational system, such as colour and brightness (visual), pitch and tone (auditory), and pressure and temperature (kinaesthetic).

The sensory-specific words (such as 'picture', 'word', 'feeling', 'smell', or 'taste') that we employ – whether they're nouns, verbs, or adjectives – are called the *predicates.* More examples of these predicates are given in Table 6-1, which you can find in the later section 'Building rapport through words'.

Hearing how people are thinking

Human beings naturally blend a rich and heady mix of the VAK dimensions, and yet people tend to have a preference for one modality over the others.

How do you decide whether you or others have a preference for the visual, auditory, or kinaesthetic dimension? To discover more about your primary modality, try out the following fun quiz on yourself and with friends and colleagues – we don't claim that the test's scientific, but it takes only a couple of minutes to do:

1. **For each of the following statements, circle the option that best describes you.**

    1) I make important decisions based on:

    a) Following my gut feelings

    b) The options that sound best

    c) What looks right to me

    2) When I attend a meeting or presentation, I consider it successful when people have:

    a) Illustrated the key points clearly

    b) Articulated a sound argument

    c) Grasped the real issues

    3) People know when I'm having a good or bad day by:

    a) The way I dress and look

    b) The thoughts and feelings I share

    c) The tone of my voice

    4) If I have a disagreement, I'm most influenced by:

    a) The sound of the other person's voice

    b) How that person looks at me

    c) Connecting with that person's feelings

    5) I'm very aware of:

    a) The sounds and noises around me

    b) The touch of different clothes on my body

    c) The colours and shapes in my surroundings

2. Copy the letters of your preferred statements onto the following grid.

1a K	4a A
1b A	4b V
1c V	4c K
2a V	5a A
2b A	5b K
2c K	5c V
3a V	
3b K	
3c A	

3. Add up how many Vs, As, and Ks you got.

4. See how you did!

Did you get mainly V, A, or K, or was your total evenly mixed? Check your preferences below and see whether our explanations make any sense for you:

✔ **V – visual:** A visual preference may mean that you're able to see your way clearly, keep an eye on things, and take a long-term view. You may enjoy visual images, design, watching sport, and the symbols involved in studying physics, maths, or chemistry. You may need to live or work in an attractively designed environment.

✔ **A – auditory:** An auditory preference may mean that you're able to tune into new ideas, maintain harmonious relationships, and that you're happy to sound people out and listen to the opinions of others. You may enjoy music, drama, writing, speaking, and literature. You may be highly tuned into the sound levels in your environment.

✔ **K – kinaesthetic:** A kinaesthetic preference may mean that you're able to get to grips with new trends, keep a balance, and hold tight on to reality. You may enjoy contact sports, athletics, climbing, and working with materials – electronics, manufacturing, hairdressing, or construction. You may be sensitive to the textures and feel of your environment.

Within Britain and America, researchers estimate that visual is the dominant style for approximately 60 per cent of the population; which is hardly surprising given the daily bombardment of our visual senses.

Beware of labelling people as visuals, auditories, or kinaesthetics – a gross generalisation. Instead, think of people as having a preference or habitual behaviour in a particular context, rather than identities. Be mindful, too, that no one system is better or worse than any other. (You can't help but operate in all the different modes, even if this happens unconsciously.) The systems are simply different ways of taking in, processing, and outputting information, as you experience the world around you. After all, everyone's unique.

Listening to the World of Words

The notion of sensory awareness isn't new, and dates back at least to the days of the Ancient Greek philosopher Aristotle, who talked about the senses in his book *On The Soul*. The nineteenth century psychologist William James was the first to discuss the primacy of modalities, which NLP refers to as the visual, auditory and kinaesthetic representational systems (check out the earlier section 'Getting to Grips with the Senses').

In the early days of NLP, the founders Richard Bandler and John Grinder, became fascinated by how people used language in different ways. The whole NLP notion of modalities came out of their seminars and study groups when they identified patterns of speech linked to the VAK senses. People represent their experience through their senses, and so NLP came to call the senses representational systems (or modalities).

The representational systems are much more than information channels coming in through the eyes, ears, or hands. The term refers to a whole complex system of activity that includes input, processing, storage, retrieval, and then output.

For example, you may take in information through your eyes – such as the image of a favourite person's face – and mentally process that information, store it for the future, retrieve the memory of it the next time you're feeling a bit blue, and say to yourself 'Never mind, things will look better tomorrow.' All of this happens outside of your conscious awareness.

The everyday language that you use provides clues to your preferred representational system, the one that you've developed through your life. In order to enhance your own communication skills, listen to the types of words that people use, and ask yourself whether these words are visual, auditory, kinaesthetic, or neutral (not sensory-specific). You can find all sorts of clever clues as to what's going on inside people's heads, and whether they're more responsive to pictures, words, or sounds. You can then go on to note what kind of language gets you the best response from a particular person.

Building rapport through words

In our own training sessions, we often test out the method of representational systems and observe how easily and quickly groups with the same preferences can build rapport. Such people find that speaking to those who 'speak their language' is naturally easier.

So what can you do when you feel that you're speaking a 'different' language and the conversation is harder? Begin by listening more carefully and identifying other people's language preference. Then you're in a great position to adjust your language pattern so that it aligns with those around you and therefore build rapport through the similarity of your language pattern.

Table 6-1 lists some of the sensory-specific words and phrases – the VAK predicates mentioned in the earlier section 'Filtering reality' – that you hear people say. You can start to build up your own lists and notice which words you say or write frequently. When you have difficulty getting through to certain people, check whether you're stuck in a rut with your own language.

Table 6-1	VAK words and phrases	
Visual	*Auditory*	*Kinaesthetic*
Bright, blank, clear, colour, dim, focus, graphics, illuminate, insight, luminous, perspective, vision	Argue, ask, deaf, discuss, loud, harmony, melody, outspoken, question, resonate, say, shout, shrill, sing, tell, tone, utter, vocal, yell	Cold, bounce, exciting, feel, firm, flow, grasp, movement, pushy, solid, snap, touch, trample, weight
It looks like. . .	It sounds like. . .	It feels like. . .
A glimpse of reality	So you say	We reshaped the work
We looked after our interests	I heard it from his own lips	Moving through
This is a new way of seeing the world	Who's calling the tune?	It hit home
Now look here	Clear as a bell	Get a feel for it
This is clear cut	Important to ask me	Get to grips with
Sight for sore eyes	Word for word	Pain in the neck
Show me what you mean	We're on the same wavelength	Solid as a rock
Tunnel vision	Tune into this	Take it one step at a time
Appears as if. . .	Music to my ears	Driving an organisation
What a bright day	That strikes a chord	The pressure's on

A few olfactory and gustatory words also exist, such as the following: fragrant, fresh, juicy, odour, pungent, salty, smell, smoky, sour, spicy, sweet, and whiff.

Many words in your vocabulary don't have any link to the senses. These words are non-sensory, and because they're 'neutral' you neither connect nor disconnect with somebody else's modality. Neutral words include the following: analyse, answer, ask, choose, communicate, complex, educate, experience, favourite, imagine, learn, question, remember, transform, think, understand, use, and wonder.

Rich or digital?

In any walk of life, people develop their own shorthand style of language with co-workers, friends, and family. Listen to a group of doctors, teenagers, or builders; they have their own way of getting the message across quickly and efficiently.

Speaking from personal experience, we can safely generalise that many business people, and especially those who work in the IT industry, stay highly tuned into their own digital style of language. Surrounded by logical technology they forget how to put any sensory-specific language into their communication (until they discover NLP, of course!).

Communication issues arise for any group of people when they step outside their peer group.

All too often, corporate-speak sends people to sleep. Just contrast the average script of a *Death by Powerpoint* presentation in corporations across the globe with the inspired 'I Have a Dream' speech of Martin Luther King, and you soon see why so many executives power nap in front of their laptops in the afternoons.

The solution lies in passion. When people live their passion and want to share it with the world, they naturally engage all their senses and this reality is reflected in the words they speak. If you analyse the speeches of Barack Obama or Winston Churchill, or the narration from a TV series by world-renowned naturalist David Attenborough, you notice the richness and use of sensory-specific words in their speech.

When people's thoughts and words are highly logical, conceptual, and devoid of sensory language, NLP calls this style *digital processing*. Documents from insurance companies are typical of digital language, as in the following example: 'The obligation to provide this information continues up to the time that there is a completed contract of insurance. Failure to do so entitles the Underwriters, if they so wish, to avoid the contract of insurance from inception and so enables them to repudiate liability.'

Bringing on the translators

Two people can sometimes struggle to communicate, despite sharing similar viewpoints, because they speak with different language styles. One may use an auditory style, for example, and another a visual or kinaesthetic style. To be an effective communicator, you need to be able to do two things: know your own preferred style or modality and also practise using other ones.

Have you ever heard a dispute that goes something like the following one between a manager and a team member in the office? To demonstrate the different language styles, we show the predicates (the sensory-specific words and expressions) in italics:

Manager: (Betty) 'I can't *see* your point of *view* about your appraisal' (visual).

Employee: (Bill) 'Well, can we *talk* about it further?' (auditory).

Betty: 'It's perfectly *clear* to me – just *black and white*' (visual).

Bill: 'If you would discuss it, it may be more harmonious around here' (auditory).

Betty: 'Just have a *closer look*. I'm sure you'll get a better *perspective*' (visual).

Bill: 'You never *listen*, do you? End of *conversation*' (auditory).

Betty, the manager, stays with visual language, and the employee, Bill, is stuck in auditory mode: they're disconnected and not making progress.

Here's how a third person – maybe Bob from human resources or another department – can help to shift the dispute:

> **1. Bob sums up the situation in *visual* mode to Betty and *auditory* mode to Bill.** The conversation goes something like:
>
> 'So, Betty, it looks like you have a *clear picture* of the situation (visual). And Bill, you've still got some important questions to *talk through* (auditory).' (Heads nod in agreement.)
>
> **2. Then Bob shifts into the third system (kinaesthetic), which is neutral ground for both arguing parties.**
>
> 'You both want to *get this moving* and *off the agenda*. So how about we all *kick around the stumbling blocks* for an hour in my office, *reshape* the problem, and finally *put it to bed*.'

One of our colleagues, Helen, was a touch sceptical about the language differences when she first became curious about NLP. Yet she experienced one of those wonderful light-bulb moments when she first discovered her own representational systems and decided to play with them at home before trying them out in her business life. She noticed how her husband, Peter, sometimes switched off and seemed uninterested when she wanted to talk about important decisions at home. She wondered whether changing the words she used would have any effect.

Helen says that: 'I'd be ready to talk to him about pretty major issues such as which schools the girls should go to or whether we should go ahead and spend thousands of pounds on redesigning the kitchen, and all I'd get was a cursory "Yup, fine" or "No, not now." I realised that having a strong kinaesthetic preference, I often began a conversation with: "Peter, how do you *feel* about XYZ?" I also noticed that he used plenty of visual language. So I thought I'd give it a go and ask him: "Peter, how do you *see* XYZ?" The difference, when I began playing with it and slipping more visual words into the conversation, was quite staggering. The change was so easy to make and, hey presto, I got his attention. It was almost magical!'

NLP suggests that everyone has the capacity to develop their sensory representational systems, by simply moving their bodies or turning off the mobile phone to see what's going on around them.

As with any system, making a change in one part causes an effect elsewhere, and that change begins by paying attention to what's happening around you.

Acknowledging the Importance of the Eyes

Body language offers wonderful clues to people's preferred representational systems. How they breathe, stand, move, their tone of voice, and tempo of speaking all tend to vary according to visual, auditory, and kinaesthetic styles. In particular, in the early days of NLP, Bandler and Grinder observed that people move their eyes in systematic directions depending on which modality they're accessing. These movements are called *eye-accessing cues*.

Therefore, when people move their eyes in response to a question, you can pretty much guess whether they're accessing pictures, sounds, or feelings. Why is noticing these movements helpful, you may wonder? The answer is that you have a great chance of knowing, even without them uttering a word, which system they're going to use and how you can talk to them in a way that makes them respond positively to you. Table 6-2 outlines what eye movements are associated with which modality.

Table 6-2	Accessing cues		
Pattern	*Eyes move to the subject's*	*What's happening inside*	*Sample of language*
Visual constructed	Top right	Seeing new or different images	Think of an elephant covered in pink icing
Visual remembered	Top left	Seeing images seen before	Think of your partner's face
Visual	Blank stare ahead	Seeing either new or old images	See what's important
Auditory constructed	Centre right	Hearing new or different sounds	Listen to the sound of your name backwards

(continued)

Table 6-2 *(continued)*

Pattern	Eyes move to the subject's	What's happening inside	Sample of language
Auditory remembered	Centre left	Remembering sounds heard before	Hear your own doorbell ring
Auditory internal dialogue	Bottom left	Talking to oneself	Ask yourself what you want
Kinaesthetic	Bottom right	Feelings, emotions, sense of touch	Notice the temperature of your toes

Figure 6-1 shows the kind of processing that most people do when they move their eyes in a particular direction. A small percentage of the population, including about half of all left-handers, are reversed – their eye movements are the mirror image of those shown.

The illustration in Figure 6-1 is drawn as if you're looking at someone else's face and shows how you see their eyes move. So, for example, if they're moving up and to your right into the *visual remembered* position, your own eyes would be shifting up and to your left if you're trying it out on yourself in a mirror.

By developing your sensory awareness – spotting those little details – you can become more attuned to how people may be thinking at different times. When you know this information, you can select your words so that they listen to you.

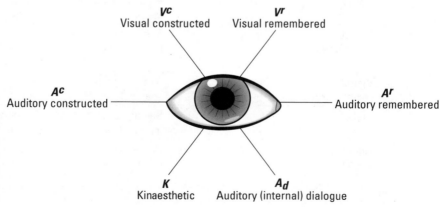

Figure 6-1:
Eye-accessing cues.

The telltale signs of a liar

How well do you think you can spot a liar? You may believe that you're totally clued up and can see instinctively when someone's fibbing, but numerous scientific studies over the last 30 years show that most people can only guess when someone is telling little white lies. Indeed, people can even be duped by the most outrageous untruths.

Years of research by Paul Ekman, world-respected for his studies of emotions, reveal that the secret lies hidden in our micro-expressions. Some 42 different muscles move in a person's face to create thousands of different micro-expressions. These expressions change all the time in all sorts of subtle ways. So subtle, in fact, that if you can discover how to focus and catch these superfast movements, you have all the information you need to spot the liars.

The trouble is that with so many possibilities, any human being has difficulty registering the discrepancies that show a false emotion – a lie. Even the latest generation of machines can't read these expressions right all the time. So who can accurately pick out the naughty tricksters? Ekman's research rates the star performers as members of the US Secret Service, prison inmates, and a Tibetan Buddhist monk.

You would expect Secret Service agents to be highly trained to spot dangerous suspects, and prisoners live in an environment of people experienced in crime and deception, and they need to distinguish who to trust in order to survive. Meanwhile, Ekman's Buddhist subject had none of these life experiences, but had spent thousands of hours meditating, and appeared to have the sensitivity to read other people's emotions very accurately from their fleeting facial expressions.

In this exercise, your aim is to notice how people's eyes move so that you can calibrate them and decide whether they're thinking in pictures, sounds, or feelings. Find a willing friend, and then use the instructions, questions, and diagrams on the Eye Movements Game sheet in Figure 6-2. Each statement on this game sheet is phrased to engage with the senses – in the past or future. Follow these steps:

1. **Get your friend to think about something neutral so that you can check what their face looks like in a neutral state.**

   Washing up or sock-sorting may be a pretty safe and mundane subject to suggest.

2. **State one instruction or question at a time from the Eye Movements Game sheet. As you do so, pay full attention to their eyes.**

3. **Pencil in arrows on Figure 6-2 to record the direction in which your friend's eyes move.**

   Your arrow marks should match up with the positions on the eye-accessing cues (shown in the earlier Figure 6-1, in the 'Acknowledging the Importance of the Eyes' section), so that they move to top, centre, or lower positions, and to the left or the right. When you've recorded your friend's eye movements, see whether their eyes go to the position that you expect based on the eye-accessing cue pattern outlined in Table 6-2 (in the earlier section 'Acknowledging the Importance of the Eyes').

Eye Movements Game

1. What does the Queen of England look like on TV?

2. What do you see when you wake up in the morning?

3. Picture a pink elephant.

4. A circle fills a triangle; how many shapes are there?

5. Remember the sound of a car horn.

6. What are the first words you said today?

7. Imagine Donald Duck saying your name and address.

8. What do you say to yourself when you've made a silly mistake?

9. How hot do you like the water when you take a shower?

10. What is the sensation of crumbs of food in your bed?

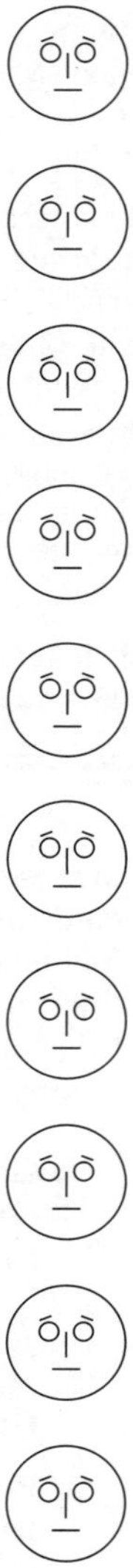

Figure 6-2:
The Eye
Movements
Game sheet.

Making the VAK System Work for You

When you become aware of the VAK dimensions (which we describe in the earlier section 'Filtering reality'), life becomes more interesting. Here are some ideas on how you can pull this technique out of your new toolkit and use it to your advantage:

- ✔ **Influencing a business meeting, training session, or presentation.** Remember that when you speak to a room full of people they all have a preference for how they take in information and you don't know what that is. Unfortunately, people don't have a label on their foreheads to inform you about what they want to know and how they want to receive it – give me the picture, tell me the words, share your feelings about this subject. So, you need to ensure that you connect with each and every person in the room by presenting your ideas with a variety of media. Vary your presenting style and aids to help the visuals see the information with pictures, the auditories to hear it loud and clear, and the kinaesthetics to experience it with feeling.

- ✔ **Making home projects fun for all.** Recognise that each family member has a different way of thinking about a major project. Perhaps you want to extend the house, redecorate a room, or redesign the garden. Not everybody wants to spend hours talking it through, with discussions that stretch late into the night. Your partner may want to pore over the drawings, whereas your children are motivated by the chance to get stuck in and get their hands dirty with paint or earth.

- ✔ **Developing your goals so that they're more real for yourself.** When you set goals in your personal or professional life, they come alive if you use all your senses effectively. Think of what the goals look, sound, and feel like when you've achieved them and at every step along the way. NLPers get proficient at imagining all the fine details of their future experiences – you may hear the phrase 'putting up a movie screen' to describe how people can create their own dream. Therefore, if you want to motivate someone (or yourself) to push out of their comfort zones, help them to explore what things may look like when the task is complete and the hard work done.

- ✔ **Helping children to learn better.** Thank goodness education has changed dramatically since we were at school, and teachers now recognise that pupils learn in different ways. As parents and/or teachers, you need to support children to understand how they learn at their best – and appreciate that the method may be different to the way you were taught or prefer to learn. Visual learners benefit from pictures, wall displays, and diagrams. Auditory learners need to hear what they're learning – through discussions, lectures, and music. Kinaesthetic learners benefit from practical sessions and role playing: they prefer a 'hands-on' approach. Teachers of groups of pupils need to provide a multi-sensory approach that caters for all styles. Children may be labelled as 'slow' when in fact the dominant teaching style doesn't fit with their preferred way of learning. All these principles apply to adult learners, too.

✔ **Increasing the impact of the written word.** When you put pen to paper and words to screen – from a job description, to customer proposal, charity letter, product advertisement, or article for your local community newsletter – you need to broaden your vocabulary to cover all the representational systems. To appeal to every reader, select words that include all three dimensions.

✔ **Connecting with clients and colleagues on the phone.** Nowadays more and more business happens on the phone and through email rather than face-to-face. You may never get to meet some of your clients or colleagues. Keep a pad by the phone and make a note of the kind of language they use – can you hear visual, auditory, or kinaesthetic language? As you listen, and then reply, phrase your sentences to match their preference.

Focus on one sense a day

While reading this chapter, you may have become more curious about yourself and those with whom you spend time – how you and they think and experience life. To enhance your skills further, you can explore your senses in different ways, for example, picking a sense theme for each day.

Perhaps you can make today an olfactory day, when you pay attention to every fragrance, smell, and aroma. Or a visual day, when you switch off the music and focus on the sights, shapes, and pictures – really see what's around you. A touch day can be fun, when you feel the surrounding textures or get in touch with your feelings at regular points in the day.

If you're a creature of habit who takes the dog for a walk every morning or drives the same route every day, notice what changes for you when you pay attention to just one sense at a time.

Chapter 7

Creating Rapport

● ●

● ●

Rapport sits at the heart of NLP as a central pillar, or essential ingredient, which leads to successful communication between two individuals or groups of people. Rapport is a mutually respectful way of being with others and a way of doing business at all times. You don't need to like people to build rapport with them. Also, rapport isn't a technique that you turn on and off at will, but something that should flow constantly between people.

Rapport is like money: you realise that you have a problem only when you don't have enough of it. The first rule of communication is to establish rapport before expecting anyone to listen to you. And this rule applies to everybody and in every situation, whether you're a teacher, pupil, spouse, friend, waitress, taxi-driver, coach, doctor, therapist, or business executive.

Don't kid yourself that you can pull rapport instantly out of the bag for a particular meeting, conversation or problem-solving session. True rapport is based on an instinctive sense of trust and integrity. This chapter helps you to spot situations when you do (and don't) have rapport with another person. We share some special NLP tools and ideas to enable you to build rapport and encourage you to do so with people where it may prove valuable for you.

Knowing Why Rapport Is Important

The word rapport derives from the French verb *rapporter*, translated as 'to return or bring back'. The English dictionary definition is 'a sympathetic relationship or understanding': rapport is about making a two-way connection. You know that you've made such a connection when you experience a genuine sense of trust and respect with another person, when you engage comfortably with someone no matter how different the two of you are, and when you know that you're listening and being listened to.

Although you may want to spend your time with people who are just like you, the world is full of a huge variety of different types of people to meet, all with special skills, opinions, and backgrounds. Rapport is the key to success and influence in both your personal and professional life, because it's about appreciating and working with differences. Rapport makes getting things done much easier and allows you to provide good customer service to others and enjoy being on the receiving end of it, too. Ultimately, rapport preserves your time, money, and energy. What a great stress-free way to live!

Recognising rapport when you see it

You can't take a magic pill to acquire rapport instantly; it's something you develop intuitively. So, in order for you to understand how you personally build rapport and what's important to you in different relationships, carry out the following steps:

1. **Think for a moment about someone with whom you have rapport.**

   What signals do you send out to that person and receive back that allow you to know that you're on the same wavelength? How do you create and maintain your rapport?

2. **Think for a moment about someone with whom you don't have rapport, but would like to.**

   What signals do you send out to that person and receive back that allow you to know that you're not on the same wavelength? What gets in the way of creating and maintaining rapport with that person?

3. **Think about your experience of the first person.**

   What can you do differently in your behaviour with the second person to help you build a stronger relationship?

You may think that the first person (with whom you have rapport) is simply easy to get on with and the second (with whom you share no rapport yet) is just a difficult person. Yet, by being more flexible in your behaviour and in your thoughts about the second person, you may find that you can build rapport through some simple actions.

Is anyone in?

Do you ever meet a new group of people and then forget their names almost immediately. Your intention is to concentrate and yet you find yourself losing focus. Or perhaps you say good morning to your colleagues and don't have time to look them in the face.

Robert Dilts tells the story of a West African tribe and the way they greet each other:

Person A says: 'I see you [name].'

Person B replies: 'I'm here. I see you [name].'

Person A replies: 'I'm here.'

Try this approach with a friend who's willing to play! It just takes a few seconds longer than 'Hi there, mate' or 'Morning!' and has the effect of making you concentrate on that other person and make a genuine connection.

You need to take time to get to know people and what's important to them instead of expecting people to adapt to you and your style. Throughout this chapter we provide tips for doing just that.

Identifying people with whom you want to build rapport

By now you may be getting curious about the people around you – those with whom you work, share a home, or socialise. Perhaps you want to get to know some key individuals better, such as the manager of a project or your new partner's family. Maybe you want to influence your bank manager, or the recruiter at that all-important job interview.

Below we provide a template to help you think about anyone with whom you desire better rapport. We ask you to write down your ideas to make you stop and think, and so that you can come back to revisit your notes at a future date. Good relationships take serious investment – time to build and nurture. You can see that the questions require you to think about your needs and those of the other person. Rapport is a two-way street.

Sometimes you have limited information about the intended person. If so, use this situation as your prompt to go out and do your research. Get curious about what makes that person tick, and who can help you find the information you need. Maybe you have a friend or colleague in common that you can identify with the help of a social networking site such as Facebook or LinkedIn.

Name: _____

Company/group: _____

What's your relationship to this person?_____

Specifically, how would you like your relationship with this person to change?
_____
_____

What impact would this change have on you?_____
_____
_____

What impact would this change have on the other person?_____
_____
_____

Is the change worth investing time and energy?_____
_____
_____

What pressures does this person face?_____
_____
_____

What's most important to the person right now?_____
_____
_____

Who do you know that you can talk to who has successfully built rapport with this person? And what can you discover from this other person?
_____
_____

What other help can you get to build rapport?_____
_____
_____

What ideas do you have now for moving this relationship forward?
_____
_____

What's the first step?_____
_____
_____

When rapport really matters

Fast-moving businesses breed stressful working conditions. Take the frenetic world of advertising: highly competitive, new young teams, artistic temperaments, large budgets, and crazy deadlines. In an industry in which people frequently work all night, mistakes are bound to happen.

In advertising agencies from London to Sydney, you can be certain that a number of client problems are brewing at any one time. Media, such as newspapers and magazines, appear on the desks of executives the world over, and what happens when your client's advertisement from last week's issue appears in place of this week's new message? All too often, anxious calls fly back and forth across the airwaves when the wrong ad appears in the newspapers, artwork goes astray, and computers crash mysteriously taking with them the latest version of an important design.

One of our advertising friends once produced a customer magazine for a corporate client in which some of the main photographs appeared in black and white: they should have been in colour. In a hurry, he hadn't checked the proofs carefully. When the print was delivered, he called the client, confessed the error, apologised, and took full responsibility for a costly mistake. As he worked for his own agency, he knew that if he had to pay for the reprint, the bill for several thousands of pounds would come straight out of his own profits.

At the other end of the phone, the young corporate marketing executive's first reaction on hearing of the error was that the whole job would have to be reprinted; she'd discuss it with her boss and get back to him.

Within an hour, the client called back to say that her boss's reaction was that it was a genuine mistake. Because of the good working relationship, the company would accept the job and let it go out. The boss had remembered the times when our friend had gone beyond the call of duty to respond at the weekend and late in the evening, so that the client achieved a product launch on time. The boss also valued the time he'd taken to understand the company's business, plus the advice and experience he'd shared on using budgets wisely.

And what's the moral of the story? Simply that investing time in building the right relationships is just as worthwhile as getting the job done.

Having Basic Techniques for Building Rapport

Having rapport as the foundation for any relationship means that when tough issues arise, you can more easily discuss them, find solutions, and move on. Fortunately, you can find out how to develop rapport.

Rapport happens at many levels and you can build rapport constantly through the following:

- The places and people you spend time with
- The way you look, sound, and behave

✔ The skills you develop

✔ The values you live by

✔ Your beliefs

✔ Your purpose in life

✔ Being true to your natural identity

Sharpening your rapport with eight quick tips

For starters, try the following immediate ways to begin building rapport:

✔ Take a genuine interest in getting to know what's important to other people. Start to understand them instead of expecting them to understand you first.

✔ Pick up on the key words, favourite phrases, and manner of speaking that an individual uses and build these aspects subtly into your own conversation.

✔ Notice how a person likes to handle information: lots of details or just the big picture? As you speak, feed back information in this same portion size.

✔ Check how a person uses the representation systems with visual, auditory, and kinaesthetic language (which you can read more about in Chapter 6), and use similar words during your conversations.

✔ Breathe in unison with the person. You can do this discreetly by watching their neck and chest to see when they inhale and exhale, and then matching your breathing to the other person.

✔ Look out for someone's overall intention – the person's underlying aim – as opposed to the exact things done or said. People may not always get it right, but work on the assumption that people's hearts lie in the right place.

✔ Adopt a similar stance to another person in terms of your body language, gestures, voice tone, and speed of talking.

✔ Respect people's time, energy, friends and favourite associates, and money. These items are important resources for you.

The next four sections contain some more advanced rapport-building techniques.

Viewing the communication wheel and developing rapport

Classic research by Professor Mehrabian of the University of California at Los Angeles (UCLA) looked at how people receive and respond to live communication. He suggests that when an incongruity exists between what you say and how you say it, 7 per cent of the message is conveyed through your words, 38 per cent comes through the quality of your voice, and a massive 55 per cent comes through gestures, expression, and posture (check out Figure 7-1).

Although opinion is divided on the actual percentages, most researchers are in agreement that messages aren't just conveyed in words, but that the tone of your voice and body language has a strong impact. If you've ever heard people say that 'everything's fine' when clearly they aren't well, you know that the impact of what you see in the other person influences you more than the words spoken.

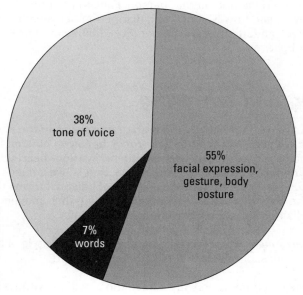

Figure 7-1:
The impact of your communication.

(Pie chart labels: 38% tone of voice; 55% facial expression, gesture, body posture; 7% words)

Clearly, first impressions count. Do you arrive for meetings and appointments appearing hot and harassed or cool and collected? When you begin to talk, do you mumble your words in a low whisper to the floor or gaze directly and confidently at your audience before speaking out loud and clear?

In terms of building rapport – *you* are the message. And you need your words, image, and speech all working in harmony. If you don't look confident – in other words, as if you believe in your message – people aren't going to listen to what you're saying.

Rapport involves being able to see eye-to-eye with other people, connecting on their wavelength. A large percentage of the perception of your sincerity comes not from what you say but how you say it, and how you show an appreciation for the other person's thoughts and feelings.

When you have rapport with someone, you can each disagree with what the other says while still relating respectfully to each other. The important point is to acknowledge other people as the unique individuals that they are. For example, you may well have different political or religious views from your colleagues or clients, but you don't need to fall out about it. People prefer all sorts of different foods to eat for supper, and yet you manage to agree to differ with your family on that point.

Hold on to the fact that you simply differ from the person's opinion and that this difference is no reflection on that person. Flick to Chapter 11 to read about logical levels and how NLP makes a distinction between beliefs and values at one level, and identity at a higher level. People are more than what they say, do, or believe.

Matching and mirroring

When you're out and about in bars and restaurants (or even the staff cafeteria, if you're lucky enough to get meals at work), have you noticed how two people look when a rapport exists between them? Without hearing the details of the conversation, you can see that the interaction is like a dance: people naturally move in step with each other. A sense of unison informs their body language and the way they talk – elegantly dovetailing their movements and speech. NLP calls this situation matching and mirroring.

Matching and mirroring is when you take on someone else's style of behaviour and their skills, values, or beliefs in order to create rapport.

In contrast, think of a time when you've been the unwilling witness to an embarrassingly public argument between a couple, or a parent and child, in the street or supermarket: not quite a punch-up, but almost. Even with the volume turned off, you soon notice when people are totally out of sync with each other, just from their body posture and gestures. NLP calls this situation *mismatching*.

When rapport helps you say 'no'

Perhaps you're one of those people who prefer to say 'yes' to everything, to be helpful and pleasing to the boss, clients, and family. You're the first person to put your hand up in committee meetings, the one who organises the school jumble sale or charity dinner, who drives the kids around, and you're always the one who ends up having to do the tasks. Discovering how to say 'no' sometimes is one of the greatest skills for modern living, if you're to protect yourself from being overloaded and then becoming sick with the stress.

At work, a manager can easily be tempted to ask the willing worker to take on more. Consider James's story.

As a maths teacher who loves his job, James was finding it increasingly hard to say: 'I'm not going to take that on.' He felt he was letting people down by saying 'no' and was in danger of making himself seriously ill through overwork. He discovered that by simply matching the body language of his head of department, he was more easily able to smile and say very politely: 'I'd love to do that, but my time is already fully committed. If you want me to take on extra responsibility, you must decide what you'd like me to stop doing to make time for this.' In this way he refused to take on a greater load than he was able to handle.

Matching and mirroring are ways of becoming highly tuned to how someone else is thinking and experiencing the world: it's a way of listening with your whole body. Simple mirroring happens naturally when you have rapport.

NLP suggests that you can also deliberately match and mirror someone to build rapport until it becomes natural. To do so, you need to match the following:

✔ Body postures and gestures

✔ Breathing rates

✔ Rhythm of movement and energy levels

✔ Voice tonality (how you sound) and speed of speech

Beware of the fine line between moving in rhythm with someone and mimicry. People instinctively know when you're making fun of them or being insincere. If you decide you want to check out mirroring for yourself, do so gradually in no-risk situations or with strangers you aren't going to see again. Don't be surprised though if it works and the strangers want to become your friends!

Pacing to lead other people successfully

Building great relationships requires that you pace other people. As a metaphor, NLP compares pacing people with running alongside a train. If you try to jump straight on to a moving train, you're likely to fall off. In order to jump on a moving train, you need to gather speed by racing alongside it until you're moving at the same speed, before you can jump.

In order to lead people – to influence them with your point of view – remember to pace them first. This approach means really listening to them, fully acknowledging them, truly understanding where they're coming from, and being patient about it.

To build rapport NLP advises you to pace, pace, and pace again before you lead. Pacing is how NLP describes your flexibility to pick up and match, respectfully, other people's behaviours and vocabulary, and where you actively listen to the other person. Leading is when you attempt to get the other person to change by subtly taking that person in a new direction.

In business, companies that succeed in introducing major change programmes do so in measured steps, allowing employees to accept changes gradually. People are unwilling to be led to new ways of working until they have first been listened to and acknowledged (that is, paced). The most effective leaders are those who pace the reality of their people's experience first.

When you watch effective salespeople in action you can see how they master the art of pacing the customer and demonstrate genuine interest. (By effective, we're thinking of those who sell a genuine product with integrity rather than the shark approach.) They listen, listen, and listen some more about what the customer's needs are – what the person really wants – before trying to sell anything. People resent being sold to, but they love to be listened to and to talk about what's important to them. An antiques dealer friend has perfected this art over many years, gently guiding his customers through his genuine affection for the articles he sells from his own home, and sharing his expertise.

When Kate bought a family car several years ago, she went to six different showrooms where salespeople rushed to sell the virtues of their car without showing any interest in how it fitted in with her lifestyle. At the time she had a young family and went on long trips with the children in the car.

The salesperson who was successful displayed superb interpersonal skills and presented a practical, family estate car. He paced Kate well, listening carefully, treating her with respect (unlike those who assumed the buying decision would be made by her husband), and trusted her with the keys so she was able to take it for a spin immediately. As she drove along, he gently gathered the information he needed to match the right model of car to her buying criteria, realising she wasn't going to accept a hard direct sell. Within half an hour she bought the car and became a firm advocate of the brand and the garage.

Building rapport in virtual communication

Twenty years ago, the Internet and email tools were confined to research labs and computer geeks. Regular business transactions involved cheques, letters, and faxes, mostly filed in hard copy: jumping in the car to visit suppliers and colleagues was all part of a day's work. Today, life's different. Of course, people still write and phone – the paperless office remains elusive – but the percentage of electronic transactions has shot through the roof. People are tweeting, blogging, and managing their lives online. If you lose your computer connection or have no access to email, you can feel lost and helpless very quickly.

Virtual teams who hold virtual meetings haven't just entered the workplace; you're as likely to join teleconferences for sharing information and speaking to social groups. People are comfortable with the virtual management of multi-cultural project teams that sit across global networks and work remotely thanks to technology – conference calls, email and videoconferencing. Expecting to get to manage our finances online or through an international support system is the norm, instead of seeing local bank staff or postal workers.

In this environment of reduced face-to-face contact, you lose the nuances of facial expressions, the body language, and the subtlety of getting to know the colleague at the next desk as you work closely with others. At its best, the virtual team spells freedom and flexibility of working practices, diversity, and a richness of skills: at its worst, it's lonely, isolated, and ineffective.

The challenge of building rapport through virtual working is now greater than ever. Little wonder that people are being recruited more for soft skills – the ability to influence and negotiate – than for technical competence.

Here are ten ways to develop rapport over the phone and in teleconferences:

- Make sure that all the locations are connected and can hear each other on the phone. Introduce and welcome people with a roll call.
- Work to a clear agenda. Set outcomes for the call and agree them with all participants.
- Check that you've had input from a mix of people. If necessary, encourage the quieter individuals to take part; say, for example, 'Mike, what are your thoughts on this?'
- Discourage small talk or separate chats at different sites: keep to one discussion, one meeting, one agenda.

✔ Speak more slowly and precisely than in face-to-face meetings. Remember you can't get clues from the body language.

✔ Listen for the style of language – check whether people have visual, auditory, or kinaesthetic preferences, and match your language style to theirs as we suggest in Chapter 6.

✔ Get attention before making your point (otherwise the first part of the message gets lost). Begin with phrases along the lines of 'I have something I'd like to mention here . . . it's about. . .'

✔ Use people's names more than in face-to-face meetings. Address questions to people by name and thank them for their contribution by name.

✔ Visualise the person at the other end of the phone line as you listen to the conversation (you may even like to have a photo of the person in front of you).

✔ Summarise and check your understanding of points and decisions continually.

Knowing How to Break Rapport and Why You May Want To

At times you may choose to *mismatch* people for a while in order to break rapport deliberately. Mismatching is the opposite of matching or mirroring (which we describe in the earlier section 'Matching and mirroring'). To mismatch someone, you aim to do something dissimilar to that person, such as dressing very differently, speaking in a different tone or at a different speed, adopting a different physical posture, or behaving quite differently from the other person.

We worked with a team of doctors who were suffering from an increase in patient workload due to the long-term sickness of one partner. In the initial assessments with them, we noticed how most of the meetings with patients were completed within the allotted one hour, and yet meetings with one partner took nearly twice as long. This particular doctor had a reputation for being especially kind and helpful with her patients; she topped the popularity bill in a patient survey. Indeed she is a great listener, and patients loved her approach. However, in order to get through her case load during normal surgery hours, she had to discover how to limit the time with each patient in a more disciplined way. She found a way to mismatch sensitively and get through her patient list.

Discovering how to break rapport sensitively

Three particular changes to your behaviour can enable you to break rapport in the short term:

- ✔ **How you look and move physically:** You can move physically away from someone, break eye contact, or use a facial expression to communicate your message. Raised eyebrows say a lot. Turning your back is even more powerful, so beware of doing this action inadvertently!

- ✔ **How you sound:** You can change your voice intonation or volume: make it louder or softer, high or low, and remember the power of silence.

- ✔ **The words you say:** Remember that useful little phrase, 'no, thank you'. Sometimes it can be the hardest to say, so practise for when you need it. In multi-cultural settings, switching to your native language when you've been working in a common language is another clear way of saying, 'I need a break now.'

You're going to want to say 'thank you' and 'goodbye for now' plenty of times. Notice which situations are easier for you to handle and those that need some practice:

- ✔ **You're closing a deal:** Salespeople momentarily break connection with a customer at the point of signing a contract. They walk away and leave the customer to look at the paperwork alone instead of becoming connected to that final signing in the customer's eyes. This approach helps to maintain rapport in the long term if a buyer's remorse sets in.

- ✔ **You have enough information:** Maybe your brain has filled up for the moment and you're heading into sensory overload. You want time to think and digest what you've heard and come back for the next instalment later.

- ✔ **You see someone else you want to talk to:** Perhaps you're at a drinks party and become stuck with the ultimate bore and someone much more attractive is at the other side of the room.

- ✔ **You're tired:** All good things come to an end, and you need to know when the time has come for the party to end and head home.

- ✔ **You're busy:** At any one time you're going to experience a number of demands on your energy. Focus and hold on to your own outcome rather than satisfying someone else's.

- ✔ **You're getting into tricky subject areas:** Sex, politics, and religion are all good subjects to avoid in a business negotiation. They also cause overly lively dinner-party conversations where you may want to blow the whistle, call time out, and agree to differ when discussions get heated.

Enough is enough

Ralph was a very competent engineer and a great storyteller. He'd travelled widely, met all the senior people in the corporation where he worked as they were climbing the ranks, and had had interesting jobs. All the newcomers in the team loved to hear his anecdotes and exploits at the coffee machine – for a while.

Unfortunately, Ralph didn't recognise the signs when people had heard enough. As colleagues were politely edging back to their desks or desperately trying to leave the building at night, Ralph would corner them and carry on with his stories oblivious to the bored stares or attempts to end the conversation. The more they tried to get away, the more he would become entrenched in the next episode: 'And let me

just tell you about. . .' You had the feeling that if you walked away and came back next year, he would just pick up where he'd left off.

In the end, team members began to avoid him. They joked about him behind his back because he refused to pick up the cues that he'd taken more than his acceptable slot. They stopped inviting him to meetings for fear he would dominate. His career progress suffered. Colleagues deliberately broke rapport, and in the end most contact, to protect their own time.

As Ralph became more and more ostracised from the team, he became more desperate to tell his stories and gather an audience around him.

Discovering how to break rapport and end a conversation is a real skill, particularly if your best friend or mother wants to chat. Do it with consideration. Give clear feedback that you'd love to talk so long as it's at the right time of day, place, and length of time. You care about them as a person, and so try and arrange a time to talk that suits you when work's over for the day.

Grasping the power of the word 'but'

Sometimes a tiny word can make a huge difference between your ability to keep rapport and break it. NLP pays attention to such details in the pattern of conversation and so offers some useful clues for you to influence communication. Work by Robert Dilts on sleight-of-mouth patterns has demonstrated the power of words to frame people's experience: NLP calls this *verbal reframing*. Even simple connective words such as 'and' or 'but' make listeners focus their attention in different ways. When you adopt the word 'but', people tend to remember what you say after it. With the word 'and', people tend to recall what you said before and after it. When you use the connection 'even though', the effect is to focus attention on the first statement, as in: '*It is snowing today* even though the weather men said it would be clear.' By changing the order of words in a sentence, you can change people's experience.

Be aware that when you make a comment to someone, that person may only notice part of what you say. Consider the following example: 'The company has returned £5 million profit this financial year, but we're closing the San Francisco operation.' If you phrase the news in this way, people may only remember what you said after the word 'but'. Now consider the following: 'The company has returned £5 million profit this financial year, and we're closing the San Francisco operation.' Phrased in this way, people may well remember what you said *before* and *after* the word 'and'.

Find out just how much difference little words can make in your daily communication with the 'Yes, but. . .' game for three or more players.

1. **Get your friends into a circle.**

2. **Round one starts with Person A offering 'a good idea'.** For example, 'It's a sunny day, how about we take the afternoon off and head out to the beach?'

3. **Person B replies 'Yes, but. . .', and offers another 'good idea' in return.** For example, 'Yes, but we have work to finish.'

4. **Person C and all the other players offer their ideas in turn, always starting with 'Yes, but. . .'.** For example, 'Yes, but we'll miss lunch.'

5. **Round two continues with Person A offering a good idea; it can be the same as in round one or a different idea.** For example, 'It's a sunny day, how about we take the afternoon off and head off to take a walk by the river?'

6. **Person B replies 'Yes, and. . .', and offers another 'good idea' in return.** For example, 'Yes, and we can have a picnic on the way.'

7. **Person C and all the other players offer their ideas in turn, always starting with 'Yes, and. . .'.** For example, 'Yes, and I'll check the footpath map.'

Notice the difference? In spite of the instruction to come up with a good idea, the use of the word 'but' seems to naturally lead the conversation to a negative place and detract from the original good idea. By contrast, the word 'and' builds one good idea upon another.

Understanding Other Points of View

Successful people enjoy the flexibility of being able to see the world in different ways. They take multiple perspectives, enabling themselves to explore new ideas. NLP offers various techniques to help people build rapport in very challenging relationships, especially where some kind of emotional conflict is happening. These techniques are also used to explore new ways of building rapport, even in relationships that are only mildly troublesome or confusing.

Exploring perceptual positions

One of the ways that NLP helps you to build rapport with others is by distinguishing at least three different points of view. NLP calls these *perceptual positions*. This approach is rather like looking at a building from all angles – coming in at the front entrance, moving round to the back door, and then looking down with a bird's eye view from a helicopter overhead:

- ✓ **The first position** is your own natural perspective, where you're fully aware of what you think and feel regardless of those around you. This position can be one of strength – when you're really clear about what you want and your own beliefs and values – but also one of incredible selfishness, until you consciously become aware of what other people want.

- ✓ **The second position** is about shifting into someone else's shoes – imagining what a situation looks like for them. You may already be really good at always considering the needs of others: for example, mothers rapidly develop this skill in caring for new offspring. You put someone else's view first.

- ✓ **The third position** involves taking an independent view, where you act as a detached observer noticing what's happening in the relationship. At its best, this position is one of maturity from where you appreciate a situation from both sides. Sometimes, however, it can mean that you're reluctant to engage fully in a situation – you merely sit on the fence.

Mastering all three perspectives puts you in a wise place that allows you to enjoy life more fully.

Get into the habit of mentally shifting your thinking into the second and third positions when you're in conversation.

Looking into the NLP meta-mirror

The meta-mirror is an exercise, originally developed by Robert Dilts, which allows you to bring together a number of different perspectives or perceptual positions. The basis of the meta-mirror is the idea that the problem or conflict you face is more a reflection of you, and how you relate to yourself, than about the other person. The meta-mirror approach allows you to step back and see the problem you're facing in a new light – hence the idea of the mirror.

The meta-mirror helps you to prepare for, or review, a number of possible scenarios:

- ✔ Difficult conversations with a teenager or family member
- ✔ Presentations at work
- ✔ Meetings with your bank manager
- ✔ Contract negotiations
- ✔ Sensitive discussions with a partner or friend
- ✔ Ways of relating to your boss or a colleague at work
- ✔ Methods of dealing with difficult clients

William was having his house rebuilt, and he was finding that the builder wasn't keeping to schedule, because he was working on a number of jobs at the same time. As he found his anger rising at this poor service, Kate led William through the three perceptual positions to plan a difficult meeting with the builder, instead of igniting the showdown that seemed inevitable as the conflict escalated.

William recognised that the builder had serious cash-flow issues and was going through a difficult time with his family. 'The exercise made me just stop and think that he wasn't deliberately messing me about. So, I took him out for a beer, explained how dissatisfied I was feeling, and we agreed a tighter schedule of stages in the build where I would release money in smaller amounts as work was completed. This arrangement turned the situation around for both of us and saved court action.'

The following exercise takes four perceptual positions. You may like to try it with the assistance of a coach or friend to help you concentrate on the process so that you work only with your issues.

To start, choose a relationship you want to explore. Perhaps you want to gain some insight into a difficult conversation or confrontation, in the past or the future. Lay out four spaces on the floor to denote four positions (as Figure 7-2 shows): pieces of paper or sticky notes are fine. Note that you must 'break state' between each position by physically moving between each space. Just shake your body a little, or look out of the window and think about what you're going to have for supper tonight!

1. **Stand in the *first position*, your point of view, imagining that you're looking at the other person in the second position.**

   Ask yourself: 'What am I experiencing, thinking, and feeling as I look at this person?'

2. **Now shake that off and go to stand in the *second position*, imagining that you're the person looking back at yourself in the first position.**

   Ask yourself: 'What am I experiencing, thinking, and feeling as I look at this person?'

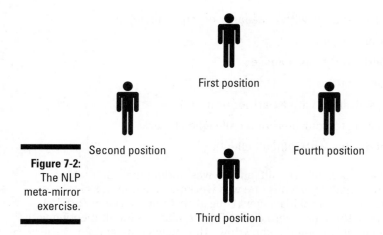

First position

Second position

Fourth position

Figure 7-2:
The NLP
meta-mirror
exercise.

Third position

3. **Now shake that off and stand in the *third position*, that of the independent observer viewing both people in this relationship impartially.**

   Looking at yourself in the first position, how do you respond to that 'you'?

4. **Now shake that off and stand in a further external space, the *fourth position*.**

   Think about how your thoughts in the third position compared with your reactions in the first position and switch them around. For example, in the first position you may have felt confused, whereas in the third position you may have felt sadness. Whatever your reactions, in your mind's eye switch them to the opposite positions.

5. **Go back and revisit the *second position*.**

   Ask yourself 'How is this different now? What's changed?'

6. **Finish by coming home to the *first position*.**

   Ask yourself: 'How is this different now? What's changed?'

Although doing these exercises can seem very strange at first, do persist. When you move *physically* into a different space, considering the different perspectives is important. Simply by moving your body to another place in the room, you unlock the thinking of the previous position. You can also do these exercises by moving between different chairs.

In NLP circles, resistance is often cited as a lack of rapport. For example, somebody may resist your attempts to get to know them better by being stand-offish and excluding you from a conversation. Or, you may resist making the effort to connect with someone who appears different from you. If you find yourself in situations where you don't always have the rapport with people that would be useful, you may need to try the following:

✔ Recognise that you're unconsciously resisting the people or the situation in which you find yourself, or that somebody else is resisting you.

✔ Consider what the reason for this may be, remembering that the unconscious mind is naturally protecting you (see Chapter 3).

✔ Refine your rapport building skills by deliberately matching, mirroring and pacing the other person until they are willing to connect with you.

Overcoming your resistance to developing rapport with someone can take some time, because you have to examine your past to understand your defensive behaviour. You may need the help of a coach or friend to gain this understanding: for example, you may have real justification for your doubts about getting too close to someone. When you discover the reason for your own resistance, you can give yourself permission to develop the rapport that you're seeking.

Chapter 8

Understanding to Be Understood: Meta Programs

*I*n 1956, George Miller carried out research on the millions of bits of data that bombard the senses of humans every second. He discovered that the conscious mind can handle only between five and nine pieces of information at any one time, which means that an awful lot of information is filtered out.

Meta programs are some of these unconscious filters that direct what you pay attention to, the way you process any information you receive, and how you then communicate it.

When you want to build rapport with someone quickly and you're forearmed, you may choose to dress, behave, or at least speak like that person. And by the latter we don't mean that you mimic someone's accent, but instead that you use the person's vocabulary. When you begin to hear other people's meta programs, you have the choice of using the same words and phrases as the person with whom you're interacting. Because people use meta programs mostly unconsciously, when you match their meta programs, what you say has the added dimension of communicating with their unconscious mind simultaneously with their conscious mind.

In this chapter we introduce you to seven meta programs that help you to communicate more effectively and more quickly; and as you experience the benefits of better communication, we hope that you're motivated to discover more about other meta programs.

Getting to Grips with Meta-Program Basics

As children, you pick up meta programs from your parents, teachers, and the culture in which you're raised. Your life experiences may change these learned programs as you get older. For instance, if you grow up being admonished for being too subjective, you may start practising detachment and learn to suppress your feelings. You can find that these attributes then affect your choice of career. Instead of entering a caring profession you may decide to use your intellect more. Your learning style may be influenced too, and you lean towards focusing more on facts and figures. If you deliver training, you may depend more on drier, chalk-and-talk systems than on getting students involved with touchy-feely experiments.

Of the many identified meta programs, we choose seven that we think are the most useful to get you started. For example, we select the *global and detail* meta program because we believe that it has great potential for conflict, and by recognising another's capacity for operating at the global or detailed end of the scale, you may be able to avoid possible problems. By understanding the other six meta programs, you can develop a greater insight into the subtle ways in which people think, which gives you the tools to influence and facilitate change by motivating not only yourself but other people too.

In Chapter 5 you can find a discussion of the introvert and extrovert meta program. The meta programs discussed in this chapter are as follows:

- Proactive/reactive
- Options/procedures
- Toward/away from
- Internal/external
- Global/detail
- Sameness/difference
- Time perspective

As you think about meta programs, keep these things in mind:

- Meta programs aren't an either/or choice. You operate meta programs all the time; however, depending on the context in which you find yourself, you focus more on one aspect of particular meta programs.

- Meta programs aren't a means to pigeonhole people; they're useful to expand your understanding of the variety of ways in which people think in order to improve communication.

- Meta programs aren't right or wrong; you simply run various combinations of meta programs depending on the context of the communication and the environment in which you find yourself.

Looking at meta programs and language patterns

If you're able to pick up on people's language, you can discover their patterns of behaviour long before the behaviour becomes apparent. Leslie Cameron-Bandler, among others, conducted further research into the meta programs developed by Richard Bandler. She and her student, Rodger Bailey, established that people who use similar language patterns portray similar patterns of behaviour. For example, people with an entrepreneurial flare may have similar patterns – outgoing, good at persuading people, strong belief in themselves, and so on – even though they may work in very different fields.

Imagine a gathering of the heads of the United Nations without any translators: very little communication would take place. A similar breakdown in communication can occur if you're unaware of the meta programs being employed by the person with whom you're trying to communicate. Learning about meta programs allows you to become proficient in translating the mental maps that people use to navigate their way around their experiences.

NLP pioneers, Bandler and Grinder, realised that people who use similar language patterns develop deeper rapport more quickly than people who use dissimilar ones. No doubt you've heard some non-French speakers complain that the French are unfriendly. Others who can speak French refute this opinion. Meta programs are a powerful way to establish rapport verbally by hearing the patterns that people are running and then responding with language that they can understand easily.

To help you understand the type of language that's characteristic of the various meta programs, we include in the following sections phrases that you're likely to hear with each meta program.

Exploring meta programs and behaviour

In the *Encyclopedia of Systemic NLP and NLP New Coding*, Robert Dilts and Judith DeLozier explain meta programs in terms of two people with the same decision-making strategies getting different results when presented with the same information. For example, although both people may make a picture of the data in their heads, one person may become completely overwhelmed with the amount of information while the other reaches a quick decision based on the feelings the pictures produce. (You can find out more about how people process the information they receive through their senses in Chapters 6 and 10). The difference lies in the meta programs that each person is running, which impacts their decision-making strategy.

A short history of meta programs

Humans have been trying to understand personality types since time immemorial. Hippocrates defined four *temperaments* based on his observations of fluids in the human body as long ago as 400 BC. He called these temperaments melancholic, sanguine, choleric, and phlegmatic. Although the Hippocratic classifications fell by the wayside, others are used a great deal.

In 1921, Carl Jung published *Psychological Types*. This book was based on his work with several hundred psychiatric patients and was his attempt to categorise his patients in order to be able to predict their behaviour from their personality. Jung defined three pairs of categories in which one of each pair would be used in preference to the other:

- An *extrovert* is energised by interacting with the outside world, whereas an *introvert* recharges their batteries by taking time to be on their own.

- A *sensor* takes in information through the five senses, whereas an *intuitor* relies more on instincts and intuition to collect information.

- A *thinker* makes decisions based on logic and objective thinking, whereas a *feeler* makes decisions based on subjective values.

Jung's personality types form the basis of the *Myers–Briggs Type Indicator*, which is one of the most widely used profiling tools today. In the early 1940s, a mother (Katherine Briggs) and daughter (Isabel Briggs Myers) team added a fourth category: a *judger* attempts to make their environment adapt to suit themselves, whereas a *perceiver* tries to gain an understanding of the external world and adapt to fit into the world.

As George Bernard Shaw said, 'Reasonable people adapt themselves to the world. Unreasonable people attempt to adapt the world to themselves. All progress, therefore, depends on unreasonable people.'

Suppose that you want to emulate Richard Branson, the founder of the Virgin group of companies. You can do so the hard way by trying to implement the processes that you think he uses. Or, with his help, you can do so more quickly and easily by modelling him; and part of the modelling process requires that you understand and use his meta programs.

The later sections in this chapter describe the behaviours and preferences associated with the different meta programs that we offer you in this chapter. By being able to recognise the meta program that people are prone to operating in a given setting, you can begin to match people's meta programs in order to become more like them and get your message heard more easily. By trying on someone else's model of the world you may gain a different perspective and add to the options available to you in other areas of your life – an added bonus.

Being Proactive/Reactive

If you're more inclined to take action and get things moving, you operate at the *proactive* end of the scale. If, however, you're inclined to take stock and wait for things to happen, you're probably more *reactive*. Some more in-depth descriptions follow:

- **Proactive:** If you're proactive you take charge and get things done. You're good at spotting solutions to situations that require constant fire-fighting. You may find yourself drawn to jobs in sales or working for yourself. You find yourself upsetting some people, especially if they're more reactive, because they liken you to a bulldozer.

- **Reactive:** If you're more reactive you may be quite fatalistic. You wait for others to take the lead or you take action only when you consider the time to be right. You may need to be careful not to analyse yourself into a paralysis.

You can exhibit proactive or reactive tendencies, depending on the context within which you're working. Robert, although very good at his job, is quite reactive about asserting himself as regards requesting promotion and pay rises. He waits for his boss to offer, rather than ask for them. He prefers to wait for instructions before working on projects, rather than initiating work. However, he loves his holidays and is extremely proactive in visiting travel agents, talking to people, and surfing the Internet when planning his holidays.

You can spot the difference between a proactive and a reactive person by the body language. A proactive person is likely to have quicker movements, showing signs of impatience. These people are likely to hold themselves erect in a 'shoulders back, chest out' posture that's ready to take on the world. A reactive person displays slower movements and may keep their head down and shoulders slouched.

According to Shelle Rose Charvet, in her book *Words That Change Minds*, when advertising for a person who you want to be proactive, you should ask the candidate to telephone instead of sending a CV. As a general rule, reactive people are less likely to call.

To discover whether someone's proactive or reactive, you can ask: 'Do you find it easy to take action when you find yourself in a new situation, or do you need to study and understand what's going on first?'

- A proactive person uses phrases such as 'just do it', 'jump to it', 'go for it', 'run with it', 'take control', and 'hit the tarmac running'.

- A reactive person is more likely to use phrases such as, 'mull it over', 'take your time', 'study the data', 'weigh the pros and cons', and 'look before you leap'.

Proactive reaction to a reactive department

The information technology (IT) department at a university in south-east England was always fire-fighting, trying to provide a service for the bursar's and registrar's departments. The two departments that used the computer systems had no communication and the IT department didn't trust the users enough to train them in the use of their systems. No documentation existed for which programs needed to be run and when. This situation had been in place for several years and was accepted as the norm. Guess what preference the staff in the IT department had? If you guessed reactive, you're right. Then a relative newcomer, with a more proactive bent, came to the department and instigated the following three simple steps:

✔ Created and maintained a list of tasks, containing operating instructions and when they were needed.

✔ Organised regular meetings between the registrar's and bursar's departments.

✔ Trained the administrative staff to produce their own reports.

These changes reduced the considerable stress that the staff of all three departments experienced, especially at peak times, and opened communication channels between the two departments using the computer systems. The self-esteem of the administrative staff really soared as they took some responsibility for running their own systems.

Moving Towards/Away From

People invest time, energy, and resources moving towards or away from something that they find enjoyable or something they want to avoid. They use their values to judge whether an action is good or bad and whether the result they get gives them pleasure or pain.

Can you remember the last time you started an exercise regime or began a new diet? Perhaps you were all fired up and eager to start, and consequently you made terrific progress: your weight began to come down and you felt so much better because of the exercise. Suddenly, though, you lost your momentum, the weight stopped going down, or worse still, started creeping up. The visits to the gym became more sporadic. As things started to go downhill you got all fired up again until. . . . You were caught in a roller coaster of being motivated and losing your focus.

'What happened?' you cry in despair. Chances are that where your health is concerned you have an *away from* meta program, which means that you're propelled to take action to get away from something, in this case weight or perhaps lethargy. Figure 8-1 illustrates how someone whose motivation to health is primarily away from may have their weight loss yo-yo over a period of time.

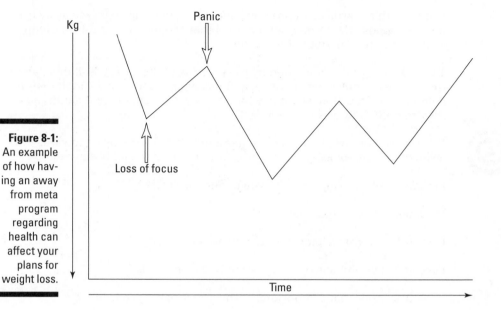

Figure 8-1:
An example
of how hav-
ing an away
from meta
program
regarding
health can
affect your
plans for
weight loss.

On the other hand, if you're drawn towards a goal, in a particular context, and are able to keep your eye on the ball, you're showing more of a *towards* propensity.

As a general rule, people move either away from or towards things. According to Sigmund Freud, your *id*, which represents your instinctive urges, moves you towards pleasure or away from pain.

Interestingly, different professions and cultures exhibit a bias for running towards or away from meta programs. Take the example of conventional medicine as opposed to alternative practices. Which preference do you think practitioners from the two camps may have? To give you a hint, conventional doctors refer to alternative medicine as 'preventative medicine'. In Romilla's assessment, conventional medicine is more prone to having an away from tendency with regards to health, the emphasis being more on curing the illness after it happens rather than on focusing on creating and maintaining good health.

People with away from patterns appear quite negative to those who run towards patterns.

Away from people have a tendency to notice what can go wrong and are very useful to employ for maintaining production plants and aircrafts, managing crises, or conducting critical analysis. These people are motivated more by the stick than the carrot. You can motivate away from people by threats of job losses and the negative consequences of not meeting financial targets.

People with towards meta programs may be seen as naïve by the away from people because the former don't always think about and cater for potential problems in the pursuit of their goals.

Towards people are motivated by the promise of the carrot. Tell them about the benefits of improving revenue and receiving a bonus and watch their eyes light up. This reaction isn't necessarily down to greed, but instead because they're excited by positive benefits.

You can find out whether a person has a preference for moving towards or away from something by a series of questions, as in the following example:

Person A: 'What's important to you about your work?'

Person B: 'I know I have security.'

Person A: 'So what's important to you about security?'

Person B: 'I don't have to worry about paying my bills.'

Person A: 'And what's important to you about paying your bills?'

Person B: 'It means I'm not in debt.'

Going to at least three levels of questions is useful because initially people may have a tendency to respond with something positive, which can hide their away from patterns. In the example above, the initial answer is towards security, although subsequent answers reveal an away from preference.

When selling a product, research the customer's language patterns. You can then elicit whether the person wants to buy the product in order to gain a benefit – such as buying a sports car in which they can have fun and feel the excitement of whizzing along with the sun roof down and the wind blowing through their hair – or to avoid a problem – for example, when buying a safe, solid family car with a focus on keeping their family safe from harm. Modify your language accordingly to save time and get results.

You move away from or towards your values. If moving away from values are not serving you, you may decide to change them. If sports at school were a painful experience and consequently sports days a humiliation, you may have problems keeping up an exercise routine. One way of releasing the emotions invested in negative memories is through Time Line Therapy® (which we discuss more in Chapter 13).

  ✔ A person with more of a towards meta program uses words such as 'accomplish', 'get', 'obtain', 'have', 'achieve', 'attain', and 'include'.

  ✔ A person who operates a more away from meta program uses words such as 'avoid', 'remove', 'prevent', 'get rid of', and 'solution'.

Discovering Options/Procedures

If you're more of an *options* person, you enjoy trying out new ways of doing things. As a *procedures* person, you display a preference for following set methodologies.

An options person loves variety. The analogy that springs to mind is that of offering a gourmet a smorgasbord or dim sum, and letting the person pick and savour the myriad delicacies on offer.

If you're a person with a preference for an options meta program, you are good at starting projects, although you may not always see them through. You're good at setting up procedures, just as long as you're not the one who's expected to follow them! Because of your penchant for testing new ways, you're unable to resist improving the most rigorously tried and tested methods or of finding some way to bend that company rule.

Don't ask options people to drive, unless you want to see the sights: they like to take a different route each time. Romilla always allows plenty of time to get somewhere new because she has a tendency for getting lost. When she gets to her destination without losing her way, she feels cheated.

Heaven help you if you're proposing to an options person! Even if the options person loves you to bits, you may have a hard time getting commitment, because options people worry about getting hemmed in, missing out on experiences, and so on. To get options people to say 'yes' to you, you need to show them all the opportunities that open up for them if they do assent.

If you have a procedures preference, you like to follow set rules and procedures, although you may prefer to have these created for you rather than design them yourself.

When you have a working procedure, you follow it repeatedly, without modification. You may feel compelled to follow each step of a procedure to the end and feel cheated if circumstances prevent you from doing so. You stick to speed limits and take personal affront when other drivers drive along using a mobile phone or with only one hand on the steering wheel.

Romilla really understood the difference between the two preferences when she was learning the healing technique of *Huna* in Hawaii. Two of her group of three wanted to sit out under the trees, by a large pond, overlooking the ocean, to work on an exercise and experiment. Richard, the third person, became extremely distressed and was ready to storm off and find another group to work with: he needed to be in the same environment where the exercise had been demonstrated and to conduct it in exactly the way he'd been shown.

You can find out which of the two preferences a person has in a given context by asking, 'Why did you choose this job?', 'Why did you choose to come to this party?', or 'Why did you choose your particular car?'

Options people may give you a list of their values that were satisfied by choosing the job, attending the party, or buying the car. You may hear their reasons for making the choice and the possibilities that the choice opens up for them.

Procedures people launch into a story or list the steps that got them the job, how they got to the party, or chose the car. For instance:

> *My Ford Puma was seven years old and I needed to change it. I bought car magazines for a few months and studied the pros and cons of comparative makes but in the end it was knowing that I'd only need to have the car serviced every 16,000 kilometres that made me decide on this make.*

✔ You may hear someone with a mainly options meta program use words and phrases such as 'play it by ear', 'bend the rules', 'possibilities', 'let's play with this', and 'try this other ways'.

✔ You may hear someone mainly at the procedures end of the scale using expressions such as 'follow the steps', 'obey the rules', 'step by step', and words like 'first', 'second (and so on)', and 'finally'.

Delving Into the Internal/External

If you trust your judgement when making decisions or knowing that you've done a good job, you operate at the *internal* end of the scale for this meta program.

If you need feedback from other people to know how well you've done, you probably have more of an *external* preference.

The crux of this meta program is whether the location for motivating yourself, judging your actions, and making decisions lies within you or with other people.

Children have an external frame of reference, which develops as they absorb the conscious and unconscious teachings of their parents and teachers. Maturity, however, usually shifts this reference point to becoming a more internal one, as you gain greater understanding of yourself and therefore trust your judgements and decisions more.

A similar transition can occur when you learn something new. You may have more of an external reference at first, needing other people to tell you how well you're doing. Experience and knowledge can then shift the reference to internal.

You have a propensity for working at the internal end of the scale, in a given context, when you question the negative feedback you receive, even if several people have said more or less the same thing. You don't need to be praised for doing a good job because you already know that you did well.

People who tend towards the internal may do well as entrepreneurs, because they don't have to wait for someone else to tell them what to do or how well they're doing it.

Bosses, if they have an internal frame of reference, need to remember to give feedback to their staff, who may have an external frame of reference and be craving praise and wanting to be told how they're doing.

If you have an external bent, however, you need to receive feedback from other people to know how you're doing and to keep yourself motivated.

Unless they explain the need for the outcomes they want in a job, internal employees may prove difficult to manage, particularly if your management style is to micro-manage. They want to do things their way and operate from their own standards. External people, on the other hand, are easier to manage as long as you understand that they do need direction and praise.

To find out where on the scale a person is, ask the following: 'How do you know you've done a good job, bought the right car, made the right decision?' An internal person may respond with 'I just know when I've done a good job', whereas an external person may respond 'My family really like the car.'

- ✔ When speaking to a person who operates from an internal frame of reference, you may gain greater leverage if you use phrases such as 'only you can be the judge', 'it's entirely up to you', 'see for yourself', and 'study the facts to help you decide'.

- ✔ When talking to someone who's more externally referenced, you may get a better response by using phrases such as 'the statistics/studies show. . .', 'they'll approve', 'the expert opinion is', and 'this has sold really well'.

Going Global or Detailed

When they start work on a project or are setting a goal, some people find that seeing the big picture is easy. Others find that getting such a global perspective is difficult, but they more easily envisage the steps required to achieve the goals, and so they prefer to work with smaller details.

Chunk size refers to the scale of a task with which a person prefers to work. A person with a *global* preference breaks tasks into larger chunks than a *detail* person, who needs to have a task chunked down into smaller, more manageable steps.

If you prefer to work at a global or conceptual level and have trouble dealing with details, you prefer a big-picture outline of what you're about to be taught when you learn something new. If your presenter launches straight into the details of the subject, you may have difficulty in understanding the new topic. You see the forest easily enough but get confused by the mass of trees. If you prefer working globally, that is, with the big picture, you may find yourself switching off or getting impatient with the amount of information that a detail-inclined presenter may give you.

When training other people, give an overview of the course before going on to talk about the specifics, to avoid losing the globally inclined people before you even get started.

If, on the other hand, you prefer eating the elephant a bite at a time, you have a predisposition for handling details. You may find that sharing the vision of someone who thinks globally is difficult. Detail people handle information in sequential steps and may have trouble getting their priorities right, because they're unable to make the more general connections to other areas within which they're working. These people are very good in jobs that require close attention to detail, especially over a period of time, for instance on an assembly line or conducting a test in a laboratory.

Detail people have a tendency to dive straight into working on a task without looking at the impact of the steps on the final, desired goal. As a result, they may not meet the actual goal or they may see the goal only after a great deal of time and energy has been spent following the steps getting to the wrong goal.

When Romilla worked in IT, weekly meetings at one multinational company were interesting to say the least. The manager was a global person and one of the programmers always gave him his progress in minute detail. The rest of the team had great difficulty in keeping a straight face when the manager's face went through its contortions of not understanding, boredom, and blatant irritation, until he would snap at one of the project leaders, 'Explain what he means.' Fortunately, the project leader was somewhere in the middle of the chunk-size range and was able to translate the details for the manager. The poor programmer sweated buckets before the meetings and his stress levels rose unbearably prior to them.

If the programmer had known the reason for his miscommunication with his boss, he might have reverse-engineered his work. Instead of talking about the code he was writing, he could have spoken, briefly, about the results his work was producing and how it was affecting the project of which the manager was in charge.

Fight, flight, freeze, and procrastination

Along with fight and flight, freezing is part of the stress mechanism. An impala caught by a cheetah goes into a state of hyper-arousal and freezes. The survival response behind this mechanism is to make the cheetah believe the impala is dead, thereby giving the impala an opportunity for escape if the cheetah stows it away for later consumption. The other reason for this survival response is that the impala doesn't feel the pain of being torn apart if the cheetah decides on an immediate feast.

Procrastination is the human equivalent of a freeze response. Are you in the habit of procrastinating? It may be that you're taking on too much and just don't know where to start.

When you're procrastinating over a particular task, the problem may be that you're overwhelmed by the size of the job to be done. Use the following process to break the task into manageable chunks:

1. **Stop!**

   If you're not already paralysed into inaction, that is.

2. **Fetch some paper and a pen.**

3. **Sit down and make a list.**

   Think about, and write down, what's really important to you.

4. **Rearrange the list in order of importance.**

   You may want to transfer some of the points to another list of actions.

5. **Get cracking!**

To discover where on the scale between global and detail someone is, ask about a recently completed project. A detail person gives a step-by-step account, for example:

> *Jim and I met for lunch on the second Tuesday last July. I remember having to ask Jim a lot of questions because he kept jumping all over the place and I had to keep him focused on each step. I was very nervous at first but felt much happier when we'd spent time on capturing all the information in a project plan.*

A global person presents things randomly, summarising the outcome, for example:

> *Tom and I met for lunch last year sometime and decided to work on building the animal sanctuary. It's really important to focus on the biodiversity. I really think people need help managing their circumstances, don't you?*

✔ A person who has a tendency to operate from a global perspective responds to words such as 'overview', 'the big picture', 'in a nutshell', 'generally', and 'essentially'.

✔ A person at the detail end of the spectrum listens better to someone using words such as 'plan', 'precisely', 'schedule, 'specifically', 'first', 'second', 'third' (and so on), 'next', and 'before'.

Recognising Sameness, Sameness with Difference, and Difference

If, when you learn or experience something new, you try and match the information to what you already know, you have a preference for *sameness*. Or, you may be someone who first notices the similarities in situations and becomes aware of the differences, in which case you have a *sameness with difference* preference.

If, however, you look at what's different from what you already know, you prefer sorting by *difference*.

As a sameness person, you have a head start as regards rapport (which we describe in Chapter 7), because rapport is all about matching someone else's physiology and thinking – probably something you do automatically. You tend to delete a lot of incoming information if you can't spot the similarities to previous situations. You may have difficulty in learning something new unless you can find patterns with which you're familiar. For example, learning a new language is easier when you can find similarities with a language you already know; Dutch may be easier for an English speaker than, perhaps, Korean. You don't like change, or even feel threatened by it, and find that adapting to changes in your work and home life is difficult. As a general rule, you dislike initiating major changes, preferring to avoid major change and procrastinate about making changes in your life when a situation gets really difficult. This means that you probably move house or change jobs very infrequently.

As a sameness with difference person, you first look for similarities in a situation and then tend to spot the differences. You like the evolutionary approach to change, preferring infrequent major changes and you may resist sudden change. In order to gain greater rapport with these people, try to emphasise things that are the same, followed by what's different, for example, 'The work is fairly similar to what you've done, however you're going to be involved with implementing new solutions.'

If you have a sameness with difference preference, you find learning new things easier than a person with a sameness preference does, but find learning new things difficult unless you can find familiar hooks on which to hang new information.

If you have a preference for a difference meta program, you thrive on change. You love a revolution in your life, thrive on frequent change, and create change for the sake of change. As with sameness people, you too have a tendency to delete vast amounts of data, except that in your case you delete information in which you can't spot the differences. Some people may find you difficult because of your tendency to always see the other side of the coin. You love learning new things, but fairly superficially, unless you have a real need to go into real depth. You have an easy rapport with other people who find focusing on differences easier, but you have to make a conscious effort to find things in common when talking to people who have more sameness or sameness with difference preferences.

One of Romilla's close family members sorts by differences. Until she discovered NLP, communications between Romilla and her family member were difficult, to say the least. Now Romilla really values his input. When working on a new project, she does all the brainstorming with friends and other family members. When she's worked out a fairly solid idea, she approaches her difference-inclined relative who can identify the omissions and problems that the brainstormers overlooked. This process saves a lot of time that would otherwise be wasted in trial and error.

To uncover a person's preferred meta program in a given context, ask about the relationship between their current job and a previous one.

A person who sorts for sameness may respond, 'There's no difference, I'm still writing programs.'

A person who runs a sameness-with-difference meta program may respond, 'I'm still writing programs for the accounting suite, but now I have the responsibility of supervising three junior programmers.'

The difference person may respond, 'I've been promoted to supervise junior programmers and everything is different.'

Ask someone the relationship between the rectangles shown in Figure 8-2. Each rectangle is the same size, but don't reveal this fact before asking the person.

A person who's operating a sameness meta program may say, 'They're all rectangles,' or 'The rectangles are the same size.'

A person who runs a sameness-with-difference meta program may respond, 'They're all rectangles but one is positioned vertically.'

A person who has a difference meta program is likely to say, 'They're laid out differently.'

Figure 8-2:
The same-
ness/
sameness
with dif-
ference/
difference
game.

If you don't have rectangles, bar mats, or coasters, use three one-pound coins and place two with their heads up and one with the tail up and ask about the relationship between the three coins.

- People with a preference for sameness use words such as 'same', 'similar', 'in common', 'as always', 'static', 'unaltered', 'as good as', and 'identical'.

- People who operate from a sameness-with-difference base use words and phrases such as 'the same except', 'better', 'improve', 'gradual', 'increase', 'evolutionary', 'less', 'although', and 'same but the difference is. . .'.

- People who operate at the difference end of the spectrum use words and phrases such as 'chalk and cheese', 'different', 'altered', 'changed', 'revolutionary', 'completely new', and 'no comparison'. To connect with them, use these phrases and others such as, 'I don't know if you agree or not. . .'

Tackling Time Perspectives

We show you in Chapter 13 that your memories have a structure and that they're in some form of a continuum: a time line linking past, present, and future. In this section, you discover that another dimension exists to the way you think about time; whether you have a propensity for focusing more on the past, present, or future. In his book, *The Time Paradox*, Philip Zimbardo explains how something that's mostly unconscious – your focus on time – has a huge influence on your life: it affects the way you make decisions and the options that you think are available to you, without your even being aware of it (as we describe in Table 8-1).

Table 8-1	Pros and Cons of Past, Present, and Future Focus	
Focus on	*Pros*	*Cons*
Past	People who remember their past positively have an appreciation of history and tradition. They have a strong positive identity, and strong foundations of patterns of behaviour and of values and beliefs.	People who focus on negative past memories may carry a lot of regret and anger, and feel less optimistic about the results they expect, and therefore get, in life; they may be afraid to make decisions because of possible damaging consequences.
Present	People who focus on the present can concentrate on the task at hand and get on with the job.	People who are too present-orientated don't learn from past mistakes in their headlong rush to complete a job and move on, and they may not make time to plan for a happy future.
Future	People who focus on the future, but in moderation, plan and are reasonably hopeful, and therefore, optimistic.	People who are always thinking of the future have a tendency to rush through life, ready for the next experience but miss out on the treasures that are to be savoured by stopping and taking stock of the good around them.

You can spot someone's time preference by listening for the verb tense they use. For example, a past-focused person may use phrases such as 'remember', 'when I was younger', 'things were better then', and 'if only I had. . .'. Someone whose focus is on the future may say 'when . . .' and 'I will. . .'. People who focus on the present adopt the present tense and talk about what's around them, for example, 'this is the way it is . . .' and 'what's happening is this'. To influence people, adapt your language to match the tense they're more prone to using.

When a time focus conflict happens in marriage

Although in very well-paid jobs, John and Sandra never seemed able to live within their means, and lived from day to day. They didn't budget, or plan for things like holidays, house moves, and what their lives would look like in five years. Money was always a bone of contention because it seemed to get frittered away on impulse buys. During a counselling session for couples, they realised that Sandra's focus was on the present while John was always dreaming about the wonderful house they would have, where they'd go on holidays, and so on, when they had the money. He had his sights set on the future. When the couple was made aware of the difference in their thinking, they decided, in the short term, to set targets for how they would budget and plan treats for themselves, even booking pretend dates. Setting small goals like this gave them practice for making bigger plans. They also gained confidence in managing their finances as they recognised they

could save money, but without having to give up things they enjoyed doing.

John still struggled to get Sandra to think beyond the month's plans. During the course of further counselling sessions, Sandra realised that the reason she 'lived for the day' was because her father had lost his business and she had witnessed him crying and saying to his wife, 'I thought I'd got it all planned, what's the use of planning?' The shock of seeing her strong Dad crying stunned Sandra and his words went straight into her unconscious, preventing her from making plans in her life. Sandra learnt that although nothing is set in stone, her unconscious memory of the past was stopping her from creating any sort of a comfortable future for herself and John. Although she still finds that trusting in the future is difficult, she's at least aware of her fears and doesn't put up barriers when John wants to make plans.

If someone is stuck in a past negative experience, agreeing with them is useful (without getting caught up in the drama of the story) because it allows you to lead them into a more positive state. Whereas, disagreeing from the start, before attaining a level of rapport, can lead to conflict that detracts from a favourable result.

The positive memories you create today are the positive memories that you can look back on tomorrow.

As with most things in life, the key to success is getting a balance. When you find yourself dwelling too much on the past, present, or future, make a conscious effort to shift your focus, until doing so becomes second nature.

If you have a tendency to focus more on past events or daydream about the future, and you want to enjoy your experiences of the present, train yourself to stop and take a really good look around your environment. Notice the people around you, the layout of a room, or what you see out of a window. Or, if you're outside, take a look at the space between the branches and leaves of the trees, the colour of the sky, the shapes of the clouds, and how doing so makes you feel inside.

Learning lessons from negative past events can help to release their hold on you. Chapter 13 shows you how to release negative emotions and limiting decisions.

Combining Meta Programs

You have a combination of meta programs that you prefer to adopt when you're within your comfort zone. Try to remember that this preference may change depending on the different circumstances in which you find yourself. For instance, a project manager may combine difference, proactive, detail, and toward preferences when at work, but choose to be more of a sameness, reactive, global person at home.

Also, realising that certain combinations of meta programs may fit certain professions better than others is important, as is understanding that many more meta programs are available that may be of use to you.

Would you want the pilot of your jumbo jet to have a high options, global, and difference meta program combination? You may well be a little nervous of being in the hands of someone who decides to skip a couple of the flight checks because the procedure is boring and seeing what happens if that red light flashes may be fun!

Would you want your prescription filled by a chemist who likes to test the result of adding a couple of extra drops of the pretty blue liquid to your angina medicine?

These examples are meant to illustrate that jobs work best when the profiles of people fit the parameters of their jobs. For instance, you may decide that the best meta program fit to fill the vacant position of a quality controller is for the person to have preferences for detail, away from, and procedures.

Developing Your Meta-Program Skills

Meta programs is one of the topics that excites the most interest in Romilla's workshops, probably because delegates realise the power of using the so-called right language: that is, the words and phrases that mean the most to the person with whom you're communicating. Using appropriate language allows you to build rapport and get your message heard better than someone who's not as skilled in the art of meta programs.

With this thought in mind, we invite you to develop your abilities by considering the following aspects:

✔ Can you identify the meta programs that you run in different areas of your life? This exercise can be particularly useful when you want to model a successful part of your life in order to improve another aspect of your life that isn't working as well.

If you find that you're better at planning your holidays than at progressing your career, is this discrepancy because you're more proactive, toward, and procedure focused when you come to plan your holiday, but you don't show these tendencies when thinking about your career? Do you feel like a very tiny cog in a very large wheel and hold yourself back from being proactive as regards your career? Perhaps you allow your boss to dictate your future, which may be due to past, negative memories (check out the earlier section 'Tackling Time Perspectives'). Working with a coach or therapist would allow you to take on-board the lessons from your past and focus on the future, in order to progress your career by putting a road map in place to follow.

Perhaps, after deciding your big career goal, you may need to be more procedure driven in order to define and attain the steps that get you there. You may also need to focus towards the goal and become more proactive in achieving it.

✔ If you're having problems with another person, perhaps you're at opposite ends of a meta-program scale. Can you identify the meta programs that you and the other person are using? For example, the global/detail meta programs can cause a lot of grief between people. If you talk about the global, big picture and the person with whom you're communicating is a details person, bite the bullet and chunk down (as we describe in the earlier section 'Going Global or Detailed'). Mismatched meta programs can result in a great deal of conflict and miscommunication. So make the effort to listen to the language that people are using and use their words when you're talking to them.

✔ If you're recruiting for a job, write down the traits for the ideal candidate when you've identified the roles and responsibilities inherent in the job. Ask yourself what questions you need to ask to establish how well an applicant fits the role, because employing the wrong person for a job can prove very costly. So, if you're employing a tax accountant you may decide that the person needs to be:

- *Proactive* to keep abreast of the changes in tax laws.

- *Procedure and detail driven* to implement the law to the letter.

- *External focused* to be receptive to the government's dictates.

- *Difference inclined* to spot any discrepancies in people's tax affairs.

Part III

Opening the Toolkit

The 5th Wave   By Rich Tennant

"Well, that's just great! We're this close to landing 'Godzilla – The Mini–Series' and you lose your emotional distance over syndication rights!"

In this part . . .

You encounter the core tools and techniques of NLP, which enable you to cope with difficult situations. In this action-packed part, you get more proficient with the tools, and are able to adapt your own thoughts and actions. From using anchoring techniques to travelling along your personal timeline, you discover the essentials that allow you to build your NLP repertoire for excellence. Roll up, roll up for a more compelling future!

Chapter 9

Dropping Anchors

I just don't know what came over me!' Are these familiar words? Ever had that feeling that your reactions to a situation have been way in excess of what was called for? Your feelings may have overtaken or even overwhelmed you. Perhaps you even say that you weren't quite yourself.

Everybody has emotional responses all the time: some are great – falling in love, joy, and pleasure – others less so – falling out of love, sadness, and pain. These experiences and feelings are what make life and work interesting and fun, as well as confusing and unpredictable. Often, in our work, we talk to managers who sigh and say if only their colleagues would leave their emotions at home. And at home, many people would prefer that their partners leave their workplace stresses at work.

Maybe you've witnessed situations when someone has 'blown a fuse' unexpectedly. Often this event happens at what, on the face of it, seems the slightest provocation. Most people can identify with the discomfort or agitation of being in a bit of a state. In fact, NLP uses the term *state* to mean to look at, and become more aware of, how you feel at any moment in time.

Taken to extremes, these feelings of being overwhelmed and being out-of-control can scare people. They can affect your career and your social life. People question whether such a person can be trusted in responsible situations or when they have to represent the company.

Fortunately, with the stabilising influence of the NLP toolkit, help is at hand to control yourself, your state at any one time, and how you affect other people. And when you discover how to do so, the effect is fantastic.

Starting Out With NLP Anchors

NLP tools that help you create positive states in yourself are known as *anchoring* techniques, based on the principle of a boat's anchor that provides stability in open water. NLP defines an *anchor* as an external stimulus that triggers a particular internal state or response.

People set anchors and respond to them all the time: for example, you know to stop your car at a red traffic light, and you find that certain foods get you licking your lips.

You may be wondering why anchors are helpful. The answer is that when you discover how to anchor, you can take all your positive experiences and memories and use them to deal with challenging situations more resourcefully.

The idea of anchoring in NLP came from modelling the techniques of the hypnotherapist Milton Erickson. Erickson often used cues as triggers to help people change their internal state. More recently, in the work of NLP co-creator John Grinder on NewCode NLP (see Chapter 1), a great emphasis is placed on getting both client and practitioner into positive states, such as a 'high-performance state' or a 'know-nothing state'.

From Twitmeyer to Pavlov, or how it all started

What the Russian psychologist Pavlov found out with his famous dog experiments was an early example of anchoring. Set a stimulus — food — and get a consistent response — salivation. Pair the sound of a bell — the conditioned stimulus — with placing the food in the dog's mouth, and soon the dog learns to respond to the bell.

Pavlov's less well-known colleague, Twitmeyer, was examining the human knee-jerk reflex in 1902, before Pavlov studied salivation in dogs. Twitmeyer took a hammer to the knee and had a bell that sounded when the hammer fell. Like so many discoveries in science, a single accidental change in an experiment leads to the most exciting breakthroughs. One day he rang the bell without dropping the hammer. And guess what? Yes, the subject's knee reacted to the sound of the bell alone.

Unfortunately for Twitmeyer, he was slightly ahead of his time and the medics of the day ignored his contribution to the science of *behaviourism* (the theory of personality that ignores the inner workings of the mind and focuses on how people are conditioned to respond to stimulation in their environment.) Fast-forward the story a couple of years to 1904 and Pavlov's work on dogs grabbed people's attention and won him the Nobel prize in Physiology.

Since then studies of animal behaviour have become increasingly more scientific and sophisticated. Every day you can read new research on the brain and increase your knowledge of human intelligence and behaviour.

Humans discover and develop behaviour in response to a stimulus: dolphins aren't the only ones who can learn amazing tricks! From conception, you're programmed to respond to certain stimuli, and you constantly move and change your state in response to your environment with an incredible flexibility of behaviour.

Setting an anchor and building yourself a resourceful state

Memories are stored as associations with the senses. Smells are particularly powerful anchors to times and events. So, for example, you smell a particular perfume and it transports you back to your first date and splashing on the cologne or aftershave. Or if you've ever been drunk on whisky, perhaps the smell of it alone is enough to make you feel nauseous. People create positive and negative anchors for themselves all the time.

NLP teachers suggest various techniques for how to set an anchor. Ian McDermott and Ian Shircore describe the following simple three-step NLP technique for taking control of your own state by establishing resourceful anchors:

1. **Get clear about the positive state you ideally want to be in.**

   Your positive state may be bold, witty, energetic, anticipatory, or enthusiastic. Be clear and specific in your own words to describe it.

2. **Recall a specific occasion in the past when you've been in that state.**

   You're looking for a comparable experience, even though the context can be very different.

3. **Relive the experience as vividly as you can.**

   Engage fully with the experience – the sights, sounds, smells, physical feelings, and internal sensations.

When you've followed these three steps and are in the highest positive state, that's the moment to set an anchor for yourself. Hand movements work well as a physical (kinaesthetic) anchor. Simply notice what your hands are doing as you engage with the experience and hold a distinct movement – such as a clenched grip, or thumb and first finger in a circle. (A handshake doesn't work because it's too mundane and habitual.) Alternatively, as an auditory anchor, listen for a sound. For those with a visual preference, create an image that symbolises the positive state.

A taste of the past: anchors in common usage

Just for a moment, look back to your very first day at school. Quietly listen for the sounds around you and how you feel to be in that new environment. Sounds and smells are particularly evocative in bringing back pictures of childhood memories – good and bad. Maybe some triggers still immediately remind you of school. What makes you recall memories of your school days? Possibly the smell of certain foods or a polished floor, the sight of a school trophy, or the sound of a bell signalling the end of lessons.

The smell of cardamom transports Romilla immediately back to her idyllic and colourful Indian childhood; yet, for Kate, merely hearing the words 'school custard' brings sights, sounds, and unpleasant tastes rushing back with a vengeance, along with anxious memories of the infant school dinner ladies forcing their charges to eat unwanted food.

If you work with adults in a training role, remember that some people had unhappy learning experiences in school, and in such cases you may come up against a natural sense of resistance. Luckily, with good teachers and trainers, most people discover how rewarding, and how much fun, continuing to learn as an adult can be, even if that wasn't their experience in childhood.

When you need to get back into a positive state, you simply fire the anchor for yourself as a stimulus to change your state. To do so, recreate the physical movement or remember the sound or image that you used as a trigger for the positive state. Another method for establishing resourceful anchors is the classic NLP exercise 'circle of excellence' described later in this chapter in the section 'Deploying stage anchors'.

Anchors need to have the following attributes:

- ✔ Distinctive – different from everyday movements, sounds, or pictures.

- ✔ Unique – special to you.

- ✔ Intense – set when you fully and vividly experience the peak of the state.

- ✔ Timely – catching the best moment to make the association.

- ✔ Reinforced – use it or you lose it; anchoring is a skill to develop with practice.

Accidentally establishing a *negative anchor* is all too easy. Take the situation, for example, where a highly stressed manager drives home from work at night and arrives at the house having had mobile phone conversations all the way from the office about work problems. As they walk in the door, their negative feelings about work peak to a high intensity. At that moment, their spouse comes and kisses them hello as they walk into the house. They may unintentionally connect their spouse kissing them with work worries, because anchors are established in this way. Then guess what? Their spouse kisses them, they begin to feel anxious, and yet don't know why.

Common sense suggests that you wouldn't deliberately set out to establish a negative anchor. So how can you avoid doing so? The key lies in recognising what triggers a negative response in you and realising that you have a choice in how you respond. If you get into the habit of responding negatively in certain situations, when you become aware of your reaction, you're in a position to decide whether that response is appropriate and helpful, or whether you want to make some changes.

Eliciting and calibrating states

Do you know when someone else is in a happy, positive state or not? What are the signals? When you meet someone and are building a relationship – socially or in business – knowing how to calibrate them is useful.

NLP defines *calibration* as the process of discovering how to read other people's responses. Good communicators learn how to heighten their skills of observation. Instead of guessing how somebody else is feeling, they notice and recognise the subtle cues and facial expressions of the people they mix with.

For example, if you know that your boss goes quiet and clenches their facial muscles when faced with a tough deadline, you're well advised to avoid a chatty social conversation when you spot those signs. Similarly, if you're negotiating a deal in business, take the time to get to know the people with whom you're negotiating. Friendly, social questions asked at the coffee machine or in the lift can help you calibrate people's body language and develop your awareness of their responses.

Try this quick game with a friend to calibrate their states. As you do so, notice the changes in their physiology – what happens to their facial movements and colour changes, as well as their body language:

1. **First notice their starting position – to check what your friend looks like in neutral.**

   To get the person into a neutral state, ask a mundane silly question like: 'What colour are your socks today?' or 'How many pens do you keep in your desk drawer?'

2. **Ask them to think for a minute about someone they really like, whose company they enjoy – paying attention to any pictures, sounds, or feelings that arise.**

   Give the person time to really get into the experience.

3. **Get your friend to stand up and shake that feeling out.**

   NLP calls this *breaking state*.

4. **Ask them to think for a minute about someone they really dislike, whose company they don't enjoy – paying attention to any pictures, sounds, or feelings that arise.**

5. **Observe your friend and compare the differences in their reaction to a positive and a negative experience.**

Some people may demonstrate a dramatic change in their body language, whereas for others the differences may be so subtle that you're hard pressed to spot them.

An NLP presupposition goes as follows: people can't *not* communicate. Like it or not, you're continually influencing other people. Just by a look or a word, you have the skill to elicit states in other people and in yourself, and it happens so easily – just by being yourself and doing what you do, with no conscious effort.

When somebody, such as a boss, parent, teacher, or partner, praises you, tells you off, or expresses joy or disappointment, you recognise that they use a particular tone of voice. Well, your own tone of voice also acts as an anchor. Varying your tone of voice is a way to change other people's states. Try out this technique when you want to change the state of an audience or an individual person you're talking to – sometimes you may need to be animated, at other times authoritative, calm, or restful.

Developing your own repertoire of anchors

One great way to work with NLP concepts is to find optimal states for yourself: simply put, the best way for you to be yourself. The idea is to develop this ability in the same way that you may acquire a repertoire of tennis or golf shots. To start, ask yourself what may be the best way for you to do the following:

- ✔ Learn effectively
- ✔ Perform at your best
- ✔ Relate to other people

Remember times in the past when you've been particularly successful in these areas. What was going on for you at the time? Where were you, who were you with, what were you doing at the time that was helpful? What was important to you?

Build a range of visual, auditory, and kinaesthetic anchors that make you feel good about yourself and other people. You may want to enlist the help of a friend and work with each other on this project.

Recognising your own anchors

What are the triggers, the stimuli, that affect you most at home or work? Make a note in the chart shown in Figure 9-1 so that you begin to become aware of the times you're feeling good and when you feel less good. Your aim is to concentrate more on your positive experiences and change or let go of the negatives.

Figure 9-1:
A personal anchor chart:
V = visual;
A = auditory;
K = kinaes-thetic;
O = olfac-tory; and
G = gusta-tory.

	AT HOME		AT WORK	
	Good	Bad	Good	Bad
V-Sights				
A-Sounds				
K-Touch/feelings				
O-Smells				
G-Tastes				

Take some time to record details of different experiences that make you feel good or bad. These experiences can be seemingly insignificant everyday events and are bound to be very individual.

You may feel good at home at the sight of a log fire or a vase of tulips on the table, the sound of your favourite CD, or the smell of a hot meal on the kitchen stove. Equally, the sight of your computer on a tidy desk, the buzz of people, or the smell of a steaming hot drink may welcome you to work in the mornings.

Alternatively, if you get angry when someone turns the TV up loud, or another email or piece of paper plops into your in-tray, you may need to find some strategies to switch the negatives into positives. Only when you identify what you do and don't like, can you start steering the minute details of your daily experience in the best direction for you.

We've organised the chart in Figure 9-1 by the different senses (head to Chapter 6 for more on these modalities). Here are some anchors to notice:

- ✔ **Visual** – pictures, colours, decoration

- ✔ **Auditory** – music, voices, birdsong, sounds

- ✔ **Kinaesthetic** – textures, feel of the physical elements, emotional vibes

✔ **Olfactory** – smells, chemicals, scents

✔ **Gustatory** – tastes, food, drink

Return to this framework every few weeks or so to help you get more of what gives you pleasure. If you have a dominant sense – for example, more visual anchors than auditory ones – check whether you're missing out and filtering information unnecessarily.

Your anchors are going to change over time. As you concentrate more and more on the things that give you pleasure, you may begin to notice that those that upset you become less relevant over time.

Here's an exercise that you may want to turn into a healthy daily habit. As you go through every day, pick out five events or experiences that have given you pleasure. Keep a private notebook of what's going well for you. Often, the small things are what make the difference – a pleasant conversation, a kind gesture, the smell of a bakery, or the sun breaking through the clouds. When you're feeling under pressure, refer to your notebook, and ensure that you spend at least part of every day on the important things that matter to you.

Going Through the Emotions: Sequencing States

Think back to yesterday. As you review the events of the day, ask yourself how you felt at different times. Were you in the same state all day? Unlikely. Just as with a temperature gauge, you may have blown hot or cold or experienced all the dimensions on the scale: you may have been cool and calm, warm and interested, hot and excited, plus any number of degrees of permutations along the way.

Humans are blessed with behavioural flexibility and the wonderful ability to change state. In fact, you need to shift states. If you operate on a constant high, you soon become exhausted. Peak performers have to be able to switch off and regenerate, recharging the batteries. Otherwise they suffer burn-out. During a presentation, for example, varying the pace and rhythm is important so that your audience stays interested. At times, you want them to be relaxed and receptive to what you're saying, at other times highly alert to the details, at other times curious and interested.

While working in one-to-one coaching sessions and facing up to difficult problems, clients regularly demonstrate a full range of emotions from extreme anger, frustration, and worry to laughter in a very short space of time. At times, when the going gets tough, the territory constantly sways to a point where someone exclaims: 'I don't know whether it's best to laugh or cry!'

Humour offers an incredibly resourceful and valuable way to change state. For example, cartoon characters often provide the ability to see the opposite perspective on your experience; to take a serious subject and put it in a new light. The skill of any leader – whether as parent or manager – lies in your ability to pace somebody through these different states and lead them to a positive outcome.

Altering states with anchors

Your states are constantly shifting, and the value of anchors is that they enable you to alter your state to a more resourceful one when you need to. Say, for example, you have a difficult decision to make, a person to meet, or an event to attend – at weddings and funerals, emotions run high and you may want to manage your feelings closely. By being in the right state, you can make the best choices and act for the best result.

As an analogy, imagine that you're sailing a dinghy in a storm, and you want to reach a safe harbour. By developing the ability to fire anchors, you can secure a calm state for yourself or switch to an energetic, risk-taking mode as necessary. An anchor, by definition, is attached to a stable position: it keeps you safe and stops you floating away. Strength and stability are the keynotes here.

Whenever you notice that you're not in a 'good' state, you have a choice. Either you stick with this uncomfortable state because, for some reason, you get some value out of it. Or you decide that you prefer to identify and shift into a 'better' state. To do the latter, you can fire off an anchor to create a more positive state for yourself. (Flip to the earlier section 'Setting an anchor and building yourself a resourceful state' for how to do so easily, in just three steps, and see Chapter 6 for more on resourcefulness.)

Constantly overriding negative anchors with positive ones can lead to problems. Negative anchors can be one way that the unconscious mind indicates to you that you need to work on an underlying issue. For example, feeling tired may be an indication that your current work patterns are exhausting you. If you continue to override this warning sign with an energetic anchor, you can become burnt out.

Getting with the baroque beat

The Ancient Greeks knew it, early psychologists used it, and modern science confirms it: music affects both mind and body. Music alters the brainwaves that demonstrate the electrical activity in your brain. When you're relaxed, your brainwaves are slower and they speed up as you become more energised. Music with around 60 beats per minute seems to be the most comfortable across cultures, because it corresponds to the beat of the human heart at rest.

Brainwaves, from alpha to delta

You have four types of brainwave, measured in cycles per second:

1. Alpha brainwaves – clear, calm, and relaxed – 8–12 cycles per second

2. Beta brainwaves – alert and problem solving – 13–30 cycles per second

3. Theta brainwaves – creative and imaginative – 4–9 cycles per second

4. Delta brainwaves – deep sleep – less than 6 cycles per second

Baroque music is especially suitable for creating a state of relaxed awareness, known as the alpha state. To explore this kind of music, look out for the largo and adagio passages in pieces composed between about 1600 and 1750 – Bach, Mozart, Handel, and Vivaldi all offer good starting points.

Here are some different ways to think about the music you play. Perhaps you're stuck in a groove with your listening taste:

- ✔ **Vary the range of CDs you listen to or the tracks you download to your MP3 player** – from baroque to classical, jazz and blues to reggae, or pop and rock to opera.

- ✔ **Change the rhythm** – compare predictable rhythms with varied and unfamiliar ones to encourage your creativity. World music is good for this aspect.

- ✔ **Instrumental or vocal?** Words can distract – solo instruments tend to encourage relaxation.

- ✔ **Intuition** – trust your own tastes. Don't struggle with a piece of music you dislike: turn it off because it's unlikely to make you feel good.

- ✔ **Start the day differently** – when you feel good in the morning, you get off to a flying start. Try swapping the confrontational news channel on the radio for inspiring and uplifting music.

Here's an exercise to work through an issue with the help of music:

1. **Think of an issue or a decision that's bothering you – rate it on a worry scale of 1 to 10 and note the score on a piece of paper.**

2. **Select three pieces of music of very different styles, from mellow to lively.**

   For example, try some baroque, jazz instrumentals, heavy rock, or soft vocals.

3. **Play the first piece of music while thinking about your issue, and then rate your thoughts on a scale of 1 to 10. Make a note of how you now see the issue and feel about it.**

4. **Play the second piece of music while thinking about your issue, and then rate your thoughts on a scale of 1 to 10. Make a note of how you now see the issue and feel about it.**

5. **Play the third piece of music while thinking about your issue, and then rate your thoughts on a scale of 1 to 10. Make a note of how you now see the issue and feel about it.**

Has your thinking shifted? Which music was most powerful for you to become more resourceful?

Walking in someone else's shoes

Another way to develop your NLP skills is to find a positive role model – someone who seems to behave how you want to – and try on that person's body language for size. For example, you can copy how they hold themselves – upright or soft, smiling or serious – and then try walking the way that they walk. You may hear of a technique called the *moccasin walk* – you imagine that you're wearing that person's shoes and try to walk as if you're treading in their footsteps.

By moving your body differently, and adjusting your posture, gestures, and breathing, you automatically change your internal state – how you think and react.

If you're a small woman copying a large man or vice versa, the moccasin walk can give you new insights into how your physical shape makes a difference to the way you influence people. Gill, one of our petite female clients, was struggling to get attention at board meetings. By becoming more attuned to the physical mass of her male counterparts, she adapted her presenting style to be more expansive – moving purposefully across the room or presentation stage as she spoke. She also now spreads out her papers and takes up a larger portion of the boardroom meeting table. Both moves are ways of marking out her territory and authority. Similarly, large men working with children often talk to children from a seated position closer to the floor, instead of towering above them – as you can spot clever politicians doing when visiting schools.

Becoming Sophisticated with Anchors

This section shows you how NLP anchoring techniques can help you face challenging and fearful situations. Perhaps you're battling with changing unhelpful behaviours such as smoking or eating the wrong foods; or maybe you want to boost your confidence to perform a skill on the sports field or make a speech in public.

Of course, NLP isn't going to turn you into an opera singer or Olympic athlete overnight – NLP can't give you the competence to perform skills you don't possess – but anchoring techniques can help you to access your innate resources to be the very best you can.

Changing negative anchors

Sometimes you need to have a way of changing a negative anchor. As a simple example, you may want to change a destructive habit. A slimmer who reaches for the biscuit tin every time they have a cup of tea has created a negative anchor. Drink equals biscuit. Or an office worker who feels anxious each day when going into work, because they once had an argument with their boss, may be heading for a stress-related illness.

Desensitising yourself

One of the most common NLP approaches to releasing a negative anchor is by *desensitising*. To start, you need to get into a neutral or disassociated state – and then you introduce the problem in small doses. So if the issue is the slimming one mentioned above, you need to get first into a strong state when you're able to say 'no, thank you' to fattening foods. Then practise being tempted while staying in the strong state. Essentially, you need to develop new habits.

Collapsing the anchor

Another strategy is to *collapse the anchor* by firing off two anchors simultaneously – the unwanted negative one plus a positive one. You release the negative anchor while holding the positive one for another five seconds. The negative state is collapsed, making way for the positive one to remain.

Jane was recently divorced and won custody of the couple's two young children. She felt uncontrollably angry every time her ex-husband called to make arrangements to visit the children. In turn, the children were becoming very anxious about weekend visits to their father and his new partner. Romilla worked with Jane to collapse the negative anchors and replace them with a series of positive ones so that she was able to manage a strong and open dialogue with her ex-husband whenever she had to look at him face-to-face or hear his voice on the phone (unwanted negative anchors). In this way, she let go of the power he held.

Lengthening the anchor chain

You can move through many different emotional states in a single day. Anchors often work well in chains, with one trigger leading to another.

Sometimes, creating a chain of anchors can be useful. Each link in the chain acts as a stimulus to the next link, building up a sequence of states. For example, think of how an opera singer prepares for a major performance, as they pace themselves through a sequence of states until they're mentally set, focused, and ready to go on stage.

You can design a chain of anchors as the route to get into a desired state when the shift from the current state to the desired positive state is too great a leap in one go.

For example, your current problem state may be Anger and your desired state Relaxed. This transition is quite a jump to achieve in one go. However, you can first step from Anger to Worry, because of the overlap in these states. Your second step can then be from Worry to Curiosity, because again similarities exist between the two states. The final step can be from Curiosity to Relaxed (see Figure 9-2). To move from step to step you need to fire off a new anchor – as explained in the earlier section 'Setting an anchor and building yourself a resourceful state' – until you reach your desired state.

Figure 9-2:
Transitioning through a chain of anchors.

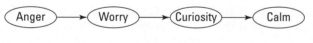

Anger → Worry → Curiosity → Calm

Curiosity and confusion are useful interim steps to achieve a change in state for yourself and others: they can often defuse emotionally charged situations.

When Kate worked on a consultancy project, one of the senior managers frequently interrupted highly charged conference calls with the statement: 'I'm confused here. Would someone please just go over that again for me.' It worked every time, as a perfect strategy to defuse the situation and raise new ideas. One person saying that he was confused made everybody else slow down and question their own understanding.

Deploying stage anchors

For many people, public speaking represents speaking under severe pressure. A number of studies, borne out by our own experiences with clients, demonstrate that some people would actually rather die than stand up and speak in public! Apparently in the US, public speaking is the number one fear; in the UK, it's in second place behind a fear of spiders.

We regularly work with clients who suffer performance anxiety, which shows itself in hot sweats, loss of voice, and stomach cramps and upsets. When dinner guests are invited to give after-dinner speeches, they often fail to enjoy the meal, because of the prospect of entertaining the audience with their wit over the coffee, petits fours, and brandy.

If ever a reason existed to use anchoring to get back in control, public speaking is it!

If you have had a particularly bad experience of public speaking, ask an NLP practitioner to do a fast phobia cure with you to desensitise the memory. (See Chapter 3 for an explanation of the NLP fast phobia cure.)

Using the circle of excellence

The NLP *circle of excellence* is a technique to help you summon up the confidence to perform a skill. You can use it when you have a fear of public speaking or when you want to boost your confidence to play your best shot in sport, as well as in many other instances.

The circle of excellence is the classic NLP technique to practise with a partner when you're providing the after-dinner entertainment. It works best if you enlist a buddy or NLP practitioner who takes you sensitively through these steps while maintaining rapport with you, and not rushing.

Think of the situation in which you have to perform, and imagine a circle on the ground in front of you about one metre in diameter. Then follow these steps, which describe the step-by step instructions that take you in and out of your circle, telling you what to do at each stage, with the help of a partner:

1. **Stand outside the circle with your partner.**

   Identify your best state. Tell your partner what that state is in your own words. Your partner says: 'Remember a time when you were [insert your exact words] . . . get back to it strongly . . . see what you saw then, hear what you heard.'

2. **Step inside the circle.**

   Relive that experience. Make it vivid, be there in it with all your senses. Feel what your hands are doing and hold or anchor that state with a hand movement at the point when the memory is most vivid.

3. **Step outside the circle, back to your partner.**

   Repeat the exercise with a second experience of your best state. In order to prepare for the future event, your partner says: 'Think of a time when this state will be useful.'

4. **Step inside the circle again.**

   With your hand in the anchored position, move into the circle; your partner asks you to see, hear, and feel how the experience can be for you now.

5. **Step outside the circle, back to your partner.**

   Relax . . . you've got it!

Repeat this exercise with more examples of your best state in order to strengthen the anchor even further. When you need to access your confident and positive state, you can imagine the circle slightly in front of you and take a small, discreet step forward into it.

Anchoring spatially

When you're giving a speech or presentation in front of an audience, *spatial anchoring* is a way of influencing your audience through anchors. When you repeatedly do the same thing on stage in the same place, people come to expect a certain behaviour from you according to where you move to on the stage. A lectern is a definite anchor – when you stand at the lectern, people expect you to speak.

While presenting, you can deliberately set up other expectations with the audience at different places on the stage. Perhaps you do the main delivery from the centre point of the stage, but move to one side when you're telling stories and another side when you deliver technical information. You may have yet another space that you step to when being humorous or light hearted. Very quickly, people come to expect a certain style input from you according to where you position yourself.

A Final Point About Anchors

Anchors may or may not work for you when you first try them. As with all the tools in this book, you learn fastest by taking an NLP class or working with an experienced practitioner. Whichever way you choose to develop your skills – on your own or with others – simply give it a go.

We encourage you to persist even if setting anchors seems strange at first. When you do take control of your own state, you expand your options and the result is certainly worthwhile. Being able to manage your emotional state is powerful, just as the famous Rudyard Kipling poem 'If' says: 'If you can keep your head when all about you are losing theirs. . .'

A fundamental NLP presupposition is that the person with the most flexibility in a situation is the one who succeeds.

Chapter 10

Sliding the Controls of Your Experience

*T*ry this experiment: think of a really pleasant experience that you've had. You don't have to share the experience so you can let rip and really get into it. As you think of the experience, do you get a picture, feel a feeling, hear any sounds? Getting all three is great, and if you can only manage one or two out of the three, that's okay too; we work with you in this chapter to help you experience all three. Can you now begin to intensify the experience? Great! Now, can you ramp it up some more?

Welcome back! As you relived the experience, how did you intensify it? Did you make the picture brighter, bigger, more colourful, or perhaps you brought it closer to you. Maybe you turned up the volume of any sounds you heard and if you had a feeling, you spread that feeling further through your body. You've just discovered how to play with your *submodalities*.

Submodalities are the basic building blocks of the way you experience your world, and therefore a very slight change in a submodality can have a significant effect on the changing of the experience. In other words, you have control over the way you choose to experience your world. You can choose to change your mind to heighten a pleasurable time or to remove the negative emotions from an unpleasant one. You can also take yourself from an undesired state, such as confused, to a better state, such as understanding.

In short, you can choose the meaning you give to what happens to you in life. This chapter tells you how.

By practising the exercises in this chapter, you become better at switching your submodalities; you discover just how easily you can change the way you think and experience the world around you. Practice can help you increase the choices in your life, whether that's to relieve stress, take the pain out of bad memories, or enhance the good times. When you set yourself a well-formed, desired outcome, for example, and pay attention to the submodalities, you make each goal more specific and clearly propel your future into motion. Have fun!

Recording Your Experiences with Your Submodalities

In NLP, your five senses – seeing, hearing, touching (also called kinaesthetic), smelling, and tasting – are called *modalities* (we describe in Chapter 6 how you experience your world through these five senses). And the means by which you fine-tune your modalities in order to change their qualities, are known as submodalities.

Examples of submodalities for your sense of sight may be the size of a picture, its brightness or colour, and whether a frame surrounds it or not. Submodalities for hearing can be loudness, tempo, or the timbre of a voice, and for feeling a heaviness or butterflies in your stomach. You get the idea?

Contrastive analysis happens when you take two experiences and compare and contrast the submodalities of each experience. If, for example, when you compare the submodalities of something you know is real – say, a dog – with something you know is fantasy – a unicorn – you notice that each has differences in its submodalities.

Grasping the Basic Info: What You Need to Know Before You Begin

Submodalities are how you give meaning to your experiences – whether something is real or false, good or bad, and so on. You can use submodalities to change the intensity of the meaning. In the exercise at the start of this chapter, you gave your experience a meaning – it was pleasant. By changing the submodalities of the experience, you were able to increase the experience and therefore the meaning of the experience – it became even more pleasant.

So now you know that you can control your memories simply by changing the submodalities of the pictures, sounds, and feelings. And just as you know that modalities can be broken down into submodalities, similarly you should be aware that the submodalities can have further distinctions. For example, a picture can be in colour and have different shades of colours, or it can be in black and white and have variations of grey. It can have a frame around it or can be panoramic. Not clear about panoramic? Imagine standing on the top of a mountain and looking at the scenery in front of you as you turn your head, slowly, through 180 degrees. What you see is in panorama. In addition, in the next section, you discover how being associated with or dissociated from a picture can have an effect on your emotions. For example, sounds can be in your head or to the side, and feelings can take on a texture.

Because you can change each of your submodalities, we provide you with a list of them in the later section 'Submodalities Worksheet', to help you record the changes. We recommend that you fill out the form before you begin to make changes so that you can always revert to the original structure of a submodality if your change raises any anxieties.

Associating or dissociating

This section helps you to understand how you can move in and out of your memories, to get more options over how you heighten or reduce the intensity of your feelings. In our experience, this aspect is a very important submodality and one that needs a little extra clarification.

When you visualise yourself in a picture, the experience is like watching yourself in a home-made film, and we call this experience *dissociated*. If, however, you're in the picture, seeing out of your own eyes, we call this experience *associated*. Being associated or dissociated into a picture can be an extremely important submodality when experiencing emotions as a result of the pictures you make.

Usually the emotions are heightened if you associate into the picture. Sometimes, people find associating or dissociating difficult. For instance, someone who has experienced a severe personal loss or been traumatised may find that associating hard and may need to work on it.

To get the feel of being associated or dissociated, create a picture of yourself sitting in the front seat of a car. When you're dissociated, you perhaps see a picture of yourself in the car, a little bit like watching yourself on television or looking at yourself in a photograph. If you want to associate into the picture, imagine opening the car door and sitting down. Now look out of your own eyes. The dashboard is in front of you. Can you see the texture and colour of the dashboard? Now look up at the windscreen. Is it splattered with the remnants of suicidal insects (or aliens, if you've seen the film *Men in Black*)?

After visualisation, some people find that dissociating is difficult. To do so, imagine stepping out of the car and onto the pavement. Turn around and look back at the car and see yourself sitting in the front seat. If you still can't dissociate, pretend that you're watching a film and you're up there on the screen, in front of the car.

If you feel that you aren't getting the hang of this exercise (or any others), feel free to leave it for the moment. You can always come back to it and give the exercise another go when you have more NLP experience embedded in your mind and muscle. Or you can find yourself an NLP practitioner or NLP practice group to work with in order to advance your skills (Appendix A is a resource list to help you make contact).

Defining the details of your memories

While you're sitting down to read this book, you're probably unaware of the feel of the seat against your back and legs, although you are now because we mention it. Similarly, you're not always aware of the qualities of your memories until we ask you to remember a time when you were, for example, brushing your teeth, playing a game, reading a book, or cooking. Then you realise that a range of qualities applies to those memories. For instance, when remembering reading a book, the picture you make of yourself, the book, or the story, may be surrounded by a frame, or it may be in black and white. Perhaps you can hear the sound of distant traffic or of the pages turning. Maybe the book you were reading made you laugh and feel uplifted and happy.

You can become aware of the qualities of your submodalities by paying attention to what you see, or hear, or feel when you recall an experience. The following sections present you with questions that can help you elicit the quality of the visual, auditory, and kinaesthetic submodalities.

We focus on just the visual, auditory, and kinaesthetic submodalities in this chapter, and put taste and smell aside for now. We do so because we believe that – unless you're a wine-, tea-, or coffee-taster – these senses don't have the same power as sight, sound, and touch. Having said that, tastes and smells certainly affect your emotional brain and you may find the smell of roasted chestnuts suddenly transporting you back to a childhood memory of falling snow and Christmas carols.

Eliciting visual submodalities

You can define the quality of a picture in terms of where it's located in space as you look at it. For instance, the image may be directly in front of you, to your left, to your right, or slightly displaced to the top or bottom. If the picture is panoramic, it looks like you're standing in one spot and turning your head to look at the view in front of you. The picture has other qualities as well, brightness, shape, and so on. You can discover how you make pictures in your head by thinking about the following qualities:

Visual Submodalities	*Questions to Discover Them*
Location	Where is it in space?
	Point to the picture.
	How close or how far away is it?
Colour or black and white	Is it in colour or is it black and white?
Associated or dissociated	Is the picture associated or dissociated?
	Can you see yourself in the picture or are you looking out of your own eyes?
Size	Is the picture big or small?
	What size would you say the picture measures?
Two- or three-dimensional	Is the picture in two or three dimensions?
Brightness	Is the picture bright or dull?
Still or moving	Is the picture still or is it a film?
	If the picture is a film, how fast is it running?
Shape	Is the picture square, round, or rectangular?
Framed or panoramic	Does the picture have a border around it, or is it panoramic?
Focused or fuzzy	Is the picture in sharp focus or is it blurred?

Eliciting auditory submodalities

Like the pictures you make in your head, the sounds you hear have certain qualities to them. You may not be aware of the attributes of the sounds you hear until you focus your mind on them by thinking of the following questions:

Auditory Submodalities	*Questions to Discover Them*
Location	Where do you hear the sound?
	Is the sound inside your head or outside?
	Point to where the sound is coming from.
Words or sounds	Can you hear words or sounds?
	If words, is it the voice of someone you know?
Volume	Is the sound loud or soft?
	Is the sound a whisper or clearly audible?
Tone	If you hear a voice, what tone does it have?
	Is it deep, rich, nasal, rasping?
Pitch	Is the sound high or low pitched?
Mono or stereo	Can you hear the sound on both sides or is it one sided?
	Is the sound all around you?
Constant or intermittent	Is the sound continuous or intermittent?
Rhythm	Does the sound have a beat or a rhythm to it?
Tempo	Is the sound you hear slow or fast?
Tune	Does the sound have a tune?

Eliciting kinaesthetic submodalities

Guess what! Submodalities to do with feelings also have qualities that help to define them:

Kinaesthetic Submodalities	Questions to Discover Them
Location	Where is it in your body?
	Point to where you can feel the feeling.
Shape	Does the feeling have a shape?
Pressure	Does the feeling exert a pressure?
Size	Does the feeling have a size?
	Is it big or small?
Quality	Does the feeling make you tingle?
	Is it spread out or knotted in one place?
Intensity	Is the feeling strong or weak?
Still or moving	Can you feel the feeling in one place or is it moving around your body?
Temperature	Is the feeling warm or cold?
Constant or intermittent	Is the feeling constant or intermittent?
Texture	Does the feeling have a texture to it?
Picture	Can you make a picture of the feeling?

Tom was prone to feeling very anxious before his weekly meetings with his manager. Consequently, he felt unable to make his case when his manager raised certain issues with him. Over a period of six months, Tom found that facing going to work became harder and harder and he was in despair when he consulted Romilla.

When questioned, Tom said that the feeling of anxiety looked like a heavy, metallic, black cube just below his sternum. Romilla asked Tom to change the colour gradually from metallic black to grey to silver. As the colour changed, the cube got lighter until Tom was left with a very 'poky' square. When Tom imagined getting hold of a corner of the square, he was able to 'pull' it out of his body and allow it to float away. Tom has gone on to use this process for dispelling other, unhelpful feelings, in different situations.

When you're playing at changing the submodalities of a memory, you need to make a list before you start changing submodalities around. If you start to get uncomfortable with the process at any point, you can then put the picture, sounds, or feelings back to how they were. In the later section 'Submodalities Worksheet', you can find a worksheet designed for this very purpose. Make as many copies as you need.

Always ask yourself whether going ahead with any change to a submodality is okay. If you discover a resistance – a feeling that makes you uncomfortable – acknowledge the feeling and thank your unconscious mind for making you aware of possible internal conflict. You can simply overcome this issue gradually, through some quiet time to yourself; or you may find that working with an NLP practitioner is beneficial.

When Romilla was working on resolving grief with a client, he didn't want to let go of the pain of loss. He believed that if he let go of the pain he would forget his father. In fact, by releasing the pain he was able to remember his father even more vividly.

Getting a little practice

Imagine you have a remote control with three sliding buttons labelled V for visual, A for auditory, and K for kinaesthetic. You can change the qualities of any pictures you make in your mind, sounds you hear in your head, or any feelings you experience in your body just by sliding the V, A, and K controls. (For more information on VAK modalities, head to Chapter 6.)

Why would you want to adjust the qualities of your memories? Supposing, years ago, you were rehearsing for a school play and your highly stressed teacher screamed at you, 'You stupid child, you blew it again!' Now you're in a job where you need to make some strong presentations to colleagues and clients. Yet every time you get started you begin to sweat and stammer and the voice in your head goes, 'You stupid child, you blew it again!' You may need to adjust the qualities of your memories because they get in the way of what you want to achieve. Imagine you slide the brightness control and the picture of the teacher gets dimmer. Then you slide the size control and the teacher gets smaller and becomes insignificant. Finally, you adjust the volume control and the scream drops to a whisper. Now you find that you can make presentations the way you always wanted.

To see how effective changing submodalities can be, try this exercise, using the worksheet in the later section 'Submodalities Worksheet':

1. **Think of someone you like.**

2. **Remember the last time you spent real, quality time with that person.**

3. **Record the qualities of the picture you see, any sounds you hear, and any feelings you get.**

4. **Change the picture you made, one *visual* submodality at a time; notice how each change affects the memory of your time together.**

5. **Change the sounds you hear, one *auditory* submodality at a time; notice how each change affects the memory.**

6. **Change any feelings that you're feeling, one *kinaesthetic* submodality at a time; notice how each change impacts the whole experience of your time together.**

Understanding Your Critical Submodalities

Some submodalities are very powerful in determining a person's response, such as the size or brightness of a mental picture. You may find that by making a picture bigger or brighter the experience is heightened. Or you may find that moving the picture to a different location or associating or dissociating into a picture (as we discuss in the earlier section 'Associating or dissociating') can affect the sounds and feelings of an experience.

A *critical* submodality is one that, when changed, alters other submodalities of an experience and also affects the submodalities of other senses. The result is that by changing, say, the brightness of a picture, not only do other qualities of the picture change automatically, but also sounds and feelings experienced in conjunction with the picture change, without conscious intervention.

Romilla was working with a client, Suzy, who was having trouble with a goal she wanted to achieve and had been struggling to reach for almost six months. When Suzy explored the submodalities of her goal, she said it was over and up to the left (if you imagine a giant clock in front of you, it was at the number 11 and almost at roof height). When asked, Suzy moved the location of the image so that it was right in front of her and about one metre away.

Suzy's reaction was phenomenal. She jumped in her chair so hard she almost fell off it and then she turned bright pink and couldn't stop laughing. Changing the location of the picture had a real impact on Suzy and brought the goal to life for her: she felt what achieving the goal would be like and the move made it much more immediate. Using some more goal-setting techniques, a delighted Suzy achieved her goal in four months.

You experience your world through your five senses: visual (eyes), auditory (ears), kinaesthetic (feelings and touch), olfactory (smell), and gustatory (taste). More than likely, you use one sense in preference to the others to collect data about your world, particularly at times of stress. This sense is called your *lead* or *primary representational system*, and it influences how you learn and the way you represent your external world inside your head.

During a coaching session, Charles discovered that his primary representational system was auditory. Also, he was more kinaesthetic than visual and felt emotions quite strongly. Charles was working to change a nagging voice that he was allowing to undermine his confidence when he was starting something new, and which kept him awake at night with its chatter. On examining the qualities of the voice, he found that it was in fact his mother talking to him and that he heard her voice inside his head. Unfortunately, she had had a rather negative way of putting things. Whenever Charles heard this voice he felt sick and a sensation like a black, shiny rock was stuck in the region of his solar plexus.

When Charles changed the voice to a whisper and moved it to just below his left ear, outside his head, he realised he didn't feel sick and he felt a warm glow in his stomach. Charles wasn't prepared to change the voice further, however, because he believed the voice served to watch out for potential problems. He just needed to change the quality so that it allowed him to get on with his life.

Making Real-Life Changes

As you experiment with the exercises in this chapter, we hope that you begin to get a pretty good idea of your *critical* submodality: the submodality that can impact on and change other submodalities. And we hope that you gain the conviction that you're in control of your experiences and can change them in order to choose how you feel. In the light of this knowledge and belief, experience real change in your life by working through the exercises in the following sections.

Just think: you can sit and program your mind on the train, in a traffic jam, or even over a boring meal with your in-laws (or should that be out-laws, just kidding!). And remember, practice makes perfect, so start experimenting, safe in the knowledge that you can't get arrested for playing with your submodalities, even in public.

Removing the pain from an experience

Can you think of an unpleasant experience you've had? We don't mean something life shattering, just an incident that, when you think of it, makes you feel less than good. Got one?

Now, using the form in the later section 'Submodalities Worksheet', examine and note the submodalities of the experience. With this knowledge, start changing the picture, sounds, and feelings that you get when you think of the unpleasant experience. What happened? You do feel better now, don't you? No? Then discover what happens when you change the submodalities of the unpleasant experience to those of the pleasant experience we asked you to recall at the start of the chapter.

Changing a limiting belief

How often have you heard yourself say such things as, 'I can't do that', 'I'm no good at maths', or 'I should learn to cook properly'? These statements are all examples of *limiting beliefs*, generalisations that you make about yourself and your world. These beliefs can disable you, holding you back, or they can empower you. Beliefs can all too easily become self-fulfilling prophesies, which start off just as a notion or a hint of an idea. Then your filters (meta programs, values, beliefs, attitudes, memories, and decisions – which we discuss in Chapter 5) begin aligning themselves like gates to let in only those 'facts' and experiences that reinforce your beliefs.

For instance, imagine that you decide that you're a little more cuddly than you want to be and so you start on a diet. Perhaps you stick to the diet for a few days, but then temptation gets the better of you. At this stage you receive a hint of the notion that 'Maybe I'm not good at following a diet.' Then you try again and submit to temptation again, until eventually you come to the limiting belief that 'I can't stick to a diet.'

1. **Think of a limiting belief you currently hold, one that you'd like to change.**

   Perhaps you believe that you have two left feet as regards dancing or that you're not a good swimmer.

2. **Think of a belief that you used to hold but which, for you, is no longer true.**

   This belief can be something such as believing in the tooth fairy. Use the form in the later section 'Submodalities Worksheet' and note the submodalities of your old belief.

3. **Think of something that you believe to be certain.**

   If you can't think of one, try the belief that 'the sun is going to rise tomorrow'.

   Again, using the submodalities form, note the submodalities of this belief.

4. **Think of a belief that you'd rather have.**

   This belief can be the opposite of your limiting belief in step 1, but restated in the positive: 'I'm a good dancer.' Perhaps you want to be better at parking – 'I'm good at parking' or want to feel more confident when speaking professionally – 'I'm a confident professional speaker.'

   With the help of the form in the later section 'Submodalities Worksheet', notice the submodalities of the belief you'd rather have.

5. **Change the submodalities of your limiting belief (step 1) to those of the belief that for you is no longer true (step 2).**

6. **Change the submodalities of the belief you'd rather have (step 4) to those of the belief of which you're certain (step 3).**

Notice how your negative belief has changed, if it hasn't disappeared altogether!

Creating an empowering belief

To avoid your beliefs turning into self-fulfilling prophecies, remember that you have control over choosing which beliefs you want to retain. In the preceding section, you discover how to let go of a limiting belief. Just imagine the usefulness of finding out how to increase your options in life by choosing to create a whole plethora of beliefs that enable you to live your life more authentically.

1. **Think of a belief that would be really useful to have: we call it a desired belief.**

   For example, 'I deserve to be successful.'

2. **Think of a belief that for you is absolutely true.**

   For example, the sun is going to rise in the morning (yes, even behind those clouds).

3. **Using the form in the later section 'Submodalities Worksheet', identify the submodalities of this absolutely true belief.**

   For example, when you think of the sun rising you may see it in front of you, about two metres away, in pale, shimmering, orange colours and very bright. You may feel warm all over and hear birdsong.

4. **Put the desired belief into exactly the same submodalities as the absolutely true belief.**

   Move the picture you get when you think of your desired belief to the same position and distance as the rising sun and give it the same colours and brightness. Then produce the same feelings of warmth and listen for the birdsong.

Getting rid of that backache

This process can be used for other symptoms such as headaches brought on by too much stress, or muscles that are stiff from maintaining the same position for too long or from overuse.

This process is great for alleviating discomfort quickly, without needing to wait for a doctor's appointment or resorting to medication, but if your symptoms persist or for peace of mind, do consult your GP.

1. **Calibrate your backache on a scale of 1 to 5.**

2. **Make a picture of the backache.**

3. **From the form in the later section 'Submodalities Worksheet', note the submodalities of the backache.**

4. **Change each attribute of the backache, one at a time.**

If the pain has a colour, what happens when you give it a different colour, such as healing blue? What happens if you see that band of steel break up into strips of ribbon, fluttering in the wind? If the pain is a dull ache, can you change the feeling to a tingle? If it feels hot, can you change that feeling into one of a cool breeze blowing over the area? These changes can reduce your backache, if it hasn't already gone.

5. **Now imagine that you're sitting in front of a cinema screen: remove the backache from your body and project a picture of the backache on to the screen.**

6. **Make the picture on the screen smaller and smaller until it becomes the size of a balloon.**

7. **Now watch the balloon float up into the sky, and as you see it floating away your backache is getting less and less.**

8. **As the balloon reaches the clouds, calibrate your backache to just a 1.**

9. **As the balloon disappears from sight, the backache fades to just the faintest memory.**

Using the swish

The *swish* is a powerful technique – based like a lot of NLP on behavioural psychology – for making lasting changes in habits and behaviours. The swish pattern is designed to change a problematic behaviour that's driven by a trigger. The idea behind the swish is to attach a self image to the trigger so that every time the trigger is activated, you see a new way of behaving and you change your behaviour effortlessly.

Say that you bite your nails. The swish enables you to use a picture of the trigger – such as seeing you run a finger along a nail and finding a jagged edge or a response to getting nervous that creates the unwanted behaviour (biting your nails) – to create a new, desired pattern of behaviour or new image (your hands looking immaculate).

You can use the swish pattern to change that feeling of exhaustion after a day's work into one of being relaxed and ready to enjoy your evening.

1. **Identify the unwanted behaviour.**

   You may want to stop biting your nails, stop smoking, or stop yourself getting angry at small transgressions.

2. **Check with yourself that going ahead with the change is okay.**

   Simply ask yourself: 'Is it okay for me to change in this context?'

3. **Identify the trigger that initiates the unwanted behaviour and make an associated picture (check out the 'Associating or dissociating' section earlier in this chapter). This image is the cue picture.**

   You may see yourself running your finger along a nail or in a situation that makes you nervous or angry.

4. **Play with the image to discover a critical submodality.**

   As you become more experienced, you'll be able to change one or two critical submodalities, but for now start off with one. You change the submodalities of the image to make the cue picture more compelling.

5. **Break state.**

   Break state means to change the state or frame of mind that you're in. You can stand up and give your body a good shake or move around the room when going from one phase of an exercise to another, allowing a natural break from the pictures and emotions of the first stage of the exercise.

6. **Think of the desired image. Create a dissociated image of you doing a preferred behaviour or looking a certain way.**

7. **Break state.**

8. **Recall the cue picture. Make sure that you're associated into it and place a frame around it.**

9. **Create an image of the desired outcome.**

10. **Squash the desired image into a very small, dark dot and place it in the bottom left corner of the cue picture.**

11. **With a *swishhhh* sound, propel the small, dark dot into the big picture so that it explodes, covering the cue picture.**

12. **Break state.**

13. **Repeat the process several times speedily.**

If you display more kinaesthetic tendencies than visual or auditory, you may find the swish more effective when you keep your hands far apart at the start of this exercise. Then, as you *swishhhh*, bring your hands together quickly.

Submodalities Worksheet

Visual Submodalities   **Describe What You See**
Location
Colour or black and white
Associated or dissociated
Size
Two- or three-dimensional
Brightness
Still or moving
Shape
Framed or panoramic
Focused or fuzzy

Auditory Submodalities   **Describe What You Hear**
Location
Words or sounds
Volume
Tone
Pitch
Mono or stereo
Constant or intermittent
Rhythm
Tempo
Tune

Kinaesthetic Submodalities   **Describe What You Feel**
Location
Shape
Pressure
Size
Quality
Intensity
Still or moving
Temperature
Constant or intermittent
Texture

Chapter 11

Working with the Logical Levels

. . . .

In This Chapter

▶ Using a core NLP model to achieve alignment

▶ Discovering your own sense of purpose

▶ Being more centred in your career, your life, and yourself

. . . .

*I*n this chapter, we introduce you to a favourite model in NLP, one that shows you how to make sense of your experience, work out the most flexible approach, and achieve the NLP ideal of understanding the outcome that you want. NLP developer and trainer Robert Dilts developed this model – known as the *logical levels* – and it has become extremely popular in NLP work.

This model is particularly helpful in several ways:

✔ Understanding what makes you tick as an individual.

✔ Comprehending how other people and organisations function.

✔ Seeing how to break an experience into manageable parts.

✔ Working with your current reality and making adjustments confidently.

The logical levels model can help you navigate a route forward during confusing times by identifying any areas of your life that aren't aligned.

Understanding Logical Levels

NLP logical levels allow you to think about any experience or situation in its component parts (check out Figure 11-1). (You may also see logical levels referred to in the NLP literature as *a series of neurological levels*.)

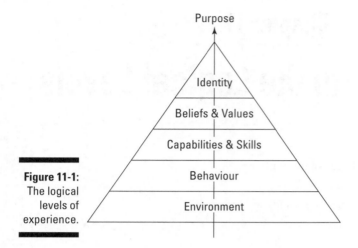

Figure 11-1:
The logical
levels of
experience.

Although we present the levels to you in Figure 11-1 as a hierarchy, looking at them as a network of interrelationships or a series of concentric circles is also helpful, because all the levels relate to each other. The visual of the model simply creates some structure and understanding about how it works.

In many instances, gathering information at the lower levels on the diagram is easier than at the higher levels. So, for example, a company would find doing an audit of the buildings (*environment*) easier than measuring whether the values of the organisation are being realised by the leaders and employees (*beliefs and values*), or assessing its image in the marketplace (*identity*). Each level impacts those above and below it; the key value of the model is that it provides a disciplined way to unpack the structure of your experience, which is the essence of NLP.

The French have an expression to describe the feeling you have when you're comfortable in yourself and everything is running smoothly: 'elle va bien dans sa peau' (literally translated as 'she goes well in her own skin'). Similarly, NLPers use the word *congruence* to describe precisely how you are when you're truly being yourself. The term means that you're comfortably on track, and consistent. The logical levels of environment, behaviour, capability, beliefs and values, identity, and purpose are all lined up. Look out for this *alignment* in organisations as well as people. When companies or individuals are going through periods of change, some misalignment is likely to exist. People may behave in unpredictable ways that aren't a true reflection of what they really believe is right or fits with their true identity.

Why is 'why?' the hardest question?

In her early career as a business writer, Kate spent many happy years of corporate life interviewing chief executives and leadership teams, interpreting their vision, and publishing their words of wisdom in an easily digestible format for employees to understand.

The 'who, what, when, where, why, and how' questions form the essential journalist's weapons. Yet, only when coming across logical levels in NLP did Kate realise just why some questions meet blank stares, even hostility, while others receive a warm welcome.

When you want to know something about a subject, work up the logical levels. Start with gathering information that relates to the environment – the where, when, and with whom. These questions are factual and so easier to answer. Then move through the what and the how. Leave the why question to last. Answering 'Why did you do that?', which rushes headlong into the realm of beliefs, is harder than answering 'How did you do that?', a much gentler approach; or even 'How did that happen?', which disassociates the person from the question.

Asking the right questions

As you begin to gather information about a person or situation, consider asking questions that apply at these different levels, beginning from the base of the pyramid illustrated in Figure 11-1:

- **Environment** refers to the factors that are external opportunities or constraints: answers the questions 'where?', 'when?', and 'with whom?'.

- **Behaviour** is made up of specific actions or reactions within the environment: answers the question 'what?'.

- **Capabilities and skills** are about the knowledge and skills, the 'how-tos' that guide and give direction to behaviour: answers the question 'how?'.

- **Beliefs and values** provide the reinforcement (motivation and permission) to support or deny your capabilities: answers the question 'why?'.

- **Identity** factors determine your sense of self: answers the question 'who?'.

- **Purpose** goes beyond self-consciousness to relate to the bigger picture about your mission: answers the questions 'what for' or 'for whom?'.

Taking logical levels step-by-step

The logical levels enable you to think about what's happening in the world around you. These stepping stones help you to understand the structure and pattern as well as the content of different issues, events, relationships, or organisations, as we explain in this section and the next.

We now look at how you can apply this model when you're facing a dilemma that needs a solution. Imagine that you're in a relationship that isn't working. You can use the concept of logical levels to help you find the best way forward. Here's how the process works:

1. **Recognise that things are out of alignment.**

   You know this situation is the case when you're uncomfortable with your partner and you know that you want things to be different.

2. **Discover what can be different.**

   Ask yourself certain questions that can help you pinpoint exactly what you want to be different. If you both simply moved to a new flat or different city would things improve? For example, does one set of in-laws make too many demands on your time and stop you from developing your relationship as a couple? Or do you have a fundamental difference in your values? Each logical level has certain types of questions. (Head to the later section 'Finding the Right Lever for Change' to help you work through the individual logical levels.)

3. **When you've identified the logical level, bring that level back in alignment with the others.**

   At the lower levels, say at environment or behaviour, you may both be able to adjust some simple habits in order to have a harmonious relationship. You may ask your partner to be more tidy at home, for example, while you share the administration of bill paying. Building your skills in an area such as talking freely about your feelings or learning DIY may take more time and effort. Also, working with an individual coach can be valuable, to help you examine your beliefs and values or develop a stronger identity for yourself.

Fran was shocked when her husband of ten years announced that he was leaving home and moving in with one of her good friends. She felt that if they were to move house (change the environment level) and spend more time together (the behaviour level) all would be well. Through some relationship work, she came to realise that her husband had always had completely different values (the beliefs and values level) from her. He was from a large, boisterous family environment, and Fran focused all her attention on her work. She never wanted to be a mother or homemaker (the identity level) and felt her sense of purpose was achieved through her work in corporate litigation. In the end, they decided to divorce and amicably go their separate ways because they each wanted a fundamentally different relationship.

Often people attempt to solve issues by changing one logical level – such as environment or behaviour – when they need to address a separate logical level, such as that of values or identity. Similarly, when you have issues with someone's behaviour, remember not to challenge their identity, and to respect their beliefs.

Employing practical uses for logical levels

You can use logical levels to bring energy and focus to many different situations. Here are just a few examples:

- **Gathering and structuring information:** Compiling a report, school essay, conducting interviews, or structuring any piece of writing.

- **Carrying out a modelling exercise:** The logical levels offer a practical framework to start from (turn to Chapter 19 for more on modelling).

- **Making a career choice:** Exploring all aspects of a career move from ascertaining the best environment, to getting your values met, to how this job connects with your passion and purpose in life.

- **Building relationships in a family:** Exploring what all members of the family want for the family to work together. This approach is especially useful when dramatic change occurs in a family's structure such as divorce or remarriage.

- **Improving individual or corporate performance:** Deciding where to make business changes that help turn around a struggling company or one going through mergers and acquisitions. Coming up with a development plan for an individual employee.

- **Developing leadership and confidence:** Stepping through the levels to get alignment and feel confident in leading a team or enterprise.

Open any toolbox – whether it's a box of coloured flipchart pens, a palette of paints, electric drill bits, or a mechanic's spanners – and some favourites always take centre stage. You keep coming back to these faithful friends and can depend on them for the feel-good factor. You'll discover that the logical levels model provides a value-added feature time and time again. The model is ever-present, like a mate helping to decipher complex information, whether you need to make sense of a business project or unravel a difficult conversation. If you keep returning to any single well-loved tool in the NLP toolkit, the logical levels model may well be the one for you.

Finding the Right Lever for Change

Carl Jung, one of the 20th century's leading thinkers in psychology, famously said, 'We cannot change anything until we accept it. Condemnation does not liberate, it oppresses.' And he was right, because the first step to coping with change is to accept that it's happening. You're then in a position to work proactively with the change and give yourself options, instead of waiting to be on the receiving end of whatever happens to you.

Three requirements need to be in place for change to happen. You must:

- Want to change
- Know how to change
- Get or create the opportunity to change

In the following sections, we delve further into the logical levels. As you explore, keep in mind one important question: 'How can you make change easy for yourself?'

We apply all the questions we raise in the following sections to you as an individual, but you can ask the same questions to assess what's happening in an organisation as well.

Environment

The environment level is about place and people – the physical context in which you hang out – and about finding the right time. If you want to become fluent in a new language, the easiest way to learn is to go and live in the relevant country for a while, fully immersing yourself in the culture, ideally by living with native speakers. Similarly, if you want to get to grips with a new software package, moving on to a project to work with a person or team that applies it in their business makes sense. Again, the new environment is conducive to learning, which is itself a type of change. The timing is also critical – you can't learn if the time isn't right for you – for example, if you're tied up with other needs.

Here are some environment questions to ask yourself when you sense that you're not in the right place or now isn't the right time for you to get what you want:

- Where do you work best?
- Where in the world do you want to explore?
- What kind of home environment is right for you – modern, minimalist, or traditional?
- What kind of people do you like to have around you? Who makes you feel good, energised, and comfortable? Who makes you feel drained? Or do you prefer to work alone?
- What time of day do you feel good – are you up with the lark in the mornings or a night owl?

Questions such as these give you the right kind of data so that you can decide what environment issues you can work on.

Behaviour

Your behaviour is all about what you say and do – what you consciously get up to. In NLP terms, behaviour refers to what you think about as well as your actions. NLP also points out that all your behaviour is aimed at a purpose, and has a positive intention for you.

Change at the behavioural level is easy to make when you have a real sense of purpose, and it fits with your sense of identity and your beliefs and values.

Ask yourself the following behaviour questions when you think that you may need to change your behaviours in order to get the results you want:

✔ Do your behaviours support your goals?

✔ Do they fit with your sense of who you are?

✔ What do you do that makes life interesting and fun?

✔ What do you find yourself saying habitually? Can you detect any patterns?

✔ What do you notice about other people's words and sayings?

✔ How aware are you of people's behaviour – for example, how they walk, the tone of their voice, and their smile?

✔ What colour changes do you observe in people as they talk?

✔ How does your breathing change, and when?

✔ What body language do you adopt in different circumstances?

✔ Does the sound of your voice fit consistently with what you're saying?

Maximising effective behaviours

In order to create positive change, developing the behaviours and habits that serve you well is a good idea. Often, small changes have an incremental effect. If you're slimming to fit into a new outfit, eating a healthy salad each day in place of your sandwiches is a valuable habit to cultivate. In the same way, if you're trying to improve your meetings at work, good behaviour for a team would be to set clear beginning and end times.

When Manuela wanted to drop a dress size in weight for her daughter's wedding day, she realised that she had to take her dieting seriously. She worked with a nutritionist who taught her about adapting her diet and gave her a record sheet to write down everything she ate, the supplements she took, and the exercise regime. She also gave Manuela a notebook to make a daily note of everything that had gone well in her day and introduced her to a motivational fitness trainer. This daily regime kept Manuela on track to regain her slim figure and have wedding photos that she's delighted to look at.

Practising the right behaviours until they become habitual increases your capability. How many great sports people or musicians are born wielding a tennis racket or violin? Tennis star Andy Murray is renowned for the dedication he puts into his gym work as well as the number of tennis balls he hits in preparation for tournaments. Olympic-medal-winning rowers can be seen out on the cold river as early as 5 a.m. when ordinary folks are tucked up safely in their beds. Top violinists begin by squeaking out the notes as they practise for hundreds of hours (often to the despair of their families!). Constant hard practice keeps top performers ahead in their games.

Modifying unwanted behaviours

What about the unwanted behaviours, the things you do and those you'd prefer not to do, silly habits such as smoking or eating unhealthily? They become hard to change because they're linked to other, higher, logical levels involving beliefs or identity:

'I'm a smoker' = a statement about identity.

'I need to have a cigarette when I get stressed' = a statement about belief.

'He's a big, strong lad' = a statement about identity.

'He can't live on salad and fruit' = a statement about belief.

To make change easier, create a new identity for yourself such as 'I'm a healthy person' and adopt beliefs such as 'I can develop the right habits to look after myself.' Chapter 3 tells you how.

Capabilities and skills

Capabilities are talents and skills that lie within people and organisations as valuable assets. These behaviours may be the ones that you do so well that you can do them consistently without any seemingly conscious effort. Like walking and talking, you learned these skills without ever understanding how you did so: humans are naturally great learning machines.

Other capabilities you learn more consciously. Perhaps you can fly a kite, ride a bicycle, work a computer, write a blog, or run a business. You have deliberately acquired these skills. Or maybe you're great at seeing the funny side of life, listening to friends, or getting the kids to school on time. All these capabilities are valuable skills that you take for granted and other people can learn. You're likely to remember the time before you were able to do these things, whereas you probably can't recall a time before you could walk or talk. These individual capabilities also benefit you in employment, because organisations build core competencies into their job specifications, defining essential skills that people need for the company to function at its best.

NLP focuses plenty of attention on the capability level, working on the premise that all skills are learnable. NLP assumes that anything is possible if taken in bite-size pieces or chunks. The HR director of one of the UK's most prestigious retailers told us that 'We recruit primarily on attitude: once this is right, we can teach people the skills they need to do the job.' Even attitudes can be acquired and changed so long as you find the desire, know-how, and opportunity to learn.

The question to hold on to is 'How can I do that?' Bear this question in mind as you go through every day. The NLP approach is that by modelling others and yourself, you become open to making changes and developing your own capabilities. If you want to do something well, find someone else who can do it and pay close attention to all that person's logical levels. You can find more about modelling in Chapter 19.

Here are some capability and skills questions and ideas to consider when you want to make an assessment of your capabilities and see where you can learn and improve:

- ✔ What skills have you learned that you're proud of – how did you acquire them?

- ✔ Have you become expert at something that serves you less well? If so, how did that happen? What skill may be better in its place?

- ✔ Do you know someone who has got a really positive attitude or skill that you want for yourself – how can you learn from them?

- ✔ What may you hear if you ask others to say what they think you're good at?

- ✔ What next? What would you like to learn?

As you build your capability, the world opens up for you. You're in a position to take on greater challenges, or to cope better with the ones you struggle to face.

Beliefs and values

You can read in Chapter 3 how beliefs and values direct your life and yet often you may not be aware of them. What you believe to be true is often going to be different from what another person believes to be true. We're not talking about beliefs in the sense of religion, but instead your perception at a deep, often unconscious, level. Your beliefs and values change over time.

Lee is an amateur club golfer with a passionate desire to launch his career on the international circuit. He believes that he has the same potential as his top golfing heroes and can create a living as a professional golfer. Such beliefs drive his capability and he's highly competent in his game. His beliefs also drive his behaviours – he can be found determinedly practising on the golf course most days of the year and he works at developing relationships with the media and sponsors. His beliefs also determine the environment where he spends much of his time – when not on the golf course, he's working out in the gym.

Over time Lee has come to understand the harsh reality of life on the competitive sports circuit and what he has to give up in order to pursue his dream. Checking how pursuing his dream impacts his ability to have other important things in his life, such as his own home, encouraged him to evolve his beliefs and values. So alongside the primary goal to reach the top, he's also developing new skills as a fitness and golf instructor, believing that he needs a range of career options if he's also going to be able to earn the money to have his own home and family as well as a precarious career in the game he loves.

Values are the things that are important to you, what motivates you to get out of bed in the morning, or not – criteria such as health, wealth, or happiness. Beliefs and values, and the way people rank them in order of importance, are different for each person and change over time. For this reason, motivating a whole team of people with the same approach is extremely difficult. One size doesn't fit all as regards beliefs and values.

Values are also rules that keep people on the socially acceptable road. You may seek money, but your values of honesty and respect for others stop you from stealing cash. Sometimes, a conflict exists between two important values – such as family life and work. You can read more about fixing this problem in Chapter 3.

In terms of making change, understanding your beliefs and values offers huge leverage. When people value something or believe it enough, that value becomes an energising force for change. They're concentrating on what's truly important to them, doing what they really want to be doing, and becoming closer to who they want to be. These people are in a place that feels right and natural. Beliefs and values drive you and influence the lower levels of capability, behaviour, and environment. So, by sticking to your values, other logical levels begin to come into alignment.

Often we coach people who move from one job to another with increasing dissatisfaction and are desperate to find a job they love. IT director John is a case in point. Every two years or so he'd get fed up, decide that he needed a change, and apply for another, similar, job with more money, a better benefits package, and in a new location, hoping that things would be better somewhere else. He simply made changes at the environmental level – new company, new country, and new people.

As he began to evaluate his own values and beliefs he realised that some essential ingredients were missing. He'd invested time and energy into taking an MBA and valued professional learning and development as important. Yet he always ended up in 'hire and fire' organisations that were too busy to invest in their staff or to work strategically: places that drained his energy. His beliefs and values didn't match those of the organisations in which he worked. When he understood this discrepancy, he took his skills to a prestigious international business school that valued his education and skills and gave him the opportunity to develop further.

Here are some beliefs and values questions to ask yourself when you sense that a conflict exists at this logical level that's hindering you getting what you want:

- ✔ What factors are important to you in this situation?
- ✔ What's important to other people?
- ✔ What do you believe to be right and wrong?
- ✔ What has to be true for you to get what you want?
- ✔ When do you say 'must', 'should', 'must not', and 'should not'? What assumptions lie behind these statements about what's possible?
- ✔ What are your beliefs about this person or situation? Are they helpful? What beliefs may help you get better results?
- ✔ What would somebody else believe if placed in your shoes?

Armed with the answers to these questions, you may want to work on your beliefs and values to ensure that they support you through difficult times. As you question your beliefs about yourself you may choose to discard some that no longer serve you well.

In business-change management programmes, you often hear talk of 'winning the hearts and minds' of people. If you're leading a group of people, you need to address their beliefs and values. When you have the right beliefs firmly in place, NLP suggests that the lower levels – such as capabilities and behaviours – fall into place automatically.

Identity

Identity describes your sense of who you are. You may express yourself through your beliefs and values, capabilities, behaviours, and environment, and yet you're more than all these factors. NLP assumes that your identity is separate from your behaviour, and recommends that you remain aware of the difference. In other words, you're more than what you do.

NLP separates the intention that lies behind your action from the action itself. For this reason, NLP avoids labelling people. Phrases such as 'men behaving badly', for example, doesn't mean that men are intrinsically bad, just that some behaviour is bad behaviour.

If you want to give feedback to encourage learning and better performance, always give very specific feedback about what someone says or does in terms of the behaviour rather than commenting at the identity level. So, instead of saying 'John. Sorry mate, but you were just awful.' Try: 'John, it was difficult to hear you at the meeting because you looked at the computer all the time and had your back to the audience.'

Here are some identity questions to ask yourself when you have a sense of conflict around your identity:

- ✔ How is what you're experiencing an expression of who you are?
- ✔ What kind of person are you?
- ✔ How do you describe yourself?
- ✔ What labels do you put on other people?
- ✔ How would others describe you?
- ✔ Would other people think of you as you want?
- ✔ What pictures, sounds, or feelings are you aware of as you think about yourself?

A greater awareness of self is a valuable insight in any journey of personal development. Too often people try to change others, when changing themselves would be a more effective starting point.

Purpose

This 'beyond-identity' level connects you to the larger picture when you begin to question your own purpose, ethics, mission, or meaning in life. Purpose takes individuals into the realms of spirituality and their connection with a bigger order of things in the universe, and it leads organisations to define their *raison d'être*, vision, and mission.

Human survival amid incredible suffering depends on true acceptance of your circumstances that goes beyond identity. Witness the resilience of the Dalai Lama driven from his homeland of Tibet, or the story of Viktor Frankl's endurance of the Holocaust in his book *Man's Search for Meaning*.

As you become older and approach different life stages, you quite naturally start to question what you're doing with your life. Sometimes a trigger inspires action and lights up your passion. A friend and logistics manager in industry, Alan, travelled to Kenya on holiday and saw at first-hand the educational needs of the country. Thus began a powerful one-man campaign that took over his life and led him to create an international charity taking educational materials into Africa, thanks to his personal passion to make a difference. On speaking to him about it, he often says 'I don't know why me. It's mad, but I just know I have to do this.' His purpose was stronger than his identity.

Here are some purpose questions to ask yourself when you want to check whether you're steering your life in the right direction:

- ✔ For what reason are you here?
- ✔ What would you like your contribution to be to others?
- ✔ What are your personal strengths that you can add to the wider world?
- ✔ How would you like to be remembered when you die?

In his book, *The Elephant and the Flea*, management guru Charles Handy conveys the passion that comes from a sense of mission and underlying purpose. He talks of entrepreneurs he's written about and his wife, the portrait photographer Elizabeth Handy, as people who leap beyond the logical and stick with their dream:

> *Passion is what drove them, a passionate belief in what they are doing, a passion that sustained them through the tough times, that seemed to justify their life. Passion is a much stronger word than mission or purpose, and I realise that as I speak that I am also talking to myself.*

When you're operating in a purposeful way, notice how you're unstoppable – you're then in the best place to gain true alignment at all the logical levels.

Figuring Out Other People's Levels: Language and Logical Levels

The intonation in people's language – the way they speak – can tell you at what level they're operating. Take the simple phrase, 'I can't do it here' and listen to where the stress (shown in italics below) is placed:

'*I* can't do it here' = statement about identity.

'I *can't* do it here' = statement about belief.

'I can't *do* it here' = statement about capability.

'I can't do *it* here' = statement about behaviour.

'I can't do it *here*' = statement about environment.

When you know the level at which someone's operating, you can help that person to make change at that level. For example, if the person's working at the environmental level, the question to ask is 'If not here, where can you do it?' If they're at the identity level, the question is, 'If not you, who can do it then?'

Teambuilding at Work and Play: A Logical Levels Exercise

We say throughout this book that NLP is experiential, which means that to get the benefit of many of the NLP exercises you sometimes have to move physically as well as mentally. As NLP developer Robert Dilts puts it, 'Knowledge is just a rumour until you get it in the muscle.'

This exercise helps you to brainstorm your team. You can lay out pieces of paper on the floor and walk through the different levels or use chairs, as in this version. You can set this exercise to some baroque music to get the ideas flowing and speed it up as a musical-chairs game – and you may want someone to capture ideas on a flipchart.

1. **Appoint one person to lead the exercise, ask the questions, and capture the answers.**

   This person is your question master.

2. **Place six chairs in a line; place a label on each chair to denote the logical level.**

3. **Sit one team member on each of the chairs.**

4. **Have the question master ask each person in turn questions according to the logical level of each chair.**

   Here are the questions to ask the team at each level:

   • **Environment chair:** 'Where, when, and with whom does this team work best?'

   • **Behaviour chair:** 'What does this team do well?'

   • **Capability chair:** 'How do we do what we do when we work well?'

   • **Beliefs and values chair:** 'Why is this team here? What's important to us?'

   • **Identity chair:** 'Who is this team?'

   • **Purpose chair:** 'How does this team contribute to the bigger picture? What is our mission to others?'

5. **After all the team members have answered their questions, let them move to a different chair; then repeat the questions.**

Keep people moving fairly promptly: they can always come around twice. When you've captured your brainstorming answers, the next step is to sift and work through the information you've gathered to spot patterns and new ideas to build on your strengths as a team.

Chapter 12

Driving Habits: Uncovering Your Secret Programs

In This Chapter

▶ Understanding the psychology behind your habits and behaviours

▶ Using strategies to improve communication

▶ Applying knowledge of strategies to overcome road rage

▶ Discovering how to spell well

*W*hen you wake up in the morning, do you brush your teeth first or shower first? Like everyone else, you have a strategy – in this case, a sequence of steps – for carrying out your routine tasks, whether you're cutting a loaf of bread, washing your hands, or completing your tax return. And like many other people, you may not even be aware that you do things on automatic pilot.

A *strategy* is any internal and external set or order of experiences that consistently produces a specific outcome.

When Romilla was studying yoga, her teacher Swami Ambikananda asked the class to gain a greater understanding of the unconscious rituals that we use. She suggested that we start our day by changing the regular sequence we have for getting dressed, eating breakfast, and preparing to go to work. Boy did that scramble the brain! Real concentration was necessary to keep the rest of the day running smoothly. Romilla felt as if she had forgotten something crucial and her brain kept trying to remember what it was. The overall experience was very uncomfortable.

You use your personal strategies for all sorts of behaviours: feeling loved; loving your partner, parent, child, or pet; hating someone; getting irritable with someone; buying your favourite perfume; learning to drive; and succeeding and failing in health, wealth, and happiness, and so on.

Perhaps you ask yourself from time to time, 'Why am I successful in some areas of my life and not as successful in others?' Well, you may find that you're simply using less-effective strategies in those less-successful areas. The great thing is that when you realise that you're running a strategy, you can more easily develop the tools to change those strategies that are less effective. Even better, you can find someone else's strategy that works well and copy it!

In this chapter you discover the mechanics behind your behaviours, and armed with this information you can add, modify, or delete your strategies to put you in the driving seat of your life.

The Evolution of Strategies

The NLP strategy model came about through a process of evolution. It started with behavioural psychologists such as Watson, Skinner, and Pavlov and was enhanced by Miller, Galanter, and Pribram, who were cognitive psychologists, before being refined by NLP's founding fathers, Grinder and Bandler.

The S–R model

Back in the early part of the 20th century, behavioural psychologists based their work on the study of human and animal behaviour. They proposed that people either respond to a stimulus or develop a response through conditioning or reinforcement. The most famous of the studies was that of Pavlov and his dogs. The dogs heard a bell that they associated with the arrival of food (stimulus) and therefore salivated (response). Ultimately, the dogs salivated merely at the sound of the bell (without the food). A behaviourist may argue that humans simply respond to stimuli in a similar way. For example, when John's baby gurgles and smiles (stimulus), John feels a warm glow (response), or when Mark sees a homeless person on the pavement (stimulus), he reaches for spare coins in his pocket (response).

Although behaviourist ideas remain influential in modifying behaviour, most people generally agree that humans have more sophisticated powers of thought.

The TOTE model

Miller, Galanter, and Pribram built on the S–R model of behaviourism and presented the TOTE (Test, Operate, Test, Exit) model, which is illustrated in Figure 12-1. The TOTE model works on the principle that you have a goal in mind when you exhibit a particular behaviour. The purpose of your behaviour is to get as close to your desired outcome as possible. You test your strategy in order to assess whether you've reached your goal. If your goal is reached, you stop the behaviour and exit the strategy. If the goal isn't reached, you modify the behaviour and repeat it, thereby incorporating a simple feedback and response loop. So, if your outcome is to boil the kettle, the test is whether the kettle has boiled; if it hasn't, you carry on waiting for it to boil, test for the kettle having boiled, and when it has you exit the strategy.

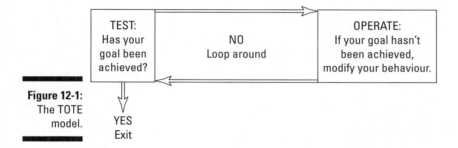

Figure 12-1:
The TOTE
model.

The flow diagram shows:

TEST: Has your goal been achieved? → NO Loop around → OPERATE: If your goal hasn't been achieved, modify your behaviour. (loops back to TEST)

YES Exit

The NLP strategy = TOTE + modalities

NLP suggests that you experience the world primarily through your five senses: visual (eyes), auditory (ears), kinaesthetic (feelings and touch), olfactory (smell), and gustatory (taste). These senses are your *representational (rep) systems*, also called *modalities*, which you can read more about in Chapter 6.

Submodalities are the different qualities that combine to make up modalities. For example, if you create a picture in your mind's eye, you're using your visual representative system or modality. You adjust the qualities or submodalities of the picture by making it bigger, brighter, or bringing it closer to you. You can discover much more about your submodalities and how they affect the way you experience your world in Chapter 10.

Bandler and Grinder included modalities and submodalities into the Test and Operate phases of the TOTE model, refining it further to create the NLP strategy model. According to Bandler and Grinder, the goal you have when you initiate a strategy to achieve a specific goal, and the means by which you assess whether or not it has been achieved, is dependent on combinations of your personal modalities. For example, when you think of your goal, you may make a picture of it, create a sound that you hear in your head, or get a feeling.

The success of your strategy ties into the success of your goal and you judge success by whether or not you feel, hear, or see what you imagined you would through the submodalities.

The NLP strategy model in action

This section shows how the NLP strategy model works for someone enacting a basic road-rage strategy. The TOTE model (take a look at Figure 12-1 in the earlier section, 'The TOTE model') is enriched by adding modalities to give you the NLP strategy model, which can be used to understand how someone operates a particular pattern of behaviour.

Figure 12-2 illustrates the process in action. Here's how the NLP strategy model works:

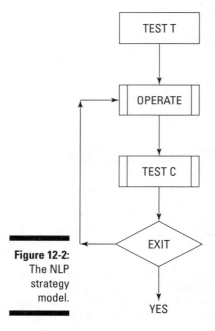

Figure 12-2:
The NLP
strategy
model.

1. **Test 1** is the initial trigger that starts off a strategy. This test is where you assess whether the information coming in from your senses complies with the data necessary to fire off the strategy. If you're prone to road rage, the trigger may be that you see someone undertaking and pushing in front of you in a traffic jam (visual confirmation), but because you're in a good mood (no kinaesthetic confirmation) you choose not to run the strategy. However, if you're in a bad mood (kinaesthetic confirmation), you fire your road-rage strategy when you get the visual

confirmation of someone cutting you up. The outcome is to make sure that the driver in front knows exactly what you think and for you to relish thoroughly the feeling of giving in to the red mist of uncontrollable rage (kinaesthetic).

2. **Operate** is the process by which you gather the data that're going to help you carry out your strategy. So for your road-rage strategy, you remember where the car horn is, where the headlight switch is, and which rude hand gesture you want to use. In this example you use the visual modality as you picture what you're going to do. You may then invoke the auditory digital modality as you recall all the juicy rude words you know. You then launch yourself into your best road-rage behaviour.

3. **Test 2** is where you compare the current data and situation with your outcome for running the strategy. Yes, you blew your horn (auditory); yes, you mouthed all your worst swear words (visual for the transgressor's benefit) and made the appropriate gestures (kinaesthetic for yourself and visual for the other driver). Yes, the red mist feels goooood as it holds you in its deadly embrace (kinaesthetic). But . . . oh no! You didn't flash your lights (visual).

4. **Exit** is where you exit your strategy. In this example, because you didn't remember to flash your headlights, you loop around to continue operating the strategy and exit when you've flashed your lights at the offending driver.

During her NLP Master Programme, Romilla was asked to break a piece of fairly solid wood with her hand, and she was worried about failing this test. Her strategy for 'psyching' herself up was to see the board breaking (visual), feel energy in her solar plexus, pulsing up her chest and down her arm (kinaesthetic), and say repeatedly, 'You can do it' (auditory digital). Here's how this approach fits into the TOTE model:

1. **Test 1:** Stepping up to breaking the board is the trigger that starts this strategy.

2. **Operate:** Romilla's strategy for psyching herself up used the visual, kinaesthetic, and auditory digital modalities.

3. **Test 2:** Testing whether she was sufficiently psyched up.

4. **Exit:** Romilla looped around to operate the strategy, building up her confidence until she was ready. When she was ready, she exited to the actual board-break strategy.

The Eyes Have It: Recognising Another's Strategy

Each personal strategy has distinct stages, such as Test 1 (Trigger), Operate, Test 2 (Compare), and Exit (as discussed in the preceding section, 'The NLP strategy model in action'), using your five senses (check out the earlier section 'NLP strategy = TOTE + modalities'). Consider the following example: Ben has just started university and uses the following strategy for telephoning home:

1. **Feels that he's missing home.** Test 1 (kinaesthetic).

2. **Makes a mental picture of his family.** Operate (visual).

3. **Says the phone number to himself.** Operate (auditory digital).

4. **Dials home.** Operate (kinaesthetic).

For the purpose of this exercise, we assume that Ben's call gets through, satisfying his Test 2, and so he exits the dial-home strategy.

When a strategy of your own is embedded in your neurology, you have little or no conscious awareness of its steps. Yet, if you know what to look for, you can figure out other people's strategies. Just look for their eye movement.

You can get a pretty good idea of how people are thinking about a topic (in images, words, or emotions) by watching their eyes (as we show in Figure 12-3). Generally, people's eyes move in the following ways (you can find out more about the secrets that your eyes give away in Chapter 6):

When they're doing this	*Their eyes do this*
Remembering a picture	Move to their top left
Creating a picture	Move to their top right
Remembering a sound or conversation	Move horizontally to their left
Imagining what a sound is going to sound like	Move horizontally to their right
Accessing emotions	Drop down and to their right
Having a conversation with themselves	Drop down and to their left

Think back to Ben and his phone call and imagine that you're watching him as he phones home. At first, his eyes go down and to his right (feeling of missing home), and then to the top and to his left (visual picture of his family). His eyes stay looking to the top and his left (as he visually recalls his family phone number) before he dials the telephone number.

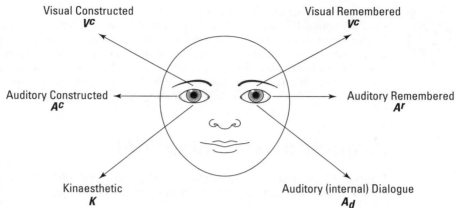

Visual Constructed
Vc

Visual Remembered
Vc

Auditory Constructed
Ac

Auditory Remembered
Ar

Kinaesthetic
K

Auditory (internal) Dialogue
Ad

Figure 12-3:
This diagram shows the eye movements when you're looking at someone who's right-handed.

How a person's eyes move depends on whether that person is right- or left-handed (Figure 12-3 illustrates a right-handed person). Left-handed people may tend to look to the top and their right when they make a visual memory. So when you're trying to figure out someone else's strategy, always check that person's responses by asking a few innocuous questions such as, 'Which route did you take to get here?' Such questions force the person into visual recall and give you a clue as to which eye strategy (left- or right-handed) is being used.

Flexing Your Strategy Muscles

Throughout your life, you continually develop strategies. You create most of the basic ones when you're young, such as walking, eating, drinking, and choosing and making friends, and you develop others as you come across new circumstances in life. Sometimes you find that a particular strategy isn't as effective as someone else's, perhaps because that person is starting from a more informed platform or had a good teacher.

For example, in your professional life, you may be very good with numbers but less so at public speaking. Perhaps your career strategy was to learn about figures through studying hard and getting lots of practice at working out budgets, but now you expect to be a good presenter without putting in the same level of study or practice.

Recognising that a strategy may have grounds for improvement is a useful tool. If, say, a colleague is cleverer at negotiating a higher salary than you for the same job, perhaps they present their successes to the boss more effectively than you. If so, maybe you should work out and implement their strategy.

Instead of being tough on yourself when you recognise a less-effective strategy, set yourself what we call a 'well-formed outcome' for an area of your life in which you want to raise your game. Chapter 4 shows how you can easily create such an outcome when you break the task down into smaller steps. If you want to learn something especially fast, find someone who already does it and hang out with them to discover their strategy (as we describe in the earlier section, 'The Eyes Have It: Recognising Another's Strategy'.

Acquiring new capabilities

Chapter 11 explains the NLP Logical Levels Model, which enables you to examine the structure of your experience in the following different ways:

- ✔ Identity
- ✔ Values and beliefs
- ✔ Capabilities and skills
- ✔ Behaviour
- ✔ Environment

Your strategies relate to the capabilities and skills level, but may also involve making changes at the other levels too. Imagine that you want to improve your strategies by acquiring new skills: in the example of the higher-earning colleague mentioned in the preceding section, you can discover how they built and maintain a rapport with the boss. They may have a very good strategy for keeping their boss apprised of progress on their projects, which you can take on board by talking to the boss of your progress each week and gaining stronger visibility.

Kay always worked in an office where she felt safe and was confident of her abilities. When she decided to set up in business for herself, she discovered that she had to develop a whole raft of new behaviours: she had to find out how to 'network' in order to spread the word of her new venture. Unfortunately, she went to networking meetings and came away without having achieved anything concrete. She was too vague about her objectives and thought only that she was going to meet new people who may prove useful in her business.

Kay realised that she needed to develop new strategies in order to connect effectively with new people. She achieved this objective by observing her friend Lindsay, who was very successful at introducing herself and making connections with new people. Kay started to adopt Lindsay's strategies (outlines of which are listed below, along with how Kay used each step) and began to make successful, new contacts.

1. **Think of the outcome you want from a networking event.** Kay decides she wants to exchange cards with at least six people who may be useful to her (and she useful to them), in a business or social context.

2. **Go up to someone and introduce yourself.** Kay says:

   'Hello, I'm Kay and you are. . . ?'

3. **Ask questions to break the ice.** Kay's questions include:

   'This is my first time here. Have you been before?'

   'How do you find these events?

   'Have you travelled far?'

   'What line of business are you in?'

4. **Stay focused on what the other person is saying as well as your outcome for the event.** Kay realises that previously she tended to get so caught up in the content of what the other person was saying that she forgot to swap cards, or she spent too much time with one person and forgot to meet people. She decides that the way to stay focused on her goal is to hold the container with her cards in her left hand instead of putting it away in her handbag. This approach leaves her right hand free to shake hands, while keeping her mind on her goal.

Recoding your programs

Strategies can be changed. In the road-rage example in the earlier section 'The NLP strategy model in action', whose agenda and best interests are you fulfilling? When you reflect on how anger and stress can physically damage your body, surely not your own. How about developing another strategy, such as the following:

1. **Test 1 – Trigger:** Someone cuts you up while driving.

2. **Operate:** Instead of accessing all your best rude words and gestures, think about the sun collapsing into a planetary nebula in about 5 billion years' time when all this angst will be completely pointless – and give yourself a little internal smile and count your blessings.

3. **Test 2 – Compare:** Does your strategy for staying positive work? If so, move to step 4; if not, return to the previous step and try an alternative strategy, such as deciding that the other person has a more urgent appointment than you. Or compliment yourself on being better organised and in control of your life.

4. **Exit:** Choose to follow your own agenda and exit.

Chinese Qigong practitioners know that the 'internal smile' technique used in step 2 improves their immune system, gets the brain working more efficiently, and can reduce blood pressure, anxiety, and simple depression.

Grasping the importance of the 'how'

NLP is interested more in process – how you do something – than in the content of your experience. So the issue isn't that you get angry when you lose at badminton (content), but rather how you go about getting angry when you lose a game (process).

Because NLP is concerned with the process of your strategy, discovering and analysing that process helps you to change a strategy that doesn't provide the desired results. So instead of smashing your badminton racket, you construct a visual image of writing a hefty cheque for another expensive racket. And because strategies can be modified, you can use the model of the way you do something successfully to improve another area in your life in which you don't feel you do as well.

Identify an area of your life in which you're successful and ask yourself, 'What strategy am I running now that I'm succeeding?' We call this exercise playing the 'as if' game. Suppose you consider yourself a fairly successful badminton player and have always wanted to take up running. Every time you start running, however, you give up because you just can't keep up the momentum. So you think about running 'as if' you're playing badminton. While examining the strategies you operate while playing badminton, you realise that your breathing and mental focus are different when you're running around the court to when you're running on the track. By adopting the strategies that you use when you play badminton when you run, you may find that you achieve your desire of becoming a more successful runner.

Tim was extremely tidy and organised at the office. Unfortunately his home was a mess: he was just unable to keep a tidy house. Romilla worked with Tim to help him identify the processes he used in the office to keep his work area tidy. He examined his strategy as follows:

1. **Test 1 – Trigger:** He saw papers and folders on his desk at work and decided he wanted to see clear space.

2. **Operate:** Tim would do the following:

    - Imagine his boss walking in and commenting on his untidiness. Interestingly, the boss's tone of voice was very similar to the one Tim's mother used when he was a child.

    - Get an uncomfortable feeling in his solar plexus.

    - Picture where the files went.

    - Get up and file away the papers and folders.

3. **Test 2 – Compare:** He looked at his desk, saw clear desk space, and experienced a warm feeling in his solar plexus.

4. **Exit:** If Tim didn't see enough desk space he didn't get the warm feeling and he proceeded to tidy up further, before he exited his strategy.

By understanding his 'tidy desk' strategy at work, Tim was able to keep a tidy home. He organised his cupboards to enable him to tidy things away. When no floor was visible, he imagined his boss walking in and ran his strategy to keep his home tidy: a very successful transference of strategies.

Using NLP Strategies for Love and Success

You behave in a particular way because you have learned a strategy, usually unconsciously, or developed a strategy to carry out a particular function. For instance, if your eyesight in one eye is weaker than the other, you may have discovered, unconsciously, to hold reading material directly in front of the stronger eye by moving your head.

The following sections show you how you can discern or be taught the modalities of others to help you discover new skills in relationships, communication, and spelling.

Ask other people questions in order to elicit their strategies: for example, ask 'How do you know when you need to go to the gym?' and then watch their eyes as they give their response (as we discuss in the earlier section 'The Eyes Have It: Recognising Another's Strategy'). This reaction gives you fairly obvious clues as to people's strategies. If you have any doubt, fine-tune the question and repeat!

Loving the deep love strategy

Everyone has a particular strategy in order for them to feel truly loved. We call this the *deep love strategy*. When someone comes along who satisfies that deep love strategy, bingo! On go the rose-tinted glasses for Mr or Ms Right.

When you meet someone to whom you're attracted or you find interesting, initially you fire all your sensory modalities (which we discuss earlier in the section 'NLP strategy = TOTE + modalities'):

- ✔ **Visual:** You make the effort to look good. Perhaps you wear the colour you've discovered the object of your interest likes. You look deeply into those gorgeous blue/green/brown eyes.

- ✔ **Auditory:** You speak in dulcet tones and say the words you think the person wants to hear.

- ✔ **Kinaesthetic:** You hold hands. You stroke the other person.

- ✔ **Olfactory:** Mmmm! Hope the perfume isn't too overwhelming. Oops! Forgot the mouthwash!

- ✔ **Gustatory:** Candle-lit dinners with herbs and spices to prove that this someone is really special.

The person you desire is hooked and you walk into the sunset hand-in-hand. But then – after some time – you experience rumblings of discontent. 'What went wrong?' you cry. Nothing really. Perhaps you and your partner just reverted to the modality you operate most naturally. So, where the wife may be craving physical contact with hugs and cuddles in order to feel loved, the husband may be proving his love by doing all he can for her, like keeping the house in good repair and washing the car and keeping it topped up with fuel.

To find a person's strategy for feeling loved, try saying words to the effect, 'You know I love you, don't you?' and 'What would make you feel even more loved?' As you do, pay attention to the eye movements we show in Figure 12-4. 'Uh, I'm not sure', with the eyes going to their bottom right (K), gives the clue that more cuddles are in order. Test your hunch. If the eyes move to the horizontal left (A^r), try asking what the person may like to hear you say.

Figure 12-4:
The eyes
reveal the
strategy.

V^r A^r A$_d$ K

Here are a couple of things to bear in mind:

- ✔ Ask your questions in a special, quiet time when just the two of you are present, and not at moments of high stress, such as in a traffic jam – we guarantee you won't like the response you get.

- ✔ Calibrate the response you get when you do something for the other person. For example, does bringing home a bunch of roses get you that special response?

In NLP, *calibration* is the process by which you read another person's response to your communication. A slap in the face is a pretty overt response and, we hope, you never repeat the words or behaviour that earned the slap. Most responses are much more subtle: a scowl, a puzzled look, flushed cheeks, a clenched jaw. A master communicator needs to be able to assess these reactions, particularly when the signals are mixed; for example, a smile with a puzzled look may indicate that the person doesn't get what you're saying but is too polite to say so.

Nothing succeeds like positive feedback in achieving your own strategy, so let other people know when they hit the mark, especially if you're aware of your beloved's deep love strategy.

Romilla knows a couple who've been very happily married for 27 years. The wife needs to have her face stroked in a specific way, with a particular look in her husband's eyes, for her to feel as if she's the centre of her husband's world; you can almost hear her purr!

Influencing people with strategies

By using your knowledge of strategies you can make yourself an irresistible communicator. When you discover people's strategies, you can use them as a framework to feed information back to people, using the steps of their own strategy. For example, suppose that you want to use a teenager's strategy to help them do their homework.

In order to feed information back using the teen's own strategy, you first need to determine what that strategy is. So you ask a question such as 'How do you motivate yourself to play football?' and watch the teen's eye movements as they answer your question. Suppose that your question elicited the following verbal response with the accompanying eye movements shown in Figure 12-4 in the preceding section:

> *I see myself in my kit, with the rest of the team [eyes move to their top left –* V^r*] and I hear everyone talking excitedly [eyes move their left, horizontally –* A^r*]. I say to myself 'we're going to win' [eyes move to their bottom left –* A_d*] and I feel really good [eyes move to their bottom right – K].*

Based on the teen's answer and their eye movements you can craft your response accordingly. You know that to motivate themselves, they remember a picture (V^r), and then they remember the excited chatter of the team (A^r). They then talk to themselves (A_d) before, finally, feeling (K) good. Based on this information you can use the following approach:

- ✔ 'Can you recall the picture of when you finished your physics homework on time last week?'

  You're asking him to make a picture of the time when he actually finished his homework, forcing him into the start of his strategy (Vr).

- ✔ 'When Mr Saunders really praised you. Do you remember what he said?'

  You're asking him to recall the words that were used in order to fire the next step of his motivation strategy (Ar).

- ✔ 'Can you remember the wonder with which you said to yourself, "For the first time, I really understand physics!"?'

  By asking them to repeat their conversation with themselves, you're directing them into the penultimate step of their motivation strategy (A_d).

- ✔ 'Do you remember how elated you felt and wouldn't it be great to finish your homework now and get that elated feeling back again?'

  In this final step you're making the teenager motivate themselves by hooking into feeling good (*K*) and suggesting that they can recreate feeling good by getting their homework finished.

You can use this technique any time you need to be really persuasive. First, ask a question and watch the eyes as the person responds, and then phrase your suggestions in language that gets you the best response.

Spelling out the NLP spelling strategy

As with other strategies, every literate person has a strategy for spelling. The good spellers have an effective strategy; the poor spellers have an ineffective strategy.

Spelling well is a very visual process. If you class yourself as a good speller, you may naturally look up to your top left (visual recall) when you visualise the word you want to spell. This action means that you've memorised pictures of words and built them into a library; you can then draw upon this store of words when you spell.

Trying to spell phonetically is usually an ineffective spelling strategy. You may be looking down and getting caught in feelings (kinaesthetic) or to the side to recall how a word sounds (auditory).

Eureka!

When Olive Hickmott came across the NLP Spelling Strategy on an NLP Practitioner course in London, it set her off on a journey of discovery. Those 15 minutes provided a totally unexpected 'Eureka!' moment, giving her the important 'how to' of spelling that had been missing all her life. Her struggle with English had adversely affected her education and her career, and meant that she didn't read for pleasure until the age of 40. She says, 'Why hadn't anyone ever told me that this was how you were expected to spell? It was one of those things that I didn't know that I didn't know.'

First she discovered how to develop her visualisation skills generally, and then how to visualise words. She has gone on to teach the methods described in her book *Spelling Means Achieving* to help others resolve areas of word confusion, such as letters jumping around the page, before they go on to achieve what they want. From spelling she has moved her work to other areas of learning difficulties including dyslexia, dyspraxia, and ADHD, and she's passionate about equipping young people with basic spelling skills at a young age before they embed unhelpful strategies.

If you spell phonetically and want to be better at spelling, try the following:

1. **Choose a word that you want to remember how to spell, and then write it in big letters and keep it to hand.**

2. **Think of a word that you can spell.**

We ask you to spell a word you know already to create a positive feeling. Sadly, when you learn to spell as a child your teachers don't always teach you the strategy to spell well. Consequently, you may get categorised as 'not the brightest student' and when asked to spell, you feel bad. Over a period of time, spelling can come to be synonymous with feeling bad. It may affect your identity, as in 'I'm a bad speller' or even worse, 'I'm a poor student'. Allow yourself to acknowledge any negative beliefs that may surface and be compassionate with yourself. You may not have got on with your English teacher and learning to spell may dredge up unwanted memories, and that's OK. Gently remind yourself that you're no longer a child under the influence of an unsympathetic teacher; rather you're an adult in control of your own life. Then give yourself permission to be as good at spelling as you can. So play with the words and go for it.

3. **Move your eyes to visual recall (usually, your top left, if you're right-handed) and make a picture of the word you know you can spell.**

Knowing you can spell the word gives you a positive feeling (satisfied, confident, happy, and so on).

4. **Bring that positive feeling into your consciousness; focus on it and enhance it; take a deep breath and enhance it some more.**

5. **Have a quick glance at the word you want to remember how to spell.**

6. **Keep hold of the positive feeling, move your eyes to your top left, and make a picture of the new word you want to spell.**

   Make sure that you make a clear, bright, big picture of the word and look at it; we mean *really look at it.*

7. **Next time you want to spell the word, move your eyes to visual recall and the word pops into your mind's eye, and you begin to believe that you can spell.**

While discussing the power of this simple spelling strategy, Kate discovered how she often uses the visual recall section of her memory to remember telephone numbers, shopping lists, and diary appointments. You can also use this method to remember where you left your keys or to help remember your multiplication tables.

Something is GHOTI-y around here

Robert Dilts, one of the most innovative gurus of NLP, relates his experience of learning to spell as a child:

My consternation grew, however, as we began with basics – such as the names of the first ten numbers. Instead of 'wun' the first number was spelled 'one' (that looked like it should be pronounced 'oh-nee'). There was no 'W' and an extra silent 'E'. The second number, instead of being spelled 'tu' like it sounded, was spelled 'two'. (As the comedian Gallagher points out, perhaps that was where the missing 'W' from 'one' had gone). After 'three' ('tuh-ree'), 'four' ('fow-er') and 'five' ('fi-vee') I knew something was wrong, but being young, I figured it was probably just something wrong with me. In fact, when 'six' and 'seven' came along I started to

build back some hope – but then they struck with 'eight' ('ee-yi-guh-hut') and I felt like the next number looked as if it should sound – 'nine' (a 'ninny').

The vagaries of phonetics also weren't lost on George Bernard Shaw. He demonstrated that the word 'fish' could be spelt 'GHOTI'. 'GH', for example, from the end of the word 'laugh', 'O' as pronounced in 'women', and 'TI' as in 'nation'. He was just making a point though: 'GH' never sounds like 'F' at the beginning of a word and 'TI' can't be used at the end of a word because it needs to be followed by a vowel in order to make the 'SH' sound.

Reproduced with the permission of Robert Dilts.

Chapter 13

Travelling in Time to Improve Your Life

. . . .

In This Chapter

▶ Understanding your time line

▶ Releasing the hold that negative emotions have on you

▶ Changing beliefs by going back along your time line

▶ Discovering how you organise time

▶ Creating your future along your time line

. . . .

Time is a core system of cultural, social and personal life. In fact, nothing occurs except in some kind of time frame.

—The Dance of Life (Edward T Hall, Anchor, 1984)

Time displays a strange, elastic quality: it goes fast when you're engaged in something interesting and stretches when you allow yourself to get bored. Are you one of the time-rich people who has all the time in the world, or are you time poor and always short of time? Perhaps having time, like money, depends on where you focus your attention. Although day and night for the rich, poor, young, and old always lasts 24 hours, the perception of time is different. Some people are stuck in the past, others have their gaze firmly staring into the future, and some people just live in the moment.

The 'American–European' perception of time is a result of the Industrial Revolution, when people had to be at work in the factories at a specific time. This idea of time has a linear format, in which one event or transaction follows another. The concept of time in Latin America, Africa, Arabic countries, and some countries in the Southern hemisphere, has a multi-dimensional structure, allowing people to operate much more 'in the moment'. Each idea of time contains strengths and weaknesses as well as the potential to cause conflict in cross-cultural exchanges and working.

When Kate worked in Zurich, a city in which you can set your watch by the trains running precisely on time, she had some fascinating conversations with a Swiss colleague who had married a Nigerian man. The marriage ended in divorce and one of the reasons cited was that husband and wife had very different attitudes to time:

> *When we lived in Africa, we'd make arrangements to visit somebody or to do something at a particular time, and then on the way we may bump into somebody else. Our detour could take days while we went off to another village or waited for another relative to appear. I could never rely on my husband to keep to commitments and he couldn't understand my haste. It was infuriating for both of us.*

Time also gives your memories meaning. With NLP techniques, you can switch the meaning you give to a memory by changing the quality of the memory as well as its relationship to time. In this chapter, we explore how employing time-line techniques enables you to work with time and memories to your advantage, including the ability to release yourself from negative emotions and limiting decisions. These tools give you the means to create the future you would rather have, without the influence of disempowering past memories.

Understanding How Your Memories Are Organised

Think of something you do on a regular basis, such as reading a book, driving to a shop, working at your desk, eating in a restaurant, or brushing your teeth. The event needs to be something that you can remember doing in the past, imagine or experience doing in the present, and also imagine doing in the future. As you access the memory or use your imagination, you code it with sensory data such as sounds, pictures, or feelings. When you access an image of the past, for example, you may also notice a difference in the quality of the pictures, to do with brightness, colour, movement, two or three dimensions, and so on. These qualities, or attributes, are called submodalities (you can read more about them in Chapters 6 and 10).

By going into the past to examine a memory and then into the future – via a pitstop in the present – you have experienced a little 'land-based' time travel. (You can experience the airborne variety a little later in the section 'Discovering Your Time Line'.)

We ask you to consider these attributes in order to help you realise that a structure exists to your memories. You instinctively know whether a memory is in the past or whether you're creating an experience in your imagination.

People view time differently: some are rooted in the past, others gaze firmly into the future, and some live in the moment. Research by Professor Philip Zimbardo shows that how you perceive time is pretty much unconscious and yet can have a significant influence on your behaviour. Understanding whether your own focus is on the past, present, or future, and getting the balance right, can have a dramatic effect on your levels of happiness and success. (Check out Chapter 8 to discover how to spot someone's perception of time.)

If we ask you to define what you're made up of, you may say 'sugar and spice and all things nice' or 'hair, skin, and blood'. But of course the whole person that makes up 'you' is much more than your component parts. The term for this reality is *Gestalt*. A Gestalt is a structure, or pattern, which can't be derived purely from its constituent parts. So, when thinking about you, someone's mind makes the leap from your components to the whole you.

Your memories are arranged in a Gestalt. Associated memories form a Gestalt, although the formation of a Gestalt may start when you experience an event that first triggers an emotional response: a Significant Emotional Event, or SEE for short. The SEE is also referred to as the *root cause*. If you experience a similar event and have a similar emotional response, you link the two events. This process continues and suddenly you have a chain.

One of psychology's founding fathers, William James, likened memories to a string of pearls, in which each related memory is linked along a string to the one before and to the one after. During any work with your time line, if you snip the string before the first occurrence, the Gestalt is broken (as the illustration in Figure 13-1 shows).

Figure 13-1:
A memory
Gestalt.

Discovering Your Time Line

Memories are arranged in a pattern. If we ask you to point to the direction from which a past memory came, where would you point? Similarly, if you were to point to something you're going to do in the future, notice where you're pointing now. Can you also point to where your present is? If you draw a line between the memory from the past, the one in the present, and the one in the future, you've created your very own *time line*.

People sometimes identify their past as being behind them and their future as in front of them. Others can have a V-shaped line, whereas some people have their past to their left and their future to their right – which is interesting because (as we discuss in Chapter 6) most people move their eyes to the left when they want to remember something and to the right when they want to imagine something that isn't real, yet. In addition, some people arrange their time line geographically, with their past in, perhaps, Cornwall, Los Angeles, or Timbuktu, and their present where they're currently residing. Their future may lie in the place to which they want to move next.

A woman who attended Romilla's workshop 'Future Perfect' (where people come to create the future they want to live) became confused while trying to find her time line. We discovered that her past was in South Africa, her present in England, and she was unable to decide about her future. We asked her to trust her unconscious and point her finger to where her future may be. She pointed to her front and slightly to the right. Romilla asked her to point to where she thought South Africa was. She pointed behind her but slightly to her left. By getting her to draw a line from where she saw her future to where she pictured South Africa, we were able to establish her time line ran in a diagonal from her left to her right.

The idea is to find a line that connects your past and future and whether you choose to do it by connecting geographical locations or simply by pointing won't affect the final result.

You may find that 'drawing' an imaginary line on the ground is easier. Then, trusting your unconscious mind, you can walk along the line, from where you think your past is to where you feel your future lies.

Walking along a time line can be difficult if spatial restrictions get in the way, for example if you're in a small room. The following exercise shows you how you can visualise your time line in your head by 'floating up' in order to get a clear view of the time line stretching out below you:

1. **Think of an event that you experienced recently.**

2. **Now take a deep breath and just relax as deeply as you can.**

3. **Imagine yourself floating up, above your present and way above the clouds, into the stratosphere.**

4. **Picture your time line below you, like a ribbon, and see yourself in the time line.**

5. **Now float back over your time line until you're directly over the recently experienced event.**

6. **You can hover there as long as you like until you decide to float back to the present and down into your own body.**

Hope you enjoyed that trial flight. Remember this process because you're going to be doing a lot of it.

Changing Your Time Line

When you've worked out your time line as described in the preceding section, ask yourself what its position is in relation to you. For instance, does the line run through your body as in the two *in-time* diagrams shown in Figures 13-2 and 13-3? Or is it out in front of you so that you can see the whole of your time line before you, as in the *through-time* diagram shown in Figure 13-4?

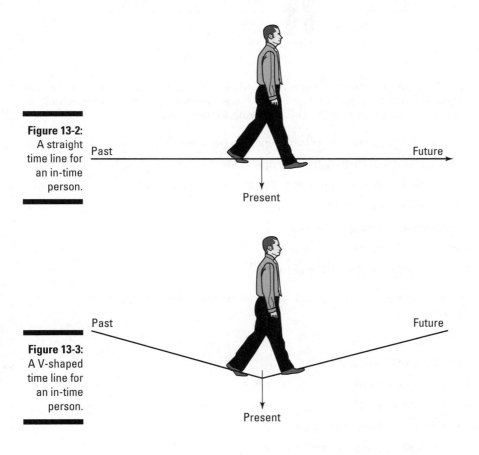

Figure 13-2:
A straight time line for an in-time person.

Past

Future

Present

Figure 13-3:
A V-shaped time line for an in-time person.

Past

Future

Present

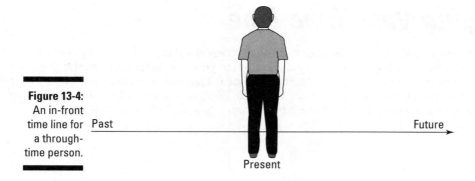

Figure 13-4:
An in-front
time line for
a through-
time person.

Past

Future

Present

The shape of your time line can influence various personality traits. If you see a through-time line, you have an American–European model of time, which means that you may display the following tendencies:

- ✔ Able to keep your emotions separate from events
- ✔ Conscious of turning up for appointments on time
- ✔ Display a strong awareness of past and future events
- ✔ Goal-orientated
- ✔ Good at planning activities
- ✔ Have difficulty living in the now
- ✔ Very aware of the value of time

As a person with an in-time line you may have the following abilities and tendencies:

- ✔ Creative
- ✔ Efficient at multi-tasking
- ✔ Engrossed in the current experience
- ✔ Feel your emotions very strongly
- ✔ Good at living in the moment
- ✔ Prefer to keep your options open
- ✔ Spontaneous
- ✔ Unlikely to plan far ahead

You can change the orientation of your time line in order to experience a different mindset, without changing any of the individual memories and events of which your time line is made up. For example, if you're an in-time person and you have to keep to a time schedule, try turning your time line so that you're through time, with all your time line in front of you. Or, if you're a workaholic and want to chill with your partner in the evening, why not pretend that your time line is the other side of your front door, and become an in-time person the moment you step through your door.

Switching time lines can cause some physical disorientation. For example, you can feel dizzy. So choose a quiet and relaxed time for altering your time line instead of when you're busy rushing around. If you feel uncomfortable while changing your time line, slow down and revert your time line to its original orientation.

If you're a through-time person and your time line is laid out in front, you can change that time line by stepping onto it so that you have to turn your head or your body to face the past or the future. Or you can float above your time line so that it spreads out below you; as you float back down to position yourself, the time line's below your feet or running through your body.

If you're an in-time person, you can step off your time line so that it spreads out in front of you and you can see your past, present, and future as a continuum, just by turning your head to your left or your right but without having to turn your body. If you prefer, you can float above your time line and when you float back down, position yourself so that your time line's in front of you.

Romilla always asks delegates on the 'Future Perfect' seminars to switch time-line orientation and to keep the different orientation over lunch, *as long as they feel comfortable*. One of the delegates, a highly in-time person, initially experienced dizziness and nausea when she put her time line out in front of her (through time) but was keen to persevere. After sitting down for a while she stabilised and went to lunch. On her return, her relief at switching her time line back to an in-time line was visible for all to see.

Apart from switching the orientation of your time line, discovering how to change the way that you space out events on it can also be useful.

John was suffering from stress. He felt as though everything was pressing in on him and that he just couldn't cope with all his work. When John went back along his time line, using Time Line Therapy® (co-created by Tad James), he remembered that he'd failed to qualify for a scholarship when he was a young boy. His mother was very scathing and judgemental. John realised that he'd been trying to please her ever since and always tried to do too much.

On examining the arrangement of his time line, John discovered that he had his present up close to his nose and his future about 15 centimetres farther in front of that. When we cleared up all the negative emotions behind his 'failure' (flip to Chapter 2 for a more empowering term, 'feedback'), John was able to move the present out to about 30 centimetres away and place his future farther along and up, about three metres away. When he stretched out his time line in his mind, he got into a panic because he felt that because he'd stretched it too far, that he'd never achieve anything in his life again. When he shortened his time line so that it wasn't as tight as it was before, but not so long that he felt panicky, he felt comfortable because he knew he would be able to plan and meet his objectives.

Simon had the opposite problem to John: he felt that he could never meet his deadlines. On examining his time line, Simon discovered that his future was so far out in front of him that he was unable to generate enough of a sense of urgency about his goals. Simon compressed his time line and imagined it as a conveyor belt. He placed goals at specific distances along the belt. When Simon made his 'to do' list for the next day, he moved the conveyor belt one notch closer. (We talk more about making 'to do' lists in Chapter 4.) This method had a real impact on Simon meeting his commitments.

Travelling Along Your Time Line to a Happier You

Your time line consists of a sequence of structured memories; pictures are in colour, sounds can be loud or soft, and feelings can make you feel light or weigh you down. (For more information on memory and the senses, turn to Chapter 6.) Your mind creates these memories in its own individual way: for example, if you experience the same event as other people – perhaps you witness an accident – each of you remembers that event differently.

As you travel your time line, examining your memories and understanding the lessons that need to be learned can release the hold that memories have on the present, which allows you to change their structure, making them smaller, softer, or lighter as necessary. Therefore, your past need no longer cast a shadow on your present – or more importantly, on your future.

Releasing negative emotions and limiting decisions

Anger, fear, shame, grief, sadness, guilt, regret, and anxiety are just a few examples of negative emotions. These feelings have value in that they make you human – and you wouldn't want to be free of the ability to experience these emotions – but at times they have a powerful, undesired impact. They can cause physical illness and have a devastating effect on the way you conduct your life.

A *limiting decision* is one that you made in the past when, for some reason, you decided that you were unable to do something, because you were too stupid, unfit, poor, or any number of other reasons. For example, you may have said: 'I can never be slim' or 'I'm bad at adding numbers.' The limiting decision limits your potential, interfering with your success.

Although you create negative emotions and limiting decisions in your past, they influence you in your present. If you can go into the past, by travelling back along your time line, and understand consciously what your unconscious mind was trying to protect you from, you can release the effect of the damaging emotions and decisions more easily.

Dealing with negative emotions can be extremely powerful and you must ensure that you have all the support you need. So, before you attempt to use the techniques in this section to release negative emotions or understand your limiting decisions, keep the following points in mind:

- ✔ In order to tackle extremely serious emotional issues, for example, the trauma of child abuse or divorce, we definitely recommend that you see a qualified therapist.

- ✔ Working with another person is best when examining time lines because that person can keep you grounded if you forget the exercise and succumb to the emotions you're experiencing. Someone else can also ensure that you follow the steps correctly.

The diagram shown in Figure 13-5 is very important to the following exercises because it clarifies the locations along your time line that you need to be aware of. The diagram is particularly useful to people who are more visual, those who create pictures in their minds.

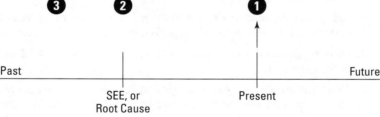

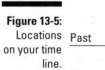

Figure 13-5: Locations on your time line.

- ✔ Location number 1 in the figure represents the position you float up to, which is directly above the present on your time line.

- ✔ Location number 2 is directly above the SEE (Significant Emotional Event) or root cause.

- ✔ Location number 3 is still way above your time line but 15 minutes before the root cause.

This exercise introduces you to a process that helps you to remove the negative emotions you may be holding on to, such as being prone to inappropriate feelings of anger. Please remember to keep an open mind to the answers that your unconscious mind presents:

1. **Find yourself somewhere safe and quiet to relax, and think of a mildly negative emotion you experienced in the past.**

2. **Check with yourself that learning from the event and releasing the emotion is okay. When you relax, ask your unconscious mind, 'Is it okay for me to let go of this anger?'**

3. **Ask your unconscious mind, 'What's the root cause of this problem, which when I'm disconnected from it, is going to cause the problem to disappear? Was it before, during, or after my birth?'**

When you ask your unconscious mind whether the root cause was before, during, or after your birth, please keep an open mind about the answer you receive. Your unconscious mind absorbs a lot of information and makes a lot of decisions without your conscious awareness. Romilla's clients have been surprised with their responses.

4. **When you obtain the root cause, float way above your time line so that you can see your past and your future stretching below you.**

   You're now at location 1 in Figure 13-5.

5. **Still above your time line, float back along it until you're above the SEE (location 2 in Figure 13-5). Take on-board what you saw, felt, and heard.**

6. **Ask your unconscious mind to learn what it needs to from the event in order for it to let go of the negative emotions easily and quickly.**

7. **Float to location 3 in Figure 13-5, which is above and 15 minutes *before* the SEE.**

8. **As you float above your time line at location 3, turn and face the present so you can see the root cause in front of you and below you.**

9. **Give yourself permission to let go of all the negative emotions associated with the event and notice where the negative emotions, if any, are now.**

   Have all the other negative emotions associated with the event also disappeared?

10. **If other negative emotions remain, use each 'out' breath to release all the emotions that are associated with the SEE.**

11. **Stay at location 3 until you feel, or know, that all the negative emotions have dissipated.**

12. **When you're ready, and by that we mean when you feel you have released the negative emotions, float back to location 1.**

    Go only as fast as your unconscious mind can learn from similar events and let go of all the associated emotions.

13. **Come back down into the room.**

14. **Just test – go into the future to when an event would have triggered the emotions you let go, and notice that the emotions have gone.**

If you don't get the results you hoped for, you may need to ask your unconscious mind to present you with the reason why you haven't let go of the emotions. The best time for this is when you're dropping off to sleep, are deeply relaxed, or meditating. If you don't get an answer that you understand, you may need to work with a coach or therapist to clear issues from your past that are stopping you from getting the results you want.

This exercise can also be used for getting rid of a limiting decision. For example, you may have decided to stay poor or unhealthy, or made some other self-defeating decision such as 'I can never be truly successful.' Follow the above process, using the limiting decision in place of the negative emotions.

Finding forgiveness

With hindsight and maturity you can forgive people from your past. Such forgiveness allows you to release all the energy you had invested in resentment, anger, or other negative emotions. You can then move on and use that energy to be more creative or loving or anything positive you may want. One useful way to accomplish forgiveness is to understand the motives of the people who hurt you and realise that, because of their own issues, they were operating from a reality that provided very limited options.

As an example, imagine that you had a burning desire to become an actor and your parents gave you a hard time about it. Now acknowledge that they were actually showing parental concern for you. They were doing their best for you with the resources they had at their disposal. Go back along your time line to when you can remember one such difficult time with your parents. You can then hover above your time line while you learn any important lessons that you needed to be aware of. You can float down into the event and give your parents a hug and let them know that you realise now that they were doing their best for you. If you find it easy, you can surround yourself in a bubble of light and just enjoy the feelings of love, compassion, and forgiveness.

Healing along the time line

Kate's friend, Tara, shared an inspiring experience with her. Tara had suffered severely with blocked sinuses since she was 18 years old. This condition was so bad that she needed antibiotics at least three or four times a year in order to alleviate the debilitating symptoms. By the time Tara attended a workshop on Time Line Therapy®, she had undergone four unsuccessful operations to clear her sinuses and been told by her doctors that she would have to live with her illness or stay on steroids.

During the workshop, Tara discovered that her symptoms became particularly severe when she felt overwhelmed by people and events. She explored the possibility that her physical symptoms were psychosomatic. By investigating any limiting beliefs and benefits she was getting from her illness, Tara realised that she had built a Gestalt (a structure) around illness. She remembered that, as a child, her brother

had received a lot of attention from their mother because he was asthmatic and the only time Tara received attention was when she had tonsillitis. Tara's father also suffered with chronic sinusitis and Tara found that her illness gave her something in common with her father. She also believed that she was unable to clear her disease by herself.

During the workshop, Tara realised that she was able to get attention from people without being ill, that she could ask for tender loving care, and that admitting to feelings of being overwhelmed was okay. She went back along her time line to where she believed the first SEE happened. She realised that it was when she first became jealous of the attention her brother received. She was able to let go of the Gestalt associated with this event and has been free of sinusitis and steroids since March 2002.

Comforting the younger you

When you travel back along your time line and find an event that involves you when you were young, you can embrace the younger you, reassure yourself that all will be well, surround your selves with light, and let your selves be healed. Now, imagine bringing all that joy and relief along your time line, right into the present.

Getting rid of anxiety

Anxiety is simply a negative emotion about a future event. In the earlier section 'Releasing negative emotions and limiting decisions', we explain how to remove a negative emotion or limiting decision by going to *before* the event that created the emotion or when you made the decision. Similarly, you can remove anxiety by going into the future *beyond the successful conclusion* of the event about which you're anxious.

Imagine what you'd see, hear, and feel when the event causing you anxiety is over and has been successful. Then, when you travel forward above your time line to beyond the successful conclusion of the event, you find that the anxiety no longer exists. Using Figure 13-6 as a reference, follow these steps:

1. **Find yourself somewhere safe and quiet to relax, and think of an event about which you're feeling anxious; check with your unconscious mind that letting go of the anxiety is okay.**

2. **Now float way above your time line so that you can see your past and your future stretching below you.**

3. **Still above your time line, float forward along it until you're above the event that's making you anxious.**

4. **Ask your unconscious mind to learn what it needs to from the event in order for it to let go of the anxiety easily and quickly.**

5. **When you have the necessary information, float farther into the future, along your time line until you're 15 minutes after the *successful conclusion* of the event about which you were feeling anxious.**

6. **Turn and look towards it now and notice that you're calm and no longer anxious.**

In the unlikely event that some anxiety remains, relax deeply and allow your unconscious mind to present you with the reason why you haven't let go of the anxiety. It may be that you need some skills to boost your confidence. If you have a history of not being your best – at least in your opinion – at similar past events, go back along your time line to uncover negative emotions or limiting decisions before doing the exercise again.

7. **When you're ready, float back to your present.**

8. **Just test – go into the future to the event and confirm that the anxiety no longer exists.**

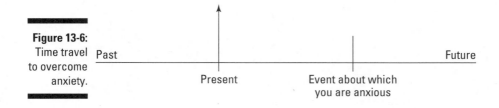

Figure 13-6:
Time travel
to overcome
anxiety.

Past

Present

Event about which
you are anxious

Future

Creating a better future

When you know how to travel your time line, imagine taking some irresistible, compelling goals and putting them into your future, and how great that would be:

1. **Find somewhere safe and quiet to relax and design your goal.**

   Chapter 4 tells you what you need to know about creating goals.

2. **Float way above your time line so that you can see your past and your future stretching below you.**

3. **Still above your time line, float forward along your time line until you're over the time by which you want to have achieved your goal.**

4. **Turn and look back to *now* and allow all the events along your time line to align so that they support your goal, noting any actions you may have to take along the way.**

5. **When you're ready, float back to your present and back down into the room.**

Always check your motives when setting and obtaining your goals, in order to ensure that they fit within all areas of your life, as we describe in Chapter 4. This process is called the ecology check. By really examining your reasons, you can ensure that no hidden negative emotions are driving you. For instance, if you're focusing on making a lot of money, you may want to know that the desire stems from wanting to be comfortably secure and able to help those less fortunate than yourself, and not because you're trying to escape a poverty-stricken childhood.

Checking your motives also helps you to identify any lurking, unconscious fears, for example: 'If I'm rich, people will only want to be friends because of my money, not because they like me.' Analysing these motives fully helps you to crystallise your exact reasons for your desire and allows you to take steps to overcome any unconscious issues.

Chapter 14

Smooth Running below Decks

In This Chapter
▶ Finding out that parts of your unconscious mind may be in conflict
▶ Discovering how to overcome self-sabotaging behaviour
▶ Experimenting with integrating parts of the unconscious mind
▶ Extrapolating personal conflict resolution to teams and organisations

Can you remember participating in or watching a tug-of-war? Both sides expend an inordinate amount of energy but don't manage to move very far. Conflict, whether within yourself or with someone else, is like a tug-of-war with two sides pulling in opposite directions and getting nowhere.

Conflict within yourself usually occurs between a conscious part of your mind and an unconscious part. Phrases such as 'I don't know what came over me', 'I just wasn't myself', 'part of me wants . . . and another part wants. . .' provide a clue to parts of your unconscious mind; parts of which you may be unaware. Take the example of a person who knows at a conscious level that smoking's bad for their health and yet continues to smoke because unconsciously they crave the companionship of their friends, most of whom smoke.

The *NLP Encyclopedia of Systemic NLP and NLP New Coding* (which you can access at www.nlpu.com) defines conflict as follows: 'Psychologically, conflict is a mental struggle, sometimes unconscious, resulting when different representations of the world are held in opposition or exclusivity.' In other words, conflict occurs when two maps of the world collide. By reconciling these two different maps, you can eliminate the conflict. This chapter shows you how.

Getting to Grips with a Hierarchy of Conflict

Conflict can take place at different levels of a hierarchy, known as *logical levels*, as follows:

- ✔ Identity
- ✔ Values and beliefs
- ✔ Capabilities and skills
- ✔ Behaviour
- ✔ Environment

When you're considering some of the conflicts you face, understanding the level at which you need to engage is helpful. For example, if as a manager you believe that people are what make your company a success but you focus more on developing your technology than your people, you may need to modify your behaviour to bring it into line with the needs of your staff and ultimately with your beliefs.

The levels of this hierarchy are also referred to as *neurological levels* because they connect with your thinking processes and therefore the brain and its interaction with your body. (You can find out all about logical levels in Chapter 11.) These neurological levels operate in a hierarchy – like the rungs on a ladder – with identity at a higher rung and environment down below. When you can identify the real logical level at which you're working, the conflict becomes easier to resolve.

Here are some examples of the conflicts you may face at the different logical levels:

- ✔ **Identity:** Often you have many roles to play in your life and work that pull you in different directions. You may want to be a good parent as well as a committed employee, or a nice, likeable person as well as a profitable manager. Perhaps you're trying to be a supportive son or daughter or a volunteer in the local community, as well as an international jet-setter.

- ✔ **Values and beliefs:** Sometimes you have a mix of beliefs that don't seem to fit well together or match your values. You may want to be happy, and yet part of you doesn't believe that you deserve happiness. You may value both health and wealth but not believe that getting them both at the same time is possible. You may value family life and global business success and be struggling to see how these items can fit together, because you have no role models of these two values sitting side by side as equals.

✔ **Capabilities and skills:** You may have a mix of great skills and abilities and yet you can't find a way to use them all in a way that satisfies you. So perhaps you struggle to find a job that satisfies your desire to build or make things with your own hands at the same time as employing your skills at managing a team of other people in order to pay the mortgage. You may be a great musician and also a qualified medic, but have to make a choice of where to put your energy.

✔ **Behaviour:** You can find yourself engaging in behaviour that doesn't seem to help you to achieve your goals. For example, have you ever had an important piece of work to do and spent hours tidying out your desk or a cupboard instead? Or maybe you wanted to diet and found that a piece of buttered toast somehow ended up in your mouth without you noticing how it got there.

✔ **Environment:** At times you may find yourself in a dilemma about the places where you hang out or the people with whom you spend time. Maybe you're mixing with the wrong sort of people – people who don't seem to have your best interests at heart or that your family disapproves of. Maybe part of you wants to move away from home and set up on your own; or perhaps part of you wants to live in the country of your birth while another part of you yearns to explore the world. You want to be in two places simultaneously and can't settle in either one.

As soon as you hear yourself or others say phrases such as 'part of me wants . . . and yet another part of me wants. . .', you can be sure that an internal conflict's going on that defies logical reasoning.

You're in total harmony with yourself when each of your logical levels is aligned with the others. Personal conflict occurs when what you're trying to achieve, or what you believe, or perhaps what you're doing is out of kilter with other levels in the hierarchy. So if you want to satisfy a goal to earn a high salary, this aim may conflict with your identity of 'I'm a good husband and father', because you don't get to spend time with your loved ones. Conflict resolution is achieved by brainstorming and asking questions of yourself and the people affected by your decisions about how you can come up with novel ways that may allow you to fulfil your goal and align your logical levels.

Drifting from Wholeness to Parts

Your memories are arranged into a pattern, or *Gestalt*, that's an association of related memories. A Gestalt may start when you experience an event that first triggers an emotional response, a *Significant Emotional Event* (SEE).

A useful way to think about this concept is to start from the premise that at some point your unconscious mind is a complete whole. When you experience an SEE, a part is created and a boundary forms around this part of your unconscious mind, separating it from the rest of the unconscious mind.

This part functions like a 'mini you', with its own personality and values and beliefs. Just like the 'conscious you', this part exhibits behaviours that have purpose and intent. Unfortunately, the behaviours can be in conflict with the actual intention of the part. For example, a person who believes they were never loved as a child may develop shoplifting tendencies because the unconscious part craves attention, even though this kind of attention isn't what the person really wants.

Understanding a part's intentions

A major NLP presupposition is that *every behaviour has a positive intent*. For example, the positive intent behind someone smoking a cigarette may be to relax. (Head to Chapter 2 for more on the main NLP presuppositions.) Sometimes the behaviour that your unconscious part makes you exhibit doesn't satisfy your underlying need.

Perhaps an alcoholic drinks to numb the pain (positive intent) of being abandoned by their spouse. The unconscious part is in fact crying out for love, but the manifested behaviour – drinking heavily – doesn't satisfy the underlying need. The answer to this problem lies in identifying and understanding the real need and satisfying it in a positive way. So if the alcoholic can come out of their stupor and recognise that alcohol isn't what they need but love is, they may dry out, clean up, learn the lessons from their failed marriage, and pick themselves up to find love.

Getting to the heart of the problem

Often a part of your unconscious mind can create problems for you. The reasons for these problems can be hard to understand logically. For example, you may suddenly develop a fear of an everyday activity like travelling or meeting people. You can reach the real, hidden purpose behind the intention of the part by peeling back and exploring each reason or intention as it surfaces. When you arrive at the true, underlying purpose of the part, you can then assimilate this purpose into the bigger whole of your unconscious mind.

The following anecdote illustrates what can happen when your unconscious mind drives the motivation of one part. Later in this chapter, in the section 'Trying the visual squash technique', you discover how to integrate two parts that are in conflict.

Oliver is a very successful business school graduate who had his career mapped out. He knew what he wanted to achieve and the time scales in which he would meet his goals. He was thrilled when he was promoted to his dream job as Vice President of Planning and Strategy in a major global corporation. Just as he was about to embark on a tour of the European sites, disaster struck. Oliver started waking up in the night with heart palpitations, breathlessness, and cold sweats. His doctor confirmed that nothing was physically wrong with Oliver.

In talking through possible reasons for his condition with his NLP coach, Oliver identified several issues connected with the promotion: he would be away from home for longer periods; he would be living in hotels; and he would be spending less time playing sport, something he was passionate about. Oliver and his coach explored each of the layers of objections that were presented and discarded them as superficial reasons for his health issues.

During a state of deep relaxation, Oliver recalled a memory of, in his words, 'failing' at maths as a young boy. Oliver's teacher and parents had very high expectations of Oliver and he felt that he'd let them down when he didn't meet the stringent exam standards. Oliver realised that, although the promotion gave him the opportunity to work at his ideal job, it was very high profile and his unconscious mind was trying to protect him from the humiliation of yet another failure. To do so, it was creating the physical problems that would ultimately get in the way of Oliver succeeding at his dream job.

By working with his NLP coach, Oliver realised that his parents and teacher had pushed him beyond his level of capability and set him up for failure. Oliver recognised that he had succeeded at his career on the merits of his abilities and he had what was necessary to be an outstanding success. He discovered that making mistakes and encountering failure was all right, as long as he was flexible enough to learn from the setbacks and use the lessons positively to move forward.

While achieving what you want in your career or a project close to your heart, you may hit a brick wall. Find yourself a quiet space and some time to explore the ways in which you may be creating barriers to your own success.

Help! I'm in Conflict with Myself

Self-sabotage is one of the symptoms you can experience when different conscious and unconscious parts of you are in conflict, where every attempt you make to reach a goal is subverted by one of the parts. We detail two of the most common methods of self-sabotage you need to keep an eye out for in this section.

Listening to your unconscious mind

As with any communication, if you understand that self-sabotage is just your unconscious mind's way of trying to communicate with you, you can assist it by examining the positive intention behind the behaviour that's stopping you from achieving your goal. You can then substitute the self-defeating behaviour with something more positive, which satisfies the intent of the unconscious mind. For instance, the smoker who wants to stop but continues smoking because unconsciously they crave the companionship of their friends who smoke, can satisfy their need for friendship by developing a new group of non-smoking friends or by undertaking a new activity that helps them develop a circle of friends with a healthier lifestyle.

Taking sides

When two parts of your unconscious mind are in conflict, the chances are that your conscious mind sides with one part or the other, making a judgement that one's bad and suppressing it by sheer force of will. The result is similar to what happens when you squeeze a balloon. If the balloon isn't blown up to capacity, as you squeeze one end the air pushes the balloon out in another direction. If the balloon is filled to capacity, you just get a bang as you squeeze. Similarly, as you suppress a part of you, the suppressed part shows up as an aberrant behaviour, physical symptom (balloon distortion), or a breakdown (the bang).

Fiona suffered so badly from eczema that she kept her body well covered. In therapy, she came to realise that the symptoms were a consequence of having been bullied at school, where all she ever wanted to do was hide. Now her unconscious mind, in its own unique way, was presenting her with a means to hide.

In Fiona's case the part that wanted to hide her from the bullies created a physical symptom, which meant she had to keep her body covered. After the therapy brought conscious awareness, previously failed medical treatments worked well. However, the eczema does flare up when Fiona is under stress, so she has developed strategies (see Chapter 12 for more on strategies) to manage her time and energy better.

Becoming Whole: Integrating Your Parts

Not all parts of the unconscious mind are in conflict with each other. You become aware of the ones that are in conflict, however, when you encounter problems such as wanting to be healthy and still craving cigarettes, or wanting to be slim but not being able to control binge-eating. You can deal with these conflicting parts as and when they surface.

More unconscious parts mean more potential for conflict, and therefore the ideal is to aspire to complete wholeness. For example, when more than two parts are involved, you can integrate them in pairs. In this section, we describe two of the more common techniques for integrating conflicting parts: the *visual squash* and *reframing*.

Trying the visual squash technique

In principle, this exercise involves identifying the parts involved in a conflict and discovering their common intention before integrating them.

As you work to integrate your parts, keep these tips in mind:

- ✔ Strive to turn a negative answer into a positive outcome. For example, if you want to do more exercise, and you get the negative answer 'I don't want to spend too much time exercising,' carry on towards a positive outcome, such as 'I want to exercise to fit in with my lifestyle.'
- ✔ Work with a qualified NLP practitioner or partner who can record your answers and prompt you with them.

Sue wanted to overcome her resistance to exercising. She did the following exercise with her friend, Gillian. The part that Sue placed on her right hand was a young child who was carefree, spontaneous, and very playful. Some of the things important to the child were freedom, playfulness, joy, and laughter, with fun being the most important. The part of Sue's unconscious that she placed on her left hand was a rather dark, dour, elderly male whose prime concern was safety. During the exercise, Sue had no trouble working with the child's hierarchy of intentions (see point 7 in the following exercise). However, when she came to work with the male part of her unconscious, Sue kept forgetting what she'd said for the earlier step and found it very helpful to have Gillian repeat her exact words to her. Because Sue didn't feel an affinity with the male part of her unconscious, she resisted 'his' responses and found having Gillian to hand very helpful.

The result of doing this exercise was that Sue realised that a part of her unconscious mind was nervous that if she exercised and got really healthy, she would stop treating her body with care. As soon as Sue became aware, consciously, of the purpose of each part, both parts discovered that their highest purpose was success.

For this exercise to be successful you have to find out what the common intention is for each part before you try and integrate them. A useful idea is to talk to the parts and have them acknowledge that each part has a positive intention for the other and that their conflict is stopping both parts from achieving their common purpose.

1. **Identify two parts of yourself that may be in conflict.**

   For instance, a part of you wants you to be healthy while another part of you puts up an almighty fight when you want to exercise.

2. **Sit in a quiet place where you're unlikely to be disturbed.**

3. **Ask the problem part to come out and stand on one hand.**

   In the example in step 1, this problem is the part averse to exercise.

4. **Imagine the part as a person and see what the person looks like, sounds like, and what feelings that person has.**

5. **Ask the non-problem part to come out and stand on the other hand.**

   In the example in step 1, this is the part that wants to be healthy.

6. **Imagine this part as a person and see what the person looks like, sounds like, and what feelings that person has.**

7. **Starting with the problem part, ask each part 'What's your positive intention and purpose?' Keep repeating the question and building a hierarchy until both parts realise that they have the same intention.**

   The part averse to exercise may say things such as, 'I get tired', 'it's important to conserve energy', or 'I want to make the world a better place.' In contrast, the part that wants to be healthy may say, 'I like the buzz I get', 'I have more energy', or 'I want to make the world a better place.'

8. **Ask each part what resources it has that the other part would find useful in attaining the common, positive purpose of each part.**

   The part averse to exercise may say things like, 'I have the imagination to design better solutions' or 'I understand the problems people may experience.' Whereas the part that wants to be healthy may say, 'I have the energy to put into changing the world' or 'I have the discipline it takes to make the world a better place.'

9. **Bring both your hands together and fully integrate the parts and their resources, seeing a new you, hearing what that new you may say, and recognising new feelings that you may have.**

10. **Using the techniques that we present in Chapter 13, go back to before your conception and travel along your time line to now, with the new, integrated you, changing your history along your time line.**

Remember that your memories are only a construction of your mind. If, in the past, you chose to make a decision – such as 'exercise is tiring' – your whole time line is based on that decision. If you then resolve this issue by integrating it with a decision you make to be healthy, you can change your time line to accommodate the new, healthy you.

Reframing – as if

The meaning of an interaction is dependent on the context in which it takes place. So by changing the context of, or *reframing*, an experience, you can change its meaning. For example, if someone criticises you for being too subjective, you can thank the person because you know that this attribute means that you're good with people or great at coming up with ideas.

This *as if* reframing is excellent for resolving conflict because it allows you to pretend and therefore explore possibilities that you wouldn't have thought of otherwise. Acting as if you have the resources now, helps to shift any beliefs that may be holding you back.

When you're in conflict, with yourself or another party, use the following 'as if' frames to help you resolve the problem:

✔ **Time switch:** Step six months or a year into the future, look back to now, and ask yourself what you did to overcome the problem.

Alan was in a well-paid job in which he was relatively happy. However, his boss had favourites in the department and Alan was getting sidelined. Alan had wanted to work for a large multinational for some time but didn't believe that his skills were good enough. Alan used the well-formed outcomes process (which we describe in Chapter 4 and Appendix C) to design his dream job. He then tried the time switch by stepping five years into the future and pretending he had his perfect job. He realised he needed to work for one of his company's competitors and two years later found himself in his dream job, working for the multinational of his choice.

✔ **Person switch:** Pretend that you're someone you respect and ask yourself what you'd do if you were able to swap bodies with the other person for a day.

Georgina admired Amanda Tapping (the actress who portrays Major Sam Carter in the television series *Stargate*). Georgina pretended to swap bodies with Amanda Tapping. She discovered that although her job supporting computer systems paid the mortgage, it failed to satisfy her on a deep level. As Amanda Tapping, Georgina discovered that she really wanted to work in films, bringing stories from people's imaginations to life. Georgina realised that life in the film world can be risky, but took the first step by enrolling for a part-time course in scriptwriting.

✔ **Information switch:** Suppose that you have all the information you need to get a solution: what would that knowledge be and how would the circumstances change?

Georgina used the information switch to break down what she would have to do to live her dream of becoming a scriptwriter. Consequently, she started evening classes in scriptwriting and working with projects for the students for a local college at the weekends. She is now at the stage where she's planning to work part-time for production companies so that she can spend more time following her dream.

✔ **Function switch:** Imagine that you can change any component in the system within which you're experiencing a restriction: for example, you aren't progressing at work or your marriage is a little bumpy. What would you change and how would this change affect the outcome?

Colin worked as an animal nurse in a busy veterinary practice; he loved his job but felt as though something was missing in his life. He sat down and used his imagination to see what element he would change. As a result, Colin's unconscious mind had him recognise that he wanted to do good where he was really needed by animals, and by people unable to afford expensive veterinary treatment. Colin now works at an animal sanctuary in India, still loves what he's doing, and feels completely fulfilled.

Resolving Bigger Conflicts

The previous sections in this chapter provide you with a pretty good idea of *intrapersonal* conflicts (within a person) and how to begin resolving them. You may also like to think about extrapolating and extending this model. You can apply the same principles of solving intrapersonal conflict to relationships and negotiations between two people, within a team, family, or social group, and between different companies and organisations. Here are some examples of these bigger conflicts:

✔ **Interpersonal conflict:** Where two or more people have differing needs that can't be satisfied at the same time.

✔ **Intragroup conflict:** Between two or more people within the group, for example, members of a team or department.

✔ **Intergroup conflict:** Between two or more groups of people, as in gang warfare or companies battling for market leadership.

In all these situations, you can use the process outlined in the following exercise to negotiate a successful outcome.

This exercise is based on the NLP process for integrating conflicting parts that we describe in the sections 'Trying the visual squash technique' and 'Reframing – as if', earlier in this chapter:

1. Imagine that you're in the role of negotiator to resolve a conflict between different parties.

2. Ask each party, 'What's your positive intention?' Keep asking both sides until you uncover some core and fundamental needs on which both parties can agree. (Please refer to the earlier section 'Trying the visual squash technique'.)

3. Ask each party to acknowledge the common ground and hold on to it.

4. Using the 'as if' frame, explore alternative solutions to the problem. (Please refer to the earlier section 'Reframing – as if'.)

5. Decide on the resources each party can bring to the table to help resolve the conflict.

6. Always keep the common aim in mind and strive for a win/win outcome.

To paraphrase Einstein, having imagination is more important than having knowledge, because knowledge boxes you into the realm of the known whereas imagination allows you to discover and create new solutions. So use your imagination for some lateral thinking to come up with novel solutions to conflicts.

Part IV
Using Words to Entrance

The 5th Wave   By Rich Tennant

DOCTOR RUNTLOWE FOUND THE APPLICANT'S COVER LETTER FOR CLINICAL HYPNOTIST TO BE MESMERIZING

In this part . . .

You explore the power of language – as we share with you the very latest techniques of the world's best communicators. You discover that the language you use doesn't just describe your experience, but also has the power to create it. If you want to know how to use stories to good effect or send an audience into a trance (and not into a deep sleep!), you find out how to do that, too.

We also provide a chapter dedicated to the most powerful questions you can ask to help you get straight to the heart of an issue without prejudicing the result for the person you're speaking to.

Chapter 15

Getting to the Heart of the Matter: The Meta Model

*H*ave you ever invited someone, even yourself, to: 'Say what you mean and mean what you say?' If only speech was that easy.

You use words all the time as important tools to convey your thoughts and ideas – to explain and share your experiences with others. In Chapter 7, we explain that in any face-to-face communication, people take just part of the meaning from the words that come out of your mouth. Your body language – all those movements and gestures – and the tone of your voice transmit the rest.

One of the NLP presuppositions to which you're introduced in Chapter 2 is that 'the map is not the territory'. This statement explains that the model that you have in your head of the world around you isn't the actual world, but just a representation you make of it. The filters of your experience and your language influence this representation of the world.

Words offer just a model, a symbol of your experience; they can never fully describe the whole picture. Think of an iceberg – the tip above the surface is like the words you say. NLP says that this tip is the *surface structure* of language. Beneath the surface lies the rest of the iceberg – the home of your whole experience – which NLP calls the *deep structure*: the way you represent the world internally, in your mind.

It's been a hard day's work

Supper table talk in Kate's family often goes as follows: 'So, has it been a hard day's work today?' In recounting the highlights of the day, the conversation invariably centres on what constitutes a hard day's work. Does a 12-hour-long stint in a warm, comfortable office surrounded by the latest labour-saving computers and coffee-making devices qualify?

The question stemmed from watching a TV documentary of motorway maintenance workers who shift traffic cones in the dead of night. The family agreed that this really was hard work in comparison with the reality of a hard day for us, as well as most of our friends and co-workers.

What's a hard day for you? In just one sentence, you can conjure up a wealth of different meanings. The qualities of the work experience when you're running a home or an office are very different in comparison with the physical reality of, say, a fire-fighter tackling blazes or a builder constructing houses and exposed to the elements in all weathers.

A statement such as 'a hard day's work' can be interpreted in numerous different ways. To get to any one speaker's precise meaning requires access to more information – the facts that have been left out. As you read this chapter, you can discover how to gain easy access to relevant information to stop you jumping to the wrong assumptions about somebody else's experience.

This chapter takes you from the surface structure and leads you into the deep structure so that you can get beyond the vague words of everyday speech to be more specific about what you mean. You meet the incredibly useful Meta Model, one of NLP's most important revelations, which clarifies the meaning of what people say. Remember that people never give a complete description of the entire thought process that lies beneath their words; if they did, they'd never finish speaking. The Meta Model is a tool that allows you to get closer access to people's experience that they code through speech.

Gathering Specific Information with the Meta Model

Richard Bandler and John Grinder, the co-creators of NLP, discovered that when people speak, three key processes happen naturally, which they labelled *deletion*, *generalisation*, and *distortion*. These processes enable people to explain their experiences in words without going into long-winded details and boring everyone to death.

These processes happen all the time in normal everyday encounters. People *delete* information by not giving the whole story, make *generalisations* by extrapolating from one experience to another, and *distort* reality by letting their imaginations run wild.

Figure 15-1 illustrates the NLP model of how you experience the real world through your senses – visual (pictures), auditory (sounds), kinaesthetic (touch and feelings), olfactory (smell), and gustatory (taste). You filter or check your perception of reality against what you already know through the processes of deletion, generalisation, and distortion. In this way, you create your personal map or mental model of the real world.

By watching and analysing two different, highly experienced therapists – at work talking to their clients – Bandler and Grinder came up with the NLP Meta Model as a way to explain the link between language and experience.

Bandler and Grinder were interested in finding the rules that determine how humans use language in order to help others develop similar skills. They were influenced by their own work in the field of linguistics, especially of *transformational grammar* (which seeks to explain the relationship between the deep structure of experience and the surface structure of language), and set out ideas on how people describe their experiences in language. They were also strongly influenced by modelling two exceptional therapists with outstanding communication skills – Virginia Satir and Fritz Perls – and they published the results in 1975 in *The Structure of Magic*.

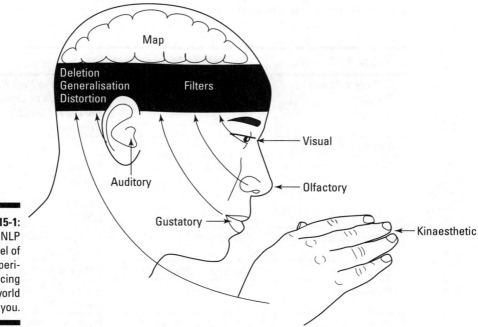

Figure 15-1: The NLP model of experiencing the world around you.

Although the early work came from the field of psychotherapy – because they wanted to enrich the skills of 'people helpers' – the models shed light equally well for non-professionals in ordinary situations, where they're simply talking with friends, family, and colleagues.

The Meta Model offers a series of questions that enable you to overcome the deletions, generalisations, and distortions that people make. Most likely, you're going to recognise some of the questions, because they're the ones you naturally ask when you want to clarify meaning. But perhaps you haven't thought about them consciously before. Asked in a gentle way and with rapport, these questions let you gather more information to define a clearer picture of what's really meant. By working with this model you can reconnect with the experiences that get lost in language.

Table 15-1 summarises some of the different ways in which you can delete, generalise, and distort an experience through the language you adopt. Don't worry about the names of the NLP patterns just yet; the important part is that you begin to tune your ears into what people say. As you discover how to spot the main Meta Model patterns that you prefer, and that others favour too, you're in a great position to respond appropriately. We also offer in Table 15-1 some suggestions of what to say when you respond, in order to gather the missing information that helps you to be sure of understanding what the other person really means.

Table 15-1	Meta Model Patterns	
NLP Meta Model Patterns	*Examples of Patterns You May Hear*	*Questions to Help Gather Information or Expand the Other Person's Viewpoint*
Deletion		
Simple deletion	I've been out	Where specifically have you been?
	Help!	What do you want help with?
Unspecified verbs	She annoyed me	How specifically did she annoy you?
Comparisons	She's better than I am	Better at what than you?
Judgements	You're wrong	Who says so and what are the facts?
Nominalisations	Our *relationship* isn't working	How do we not relate to each other?
	Change is easy	Changing what is easy?

NLP Meta Model Patterns	Examples of Patterns You May Hear	Questions to Help Gather Information or Expand the Other Person's Viewpoint
Generalisation		
Modal operators of possibility	I *can't* . . . it's not possible	What stops you? Is that true?
Modal operators of necessity	We *have to* do this . . . we *should*, *ought to*	What would happen if we didn't? Who says we should?
Universal quantifiers	He *never* thinks about my feelings We *always* do it this way	Never, ever? Every single time? What would happen if we did it differently?
Distortion		
Complex equivalence	With a name like that, he must be popular	How does having this name mean that he's popular?
Mind reading	You're going to love this	How do you know that? Who says?
Cause and effect	His voice makes me angry	How does his voice make you angry?
	I made her feel awful	How exactly did you do that?

Deletion – you're so vague

When you're listening, you naturally ignore many extra sounds, saving you the effort of processing every single word. When you speak, you economise on all the details that you could share. This practice is called deletion, because details have been removed. Figure 15-2 shows some everyday examples of deletion.

Figure 15-2:
The language of deletion.

'You were good.'

'This is important.'

'Just do it!'

'I'm scared.'

'I don't know.'

Your central nervous system is being fed millions of pieces of information every second. If you needed consciously to evaluate every bit of this information, imagine the time and energy you'd need; it would be an impossible task with full information overload!

To help you operate at peak efficiency, deletion delivers a valuable critical screening mechanism. Deletion is selective attention. Deletions in your language encourage you to fill in the gaps – to imagine information to complete what's missing. If someone says to you 'I bought a new car,' you then begin to guess more information. If that person doesn't tell you what type of car, you then create your own ideas about the make, colour, and age, based on what you've already decided about its use and the person's preferences. So if you think that the person's a lively, fun-loving character, you may decide that they bought a sports car. If you think they're safe and cautious, you may decide that they bought a conventional and practical car.

The downside of deletion is that it can restrict and limit your thinking and understanding. For example – you can develop the habit of deleting certain information and signals from others. Compliments and criticism are the classic example. Some people are experts at deleting compliments they receive and noticing only the criticism. So, too, they ignore success and notice only failure. If this habit rings a bell for you, set about breaking it now.

In a coaching session, Meera confessed to her coach that 'I'm extremely lazy.' This statement intrigued her coach who had heard about Meera's exhausting workload as a partner in a City law firm. Her coach asked her to keep a diary of 'how specifically she was lazy' for a whole week. At the end of the week, when they evaluated the diary together, Meera spotted that the expectations she placed on herself were sky high and leading to almost certain burn-out. What she saw as 'laziness' was in fact the essential recovery time that she gave herself, and she needed to reframe her limited perception to recognise its value, just as a high-performing athlete needs time off the sports track to boost energy.

To gather deleted information, you can ask these useful questions:

- Who? What? When? Where? How?
- What precisely?
- What exactly?

Notice that 'why?' doesn't figure in this list of questions. That's because 'why' forces people to question their personal judgement and purpose rather than recover lost information.

Abstract nouns and the wheelbarrow test

The Meta Model is very useful in the way that it helps you clarify vague statements. If you say to someone 'Love is so painful,' that person needs more information to understand what's going on in your life.

Abstract nouns – such as love, trust, honesty, relationship, change, fear, pain, obligation, responsibility, impression – are particularly difficult to respond to. NLP calls these words *nominalisations* – where a verb (for example, to love) has turned into a noun (love*),* which is hard to define in a way that everyone agrees on. In order to extract more meaning from your statement, another person needs to turn the noun back into a verb to help get more information and then reply. Therefore, that person's response to your statement above may be: 'How specifically is the way you love someone so painful?'

Imagine a wheelbarrow. If you think of a noun and can picture it inside the wheelbarrow, it's a concrete noun – a person, a flowerpot, an apple, a desk are all concrete examples. Nominalisations are the nouns that don't pass the wheelbarrow test. You can't put love, fear, a relationship, or pain in your wheelbarrow! Instead, when you rephrase these words as verbs, you put the action and responsibility back into the language. This helps people who speak in nominalisations to connect with their own experience, and thus find more options, rather than distancing themselves from it.

Generalisation – beware the always, musts, and shoulds

Think about when young children get on a two-wheeled bike for the first time. They pay tremendous attention to keeping their balance and steering. Perhaps they need stabilisers until they master the skill. Yet, some weeks or months later, they're competent and don't have to relearn each time they cycle away – because they generalise from one experience to the next.

Your ability to generalise from past experiences is an important skill that saves huge amounts of time and energy in learning about the world. These generalised experiences are represented by words. Think of the word 'chair'. You know what one's like: you've sat on many and seen different types. As a child, you discover that the word represents a particular chair. Then you make a generalisation. So the next time you see a chair, you're able to name it. Now, whenever you see a chair, you understand its function.

Although vitally important to communication, the skill of generalisation can also limit your experience of options and differences in certain contexts. When you have a bad experience, you may expect it to happen time and time again. A man who experiences a string of unhappy romantic encounters may conclude that 'all women are a pain' and decide that he's never going to meet a woman with whom he can live happily.

Romilla and Kate were driving from a meeting on the motorway one afternoon when Romilla ably demonstrated her natural ability to generalise and said: 'Have you noticed how *everyone's* driving my car?' Surprised, Kate asked how that was possible. Romilla pointed out that she'd seen 15 new Minis in the last ten minutes. She'd fallen in love with this car and was deciding whether to buy one. All she was able to see were the possible colour combinations of this new car. Kate hadn't noticed a single one of them – she wasn't interested in a new car at all – just concentrating on getting through the traffic and out of London.

You can hear all sorts of generalisations about particular cultures or groups:

- ✔ 'Americans talk loudly.'
- ✔ 'British drink tea.'
- ✔ 'Italians are wild drivers.'
- ✔ 'Politicians can't be trusted.'
- ✔ 'Scots are prudent with money.'
- ✔ 'Unmarried mothers are a drain on society.'

Such rigid, black-and-white thinking, which allows for no grey scale in between, creates unhelpful generalisations about other people and situations: and it's the breeding ground for discontent and prejudice. Stop and listen to what you say. When you hear the verbal clues about generalisations in words like 'all', 'never', 'every', 'always' (Figure 15-3 shows several examples of everyday generalisations), challenge yourself. Is *everyone* like that? Do *all* clients do that? Must we *always* do it this way?

Figure 15-3: The language of generalisation.

When you hear someone (or yourself!) generalising, ask the following useful questions. They make you stop and think about whether you're limiting your options unnecessarily and encourage you to take a broader perspective:

   ✔ Always? Never? Every?

   ✔ Just imagine you could, what then?

   ✔ So what happens if you do. . . ?

   ✔ What stops you?

Charlie was moaning to Kate that she was struggling to lose weight in spite of having a good basic diet and not liking sweet food. When Kate asked her friend Charlie about what she actually ate, she heard the following: 'Well, I always eat porridge, I've had the same breakfast for 20 years; then I always have a jacket potato with cheese or beans at lunchtime; and for supper I always have soup and bread. I never eat after seven in the evening.' Having heard the generalisations in her language, Kate asked what would happen if she tried some different foods, and Charlie went off to investigate fresh meal options. A month later, Charlie had lost more than three kilograms and had had fun exploring food aisles in the local supermarket.

To begin to explore your own thinking on what's possible and impossible, here's an easy exercise to do in just ten minutes. Beware – it may change your life forever!

1. **Look at the following phrases and jot down some of the statements you've made in the last week (to yourself as well as to others) that start with these words:**

    'I always. . .'

    'I must. . .'

    'I should. . .'

    'I never. . .'

    'I ought to. . .'

    'I have to. . .'

2. **Now stop.**

3. **Go back to your list and for each statement ask yourself three questions:**

    'What would happen if I didn't. . . ?'

    'When did I decide this?'

    'Is this statement true and helpful for me now?'

4. **Review your list in the light of the questions you asked.**

5. **Create a revised list for yourself that replaces the words 'always', 'must', 'should', 'never', 'ought to', and 'have to' with the words 'I choose to. . .'.**

By completing this exercise you're examining some of the types of generalisations that you make (which NLP calls *modal operators* – as in *'should', 'ought to',* and *'have to'* – and *universal quantifiers* – as in *'always'* and *'never'*. See Table 15-1). Then, in step 3, you ask the Meta Model questions to explore options for yourself. By revising the statements in step 5, you put yourself back in control of your own decisions and behaviour.

Distortion – that touch of imagination

Disraeli was right when he said, 'Imagination governs the world.' Distortion, the process by which you change the meaning of the experience when it comes up against your own map of reality, is one such example. Figure 15-4 shows some everyday examples of distortion.

Figure 15-4:
The language of distortion.

Distortion supports your ability to explore your own inner world, your dreams, and lets your imagination run wild. That's fine when you want to explore your creativity.

The problem with distortion, however, is that most people don't realise that the distortion doesn't necessarily represent the truth: instead, it just represents their own perception. For example, have you ever come out of a meeting with a group of people and all had a different understanding of what happened? Or been to the cinema or theatre with a group of friends and come away with a completely different viewpoint about the film's message when you chat to your friends about it? Distortion happens when you take one aspect of an experience and change it according to what's happening for you in your life at that time.

Tennis anyone?

At times, when people want something very badly, they believe that thing to be true even when the evidence is against them. As a tennis coach, John Woodward finds that the most frustrating people in the junior tennis leagues are the competitive parents.

'They so desperately want their children to win that they become blind to the facts of the game. They see what they want to see, even if it's not true, to the extent that as they watch their children play matches, they give faulty line calls in favour of their own budding tennis star.

Grandparents are even worse! I once saw a grandfather attack his grandson's tennis opponent with his umbrella because he was convinced that his grandson had won a shot that everybody else saw as out.'

Reproduced with the permission of John Woodward.

Another example of distortion is attempting to read other people's minds. You can never know what other people are truly thinking, even though they may give out interesting clues. When negative distortion is combined with generalisation the result can be quite debilitating. For example, a child comes home from school and says: 'Everyone stares at me every time I walk into the classroom and they all think I'm stupid.'

Beware of making judgements about what other people think until you gather specific information and review the facts.

Here are some useful questions to ask when you want to check for distorted meanings:

- ✔ 'How do you know?'
- ✔ 'How exactly does X lead to Y?'
- ✔ 'Who says?'

Using the Meta Model

The Meta Model questions give you powerful verbal tools in business, coaching, education, therapy, and in life. They let you use language to gain clarity and get closer to somebody's experience. You can adopt the Meta Model when you want to do the following:

- ✔ **Clarify another person's meaning:** When you need to be exactly sure what the other person has in mind. Are you both on the same wavelength or making assumptions that you don't really understand?

✔ **Get more information:** When you need to understand, for example, the objectives and scope of a new project.

✔ **Open up more options:** When you need to explore different ways of doing things for yourself and for others.

✔ **Spot your own and other people's limitations:** When you need to work through beliefs and unhelpful habitual behaviour.

Taking two simple steps

When you use the Meta Model, challenge distortions first, and then generalisations, and then deletions. If you begin with deletions, you may get more information than you can handle.

To use the Meta Model, follow these simple steps:

1. **Listen to the words and spot the pattern (distortion, generalisation, or deletion).**

   Refer to the section 'Gathering Specific Information with the Meta Model' earlier in this chapter for an explanation of the language clues that help you recognise which pattern is being used.

2. **Intervene with the right question.**

   For distortion, ask:

   > 'How do you know?'

   > 'What's the evidence?'

   For generalisation, ask:

   > 'Is that always the case? Every time? Never?'

   > 'What if. . . ?'

   For deletion, ask:

   > 'Tell me more. . .'

   > 'What, when, where, who, how?'

Remembering a few caveats

You can ask questions in two basic ways: one is considerate and valuable and the other sounds more like an interrogation by the Spanish Inquisition. So here are some important points to bear in mind (you don't want to fall out with your best friend!):

✔ Bear in mind that rapport always comes first. Without rapport, nobody listens to you. For information on building rapport, head to Chapter 7.

✔ Remember that people need to trust you before they're ready to open up on difficult issues. So pace their timing. You can find more information on pacing and leading people in Chapter 7.

✔ Make sure that you're clear about what you're trying to achieve – your outcome – while you ask questions, otherwise you can get overloaded with irrelevant information and cease to be helpful.

✔ Soften your voice and be sensitive in your questioning. Feed the questions gently into conversations and meetings rather than firing them like a market researcher in the street.

✔ Try the Meta Model out on yourself before you rush off to sort out your family and friends uninvited. Go steady. Like Tom in the following example, they may wonder what's happening and not thank you for your new-found interest.

On Friday nights Andrew winds down after a busy week working in the City with a beer at his favourite pub in the picturesque village where he lives. After taking an NLP training course, he was enthusiastic to try out the Meta Model. His drinking partner, Tom, an architect, talked about the week he'd had, and especially about a major argument with a colleague over an important project.

As Tom began his tale with 'I'll never work with him again,' Andrew questioned the generalisation with: 'What never? Are you sure? What would happen if you did?'

Tom looked puzzled and responded with: 'Our partnership isn't going to work; communication has just broken down.'

Delighted to spot not one but two nominalisations in one sentence (check out the earlier sidebar 'Abstract nouns and the wheelbarrow test' for a description of nominalisations), Andrew jumped in with: 'How would you like to be a partner with this guy? And how may you be able to communicate?'

To which Tom was aghast and said: 'Look, you're normally on my side. What's going on?'

In his keenness to try out NLP, Andrew forgot to match and pace his friend and ease in gently with some subtle use of the Meta Model. All Tom really wanted that night was to have a good moan to a friend who would listen and sympathise.

The value of the Meta Model lies in gaining clarity. Watch out for the danger of getting more information than you can handle. Instead, pause to consider the outcome you're seeking before asking the next question.

Chapter 16

Hypnotising Your Audience

*I*magine scenario one. You're driving along the road on an ordinary kind of day. This stretch of road is familiar, one that you've travelled dozens of times. You know where you're going. You reach your destination, stop the car, and notice that you have no clear recollection of travelling the last few kilometres.

Now imagine scenario two. You're sitting with a group of people: perhaps you're attending a meeting or lesson of some kind. You wake with a start when someone turns to you and asks you a question: 'What are your thoughts on this?' Oh dear. Your attention has wandered. You haven't a clue what the discussion is all about.

So what's happening in these two scenarios? Nothing extraordinary. You're simply experiencing an everyday trance, as if your brain is operating like a computer in sleep mode. You're daydreaming, which is an excellent example of your ability to delete the details of what's happening around you and sink into the relaxation pattern of the trance. Scenes like these ones happen the world over, every moment of the day.

In this chapter, we dip our toes into the world of trance and talk about how to turn it to your (and other people's) benefit. Specifically, we look at the language patterns you can choose to adopt in order to communicate more effectively with other people, by getting through to the unconscious part of their minds.

Milton H Erickson – the master at work

As a compelling teacher and therapist, Milton H Erickson (1901–1980) inspired and fascinated those who came to learn from him or be healed. His mastery of therapeutic skills brought positive results for many people and led him to become the most influential hypnotherapist of the 20th century.

He had a profound effect on John Grinder and Richard Bandler, the founders of NLP. They modelled Erickson in 1974 and then published several books that demonstrated the language patterns they noted. These patterns form the basis of the Milton Model in NLP, which deliberately adopts language in which the meaning is vague. The Milton Model is in contrast to the Meta Model, explained in Chapter 15, which aims to elicit more specific information.

Erickson excelled at inducing trances in his patients and effecting real change that healed people. He paced the existing reality of his clients, patiently describing what they must be experiencing before introducing suggestions and leading them to new thinking. His therapeutic style was much more *permissive* than earlier hypnotherapists. By permissive, we mean that he adopted a flexible approach that worked with the existing map of his clients – always respecting their reality and using it as the starting point for his work. He gently took clients into a trance by making general comments that they couldn't help but agree with, rather than saying 'You will go into a trance now.' He believed that clients already had the necessary resources and saw his role as the therapist as enabling the client to access them.

Discovering the Language of Trance – the Milton Model

Humans have an amazing capacity to make sense of what people say – even when it's utter gobbledygook. Sometimes, being artfully vague is valuable – when you're non-specific in the content of what you say you enable other people to fill the gaps for themselves. When your language construction is deliberately vague, people can take what they need from your words in a way that's most appropriate for them.

The *Milton Model* is a set of language patterns that you can use to take somebody into a trance state, an altered state of consciousness, in which they can access unconscious resources, make changes, and solve their own problems. The Milton Model is named after Milton H Erickson, one of the most influential of all hypnotherapists (read more about him in the earlier sidebar 'Milton H Erickson – the master at work').

The Milton Model uses all the same patterns as the Meta Model, except in reverse (head to Chapter 15 for details on the Meta Model). Whereas the Meta Model aims to gather more information, the Milton Model aims to reduce the detail, deliberately adopting vague language that can be acceptable to different people. Table 16-1 outlines the main differences between these two models.

Table 16-1	Milton Model versus Meta Model
Milton Model	**Meta Model**
Makes language more general	Makes language more specific
Moves from surface structure to deep structure	Moves from deep structure to surface structure
Looks for general understanding	Looks for precise examples
Aims to access unconscious resources	Aims to bring experience to conscious awareness
Keeps client internally focused	Keeps client externally focused

Comparing language patterns and the Milton Model

In Table 16-2, we highlight some of the key language patterns of the Milton Model. Just as in the Meta Model – Bandler and Grinder's earlier explanation of language – the Milton Model identifies three key types of pattern. You see the same deletions, generalisations, and distortions that happen in normal speech (which we explain in full in Chapter 15) – the ways in which people make sense of their everyday experiences and transform them into language.

Table 16-2	NLP Milton Model Patterns
Patterns	**Examples of the Vague Language You Can Use to Challenge Deletions, Generalisations, and Distortions and Take a Person into a Receptive State**
Deletion	
Simple deletion (misses out part of the message)	You're ready to listen
Unspecified verbs (doesn't say how the action is carried out)	As you make sense of this in your own time. . .

(continued)

Table 16-2 (continued)

Patterns	Examples of the Vague Language You Can Use to Challenge Deletions, Generalisations, and Distortions and Take a Person into a Receptive State
Unspecified referential index (doesn't say who is being referred to)	Some people will have been important to you
Comparisons (misses out what is being compared)	You're feeling more and more curious
Nominalisations (an abstract noun that is turned into a verb; see Chapter 15)	You're gaining new insights, building new friendships
Generalisation	
Modal operators of possibility (shows what you can and are able to do)	You can become more successful . . . you're able to discover new ways
Modal operators of necessity (states what you must, you have to do)	You must take this forward to where it has to go
Universal quantifiers (all, everything)	Every time you feel like this. . .
	All the skills you need are easy for you to learn
Distortion	
Complex equivalence (one situation means the same as another)	This means that you're getting all the help you need
Mind reading (interpreting another's thoughts)	I know that you're becoming more interested
Cause and effect	On each breath, you can relax even more

As the comparison of the two models in Table 16-1 shows, the Milton Model makes statements that are deliberately very general; the effect of this approach is to relax the person you're speaking to. In contrast, the Meta Model essentially invites the other person to retrieve specific details that are missing.

Meeting other aspects of the Milton Model

As well as the language patterns described in the preceding section, Erickson also used a number of other linguistic devices to assist in communication with his clients. We discuss three such devices in the following three sections.

Tag questions

A tag question is added to the end of a statement to invite agreement. Tag questions are a deliberate and very effective device that distracts the conscious mind of recipients with something they can agree with. The effect is that the statement in front of the tag question goes directly to the unconscious mind and is acted upon:

- ✔ This is easy, isn't it?
- ✔ Your health is important, you know?
- ✔ You can, can't you?
- ✔ It's time to relax, don't you know?

Even if you never read or discover anything more about hypnosis, remember two of the most powerful words in the English language that are also examples of tag questions: *that's right*. Don't take our word for it; just try them out; you'll find that it's virtually impossible for someone to disagree with you.

Embedded commands

Embedded commands or questions are sentences that are constructed so as to contain within them the outcome that Erickson wanted from the client, as with the italicised parts of the following sentences:

- ✔ 'I'm curious about whether *you will learn to relax and let yourself be comfortable* in a few moments.'
- ✔ 'What is interesting is *when did you last learn so easily*?'

The purpose of the embedded command is to send directions straight to the unconscious mind, without the conscious mind blocking them. Erickson used his tone of voice to mark the commands out from the rest of the sentence: for example, by deepening his voice for the command element.

As you adopt lessons from communicators such as Erickson, remember that although what you say is important, the way you behave (body language, tone of voice, and so on) has the most effect.

Double binds

Double binds give people a choice, but limit it. You cover the options and assume that the result you want is going to happen:

- ✔ 'When will you clean up your clutter, before you've had lunch or after?' (A typical one to use with messy teenagers or housemates!)
- ✔ 'Would you like to order it in blue or in green?' (How about this one in a sales situation?)

The tale is in the telling

Part of Erickson's therapy was to create stories – teaching tales – which helped people to make sense of their situations in new ways. Erickson was confined to a wheelchair, and yet he carried out an extensive therapeutic practice, travelling widely and teaching and giving seminars right to the end of his life.

Vast libraries of transcripts of Erickson's tales and seminars are available to purchase (see www.tranceworks.com), which make fascinating reading. Yet, those fortunate enough to have met Erickson in person point out that the written word conveys just part of the man's intuitive approach to clients. If you think about the communication equation we talk about in Chapter 7 on creating rapport, you may remember that words play only a small part in any communication – something like 7 per cent of the effect. Erickson's smiles, gestures, the tone of his voice, and his instinctive respect for and curiosity about his clients are the missing ingredients in the written stories.

Finding your own preferred model

To help you understand the differences between the Milton Model and the Meta Model, try this little role-playing exercise with a willing friend. One of you acts as the salesperson and the other as the customer:

- ✔ **The salesperson:** Imagine that you're a salesperson and your task is to sell an object or service to your partner. Your job is to persuade the customer to buy *without giving the person any details of what you're really selling* – see how interested you can get your partner while you remain artfully vague in the style of the Milton Model.

- ✔ **The customer:** Imagine that you're a customer and your job is to *get more specific information out of the salesperson* who's trying to sell to you. Challenge the vague language using tips from Chapter 15 on the Meta Model patterns to elicit detail from the generalised speech.

Afterwards, ask yourself which role felt most natural to you? Do you prefer to see and discuss the sweeping big picture or do you feel more comfortable when you talk about detail?

Understanding the art of vagueness and why it's important

As you gain familiarity with the Milton Model, you can do what others before you have done: start to notice some of the language you hear as you listen to everyone you meet. You can notice that most people have mastered the ability to communicate at a general level. In other words, most people have mastered the art of vagueness, which allows you to go inside so easily, does it not?

Vagueness is everywhere! Just consider these statements:

- ✔ 'We can work it out.'
- ✔ 'Things can only get better.'
- ✔ 'It doesn't have to be like this.'
- ✔ 'Someday, we'll all be free.'
- ✔ 'We all have our problems.'

Phrases like these are equally at home on the lips of politicians and pop stars, clairvoyants, and copywriters. You hear them on the radio every morning and they pop out from the newspaper in your daily horoscope as well as the advertisements on your computer screen for the latest must-have products. They send you into a relaxed state. You can't help but agree with such highly generalised statements.

The power of using vague language lies in the fact that you get people into a different state. Such language distracts people from the outside world, so connecting with everybody in a group or getting rapport with someone you don't know well becomes easier. When you're vague, the following happen:

- ✔ Your listeners find their own answers, which are more powerful and long lasting for them.
- ✔ You don't instil your own ideas or put inappropriate suggestions in the way.
- ✔ Your clients feel more in control, because they're free to explore different possibilities that you may never have thought of.

In addition, being vague also opens up your own map. Remember that the language you adopt affects you too – not just other people. So often people impose their own limits by the way in which they talk about themselves – those naughty thought viruses like 'I'm not good enough' or 'I'll never be able to do that' jump out and block their route to success. The Milton Model can combat such thoughts and help you do the following:

- ✔ Arouse your natural curiosity
- ✔ Discover more empowering ways of acting
- ✔ Find times when you were at your best and return you to that resourceful state
- ✔ Think more clearly

NLP has adopted the idea of *chunking* from the world of IT; the term simply means breaking things into bits. Illustrated in Figure 16-1, this NLP concept says that information needs to be in chunks of the right size for you to process it: tiny details or the bigger picture, whatever is appropriate for the person to whom you're speaking. Chapter 15 on the Meta Model, this chapter, and Chapter 17 on telling stories all explore the different ways in which giving people information at the right level of detail or chunk size aids communication.

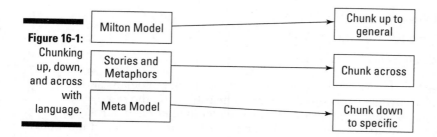

Figure 16-1: Chunking up, down, and across with language.

The Milton Model is a style of communication that moves upwards and focuses ideas at a highly general level; the Meta Model has a downward direction, concentrating on very specific details. When you use stories and metaphors, you're simply moving sideways – chunking laterally – to match the same level of detail but using stories to help people make new connections.

Going Deeper into Hypnosis

Hypnosis has existed since the eighteenth century – its original founder is usually accepted to be Franz Anton Mesmer (whose name is the origin of the word *mesmerise*). Hypnosis – or trance – is a natural state of focused attention, one in which you become *en-tranced*, where your main focus is on your internal thoughts and feelings rather than the external world around you.

Thanks to the more recent influence of Milton Erickson (check out the earlier sidebar 'Milton H Erickson – the master at work'), NLP views hypnosis and everyday trance as a safe and valuable route to your *unconscious* (which in this context means other than conscious). Your unconscious signifies the thoughts, feelings, and experiences of which you're currently unaware.

Erickson said that his patients were having problems because they were out of rapport with their unconscious minds, suggesting that good mental health involves a rapport between the conscious and unconscious minds. His style of hypnosis enlists the help of the unconscious mind to facilitate changes in patterns of thinking and behaviour, and works by a therapist talking to somebody in such a way that the person becomes self-reflective. In this altered or dream-like state, the mind is relaxed. When the unconscious mind becomes more available, the therapist helps a client make changes, whether that's giving up smoking, letting go of a phobia or fear, or making other positive changes to improve the person's confidence and well-being.

In Chapter 5, you can read about George Miller's conclusion that the conscious mind can cope with only seven chunks of information, give or take two pieces at one time. Change in your thought and belief processes takes place at an unconscious level. The Milton Model allows change by pacing the person's reality, and by that we mean truly acknowledging and respecting the qualities of somebody else's experiences that are likely to be different from your own. The model distracts the conscious mind and lets people access their unconscious mind.

When under hypnosis, some people go deep into the experience, others less so. Your brain becomes less active and muscle movement, blinking rate, and swallowing reflexes all slow down.

Getting comfortable with the idea of hypnosis

Words are powerful – they conjure up all kinds of memories and sensations and stir imaginations into action. If we say one word to you, *hypnosis*, what does your mind conjure up? If we ask you to let us hypnotise you, would you ponder the question for a second and answer 'fine', or back away shaking your head. What reaction sticks in your mind?

If you've ever experienced hypnosis, you're likely to remember a pleasant and relaxing state of being. If you haven't, you may be curious or even downright terrified. 'Don't start fiddling with my mind,' we hear you say!

Some stage hypnotists give hypnosis a bad name by the way that they encourage people to perform all kinds of embarrassing acts to entertain others. Such shows engender fear about the huge control of a hypnotist over the minds of the subjects. Little wonder, therefore, that many people are sceptical as regards hypnosis.

If this scepticism applies to you, you may appreciate another way of looking at hypnosis. Simply think about it as a dream-like state in which the possibility of change becomes more available. The *Collins English Dictionary* defines hypnosis as 'an artificially induced state of relaxation and concentration in which deeper parts of the mind become more accessible'.

When you're stuck with a problem, hypnosis simply accelerates the process of getting to the solution and help you need.

The truth is that hypnosis works only if you're a willing participant in the process. Kate once found herself in a room of over 100 people who were entranced by a group hypnosis exercise, and she was virtually the only person not following the embedded commands of the presenter. She watched in surprise as others moved on to the stage taking their chairs with them. Later, she realised that she distrusted the person running the session and had naturally protected herself from taking part. Remember that only you have the power to control your thoughts, actions, and words.

As with any therapy or similar service, check out the professional qualifications of your hypnotherapist and ask for references. Take the same safety measures that you'd use when going on a blind date. In particular, be cautious of entering a private home or space where you're alone with the person. If in doubt, taking a friend with you is a wise move.

Contrary to popular myth, under hypnosis people are in complete control of their situation. The hypnotherapist acts merely as a facilitator and the client rejects any suggestion that they don't consider appropriate.

When hard switches to easy

Registered hypnotherapist, Tom McGuire of Seven Colours, Ltd, applies the Milton Model language patterns to diverse applications – from discovering how to release anxiety to breaking habits, controlling pain, and enhancing performance in sport or public speaking.

'At times we may wrestle with problems using all our conscious resources and yet find ourselves unable to reach a satisfactory solution,' Tom says. He cites the example of weight management: 'I acknowledge the fact that the client has tried really hard in the past to lose weight. I make a point of using the word "hard" and associating that with the methods they have used in the past. I then go on to explain that using the unconscious mind is an easy way to get the results, and they begin to activate images in their own mind about how they will feel and look.'

'The Milton approach is to assume that their unconscious mind already knows how to lose the weight. We enlist the help of the unconscious mind to achieve it. No need to force it to help. Because we do not go into detail about how it will be possible, the patient becomes curious. This curiosity provides the fuel to drive the unconscious.'

'Many clients have told me that they have found themselves putting food back onto the supermarket shelf when shopping, only realising after they have done it. Sometimes they tell me that they haven't felt hungry and so forgot about food altogether between meals. The thought of food sometimes drifts into their mind but then drifts out again. No fighting, just curiosity. To me, this flexible, indirect approach embodies the Milton Model and shows the utmost respect for the client.'

Reproduced with the permission of Tom McGuire.

Experiencing everyday trances

Throughout the day you move through a series of trance-like experiences, naturally going in and out of a trance several times a minute. Humans have a fantastic protection mechanism to cope with the overload of information!

One upside is that your trance allows you to meditate, plan, rest, and relax. Daydreaming lets you open your mind to new ideas. It also enhances your natural creativity – the trance state is when you make new connections between ideas and solve problems for yourself.

The downside comes when you constantly replay anxieties and aren't reacting healthily with the external world. Perhaps you need a break or some outside help if this situation applies to you. Therapy helps people break negative trances. In fact, often hypnosis work is about bringing people out of a trance and back to reality.

What do you do to truly relax? To get yourself into that comfortable, easy state where all is well with the world? Ask the same question of any number of friends, family, and colleagues and you get quite different suggestions. Relaxation is a light, everyday trance that gives you some downtime to balance out the highs.

Here's a simple way to induce a trance in yourself and others. Get with a group of people. Spend 20 minutes telling each other of all the things you do to relax. As you explain what you do, speak in a calm and gentle voice, consider what you might like to try yourself from other people's suggestions and notice that just talking about relaxation in this way creates a light trance in the whole group.

Our challenge to you is to ask yourself whether you're spending time relaxing and allowing yourself to daydream. Building relaxation time into your diary each day and each week is a vital life-giving tonic. Become aware of your own trances and make a choice not to get drawn into the negative ones.

When Kate asked a friend, a teenager with a strong *away from* meta program (you can read more about meta programs and how those with 'away from' tendencies talk more about what they don't want than what they do want in Chapter 8), what he most likes to do to relax, his response was as follows:

> *I just find a good book and escape to somewhere pleasant and private. It's great when you're annoyed about something, because you're distracted by what you read, you get involved with the characters, and then you forget what you're angry about.*

A mere two hours later that evening after receiving this suggestion, Kate had come away from a late phone call feeling tense, having absorbed some strong negative vibes from an anxious client; she knew that she wouldn't be able to sleep until she was fully relaxed. She didn't want to get into a negative trance running her client's problems through her head. So she took her friend's advice, picked up a new novel, sank into the sofa, and became so engrossed that the angst quickly slipped away – and a good night's sleep followed. In NLP terms, she 'chunked up' from the specifics of the client's issues to a more general sense that 'all is good with the world', deleting the details. Sometimes the simplest solutions to interrupt our trances really are the best.

The common piece of advice to sleep on a problem, and a course of action will present itself in the morning, contains an essential truth. When you allow your conscious mind to rest, the unconscious mind is given the opportunity to process or retrieve information, and then the brain can really get to work in a positive way. So, next time you're struggling with an issue, as you go to bed ask your unconscious mind to help you find the answer, and notice what comes to you in the morning when you wake.

Groupthink

Have you ever noticed how group reactions to an event are bigger and more powerful than the sum of the individual parts? Perhaps you've been to a rock concert, religious gathering, big sporting occasion, or been caught in a serious airport delay. People have the ability to get into a group trance of mass hysteria – for better or for worse, like the whirling dervishes.

Groupthink is a term coined by Irving Janis to characterise situations where people are carried along by group illusions and perceptions. As a Yale University social psychologist, Janis was fascinated with the question of how groups of experts, especially in the White House, were able to make such terrible decisions.

One of the most famous examples is found in the abortive invasion of Cuba at the Bay of Pigs by 1,200 anti-Castro exiles. Launched on 17 April 1961 by the Kennedy administration, it almost led to war. 'How could we have been so stupid?' President Kennedy later remarked. In retrospect, the plan looked completely misguided, and yet at the time it was never seriously questioned or challenged. Kennedy and his advisors had unwittingly developed shared illusions that stopped them thinking critically and engaging with reality.

Janis believes that when overcome by groupthink, chief executives or their advisors aren't stupid, lazy, or evil. Instead, he sees them as victims of 'a mode of thinking that people engage in when they are deeply involved in a cohesive in-group, when the members' strivings for unanimity override their motivation to realistically appraise alternative courses of action.'

When people operate in a groupthink mode, they automatically apply the 'let's preserve group harmony at all cost' test to every decision they face.

Chapter 17

Telling Tales to Reach the Unconscious: Stories, Fables, and Metaphors

We want to tell you a story. Nan-in, a Japanese Zen master in the Meiji era, received a university professor who came to inquire about Zen Buddhism. Nan-in poured them both some tea. He filled up his visitor's cup, and then kept on pouring. The professor watched until unable to restrain himself. 'It's overfull. No more will go in,' he said.

'Like this cup,' Nan-in said, 'you're full of your own opinions and speculations. How can I show you Zen unless you first empty your cup?'

What was happening for you as you read those words? What came into your head? Your response to this little story is unique to you, and if you ask a group of people for their reactions to a story, you're going to get totally different responses. Stories get to the parts that other words don't reach. They speak to you at an unconscious level.

Through stories you can get your message across in a way that's much more effective than any logical argument, because they connect to people's experiences, memories, and emotions. In NLP terms, stories help build rapport. They enable you to convey information indirectly, pace someone's current reality, and then lead that person on to a new, healthier reality. You can move away from problems to different outcomes and open up new possibilities. So when you're sitting comfortably, we will begin. . . .

Processing Stories and Metaphors

Your brain is a natural pattern-matching machine (in Chapter 3 you can find more details on what goes on inside your mind) and you're constantly matching and sorting things. When you hear something new you make connections and say: 'Aha. This is like *this*. This reminds me of *that*.' Your brain naturally recognises patterns, and for this reason stories and metaphors transport you to a different place and put you into the type of trance that we describe in Chapter 16 – a deeply relaxed state in which you're very resourceful and your brain becomes naturally responsive to presented patterns.

NLP defines metaphors broadly as stories or figures of speech that imply a comparison. NLP suggests that stories and metaphors work as valuable communication tools because they distract the conscious mind and overload it with processing. Meanwhile the unconscious mind steps in to come up with creative solutions and the resources you need. Thus you're able to make new meanings and solve problems.

Understanding the Stories of Your Life

You live in a world of stories, and you're an accomplished storyteller. Don't believe us? Consider this. When you recount the day's events to a friend or partner, you're telling a story. When you gossip on the telephone to your mates, or describe a business process to a client, you're telling a story. Events don't have to be make-believe to qualify as a story.

Getting to grips with storytelling basics

Whether they relate actual or imaginary events, good stories have four key ingredients. Think about a child's fairy-tale handed down through generations, such as *The Wizard of Oz*, *Little Red Riding Hood*, or *Cinderella* and see if you can recognise these elements:

- **Characters:** You need a hero, plus goodies and baddies along the way
- **Plot:** The storyline of the journey that the hero takes
- **Conflict:** The challenge or difficulty that the hero faces
- **Resolution:** The result or outcome that happens at the end of the tale (we hope it doesn't end in tears!)

The travelling storyteller

Throughout history, people have told stories, myths, and legends, and used metaphors to communicate a message. The oral tradition preceded the written word and multimedia as a critical form of communication. Storytellers were typically travellers who moved from town to town, passing on important information by word-of-mouth. Without the luxury of email and PowerPoint, they used rhythm, rhyme, and visualisation to aid memory. The more fantastic and outrageous the story, the more likely people were to remember it.

Stories engage the left side of the brain to process the words and the sequence of the plots and the right side in terms of imagination, visualisation, and creativity.

Many stories are told solely to entertain, but you can use stories for a number of purposes:

✔ To focus concentration

✔ To illustrate a point

✔ To get over a lesson that people remember

✔ To sow new ideas

✔ To get people to recognise their own problems

✔ To make a complex idea simpler

✔ To change people's mood

✔ To challenge behaviour

✔ To have fun

Working on your storytelling

Stories and metaphors work in business communication just as well as in a social or spiritual context. You learn from the experiences of other people and take meaning from metaphors. Businesses tell stories to do the following:

✔ Communicate information

✔ Convey values of the organisation

✔ Educate people

> ✔ Give the listener the benefit of the company's wisdom
>
> ✔ Help teams to evaluate options and make decisions

Stories engage people more fully, which is why customer examples, testimonials, and case studies work so well to reinforce a business message. They're so much more powerful than a pure product promotion.

In many businesses, stories develop about the history of the birth of the company, which keep people in touch with the fundamental values. During our early days working at Hewlett-Packard (HP), all the employees connected with the story of how Bill Hewlett and Dave Packard started out in a Californian garage, the struggles for survival on the way to success in Palo Alto, and their continual dedication to the core principles that were written down and related to all 100,000 employees as *The HP Way*.

Corporate tales such as these engage people and align them to a common sense of purpose. They help to retain the same sense of teamwork and unity of a smaller business even as an organisation grows into a corporate giant. In HP, employees respected the founders because they were able to identify with two fellow human beings who became renowned corporate leaders thanks to their skills, grit, and determination. They felt that Bill and Dave continued to value people as well as business performance in a way that was outstanding in the demanding 'hire and fire' world of business culture.

We remember one ex-CEO, Lew Platt, speaking at an HP Women's Conference and telling the story of bringing up his children as a single parent after his wife died. He talked about the worry of getting a phone call telling him that his child was sick just as he was going into an important business negotiation. Lew knew how to connect with the heart of an audience by speaking from his own experience.

Storytelling isn't a skill to confine to business leaders. At work, you can begin to develop your own stories as a tool for getting your message across to colleagues and clients as well as to your bosses. But don't make your stories long-winded or amazingly elaborate. You may begin by noting some of your successes or interesting experiences and building them into a relevant anecdote to pull out of the bag at the appropriate moment.

Stories from your own experience can dramatically enliven an explanation of a dry subject such as customer service, quality control, software programs, or safety procedures.

In a similar vein, if you want to influence customers to buy your product or make the right decision, they're more likely to listen to you when you tell them how another customer solved a similar problem. This less forthright approach can be more effective than putting forward a direct opinion on what you want them to do.

So, too, if you want to manage your career progression positively, don't wait until your annual performance review for your boss to hear how you're doing. As some of our successful clients have discovered, a few stories that demonstrate achievements fed into conversations as a weekly diet over lunch or coffee can be much more effective.

Passing on a gift to the next generation

The storytelling tradition – from Greek myths, Arthurian legends, and Aesop's Fables through to modern writers – forms part of the rich human heritage that connects past, present, and future generations. Similarly, the stories you tell about your life (or hear about the lives of others in your family) perform the same function – they connect generations as well.

What stories do you love to hear and tell about your life? Perhaps you've heard family stories about when you were born, your first day at school, or the important events and people in your early life. Truth can be stranger and more entertaining than fiction. And the tales get told and retold, each time with fresh embellishment.

Family tales that get handed down by word-of-mouth become lost as families split and generations pass away. When Kate's neighbour, Margaret, retired, she took her interest in her family ancestors further than just compiling the family tree. Her more permanent legacy to her family is a fascinating bound collection of stories. Alongside the tree, she collected anecdotes from all living members of the family. She published them for the family and later generations to enjoy and understand more about their heritage. If you were to do the same, what stories would you like to record for posterity?

Here's a game of anecdotes that may enliven a family get-together. Write out five cards each with one of the following words: farce, thriller, comedy, tragedy, TV soap. Take a card, think of a family anecdote, and tell a story in the style that's written on the card.

Grasping the Power of Metaphors

Just as people tell stories all day, your ordinary conversations are richly embroidered with metaphors. Consider these examples (with the metaphors in italics):

- ✔ 'Look, it's a *jungle* out there!'
- ✔ 'He was *putty in their hands.*'

> ✔ 'She's a *pain in the neck*.'
>
> ✔ 'He's a *breath of fresh air*.'
>
> ✔ 'We can *cut the atmosphere with a knife*.'

Some people say that, although a picture is worth 1,000 words, a metaphor is worth 1,000 pictures.

Using metaphors in NLP

The word metaphor is derived from the Greek, and literally means 'to carry across'. Metaphors make a comparison, a parallel between two sometimes unrelated terms, and can be a powerful and innovative way of describing a situation; they can help listeners to reflect on themselves or to see a difficult situation in a new light, perhaps providing a novel way of resolving the problem.

In NLP, metaphors are used in a broader sense than that defined in English grammar – they are used to help people move across from one context to another. NLP calls this movement *chunking across or chunking sideways*. As explained in Chapter 16, chunking is about moving up and down levels of detail (up to the big picture or down to specifics) in order to communicate with somebody at the most appropriate and effective level.

As Nick Owen describes in his book *The Magic of Metaphor* (2001, Crown House Publishing): 'Metaphors are not simply poetic or rhetorical embellishments, but powerful devices for shaping perception and experience.'

In one of Kate's presentation workshops, Janet was looking at creative ways to liven up a presentation to a group of teenagers. As a careers advisor, Janet's work takes her into schools where she needs to inspire groups with all the options of apprenticeship schemes.

At first, she stood up and explained the options open to the students in the hope that they'd listen because of her strong enthusiasm and in-depth knowledge. Later, as she thought about ways of refining her presentation with stories and metaphors, Janet hit on the idea of using the metaphor of a mobile phone – something with which all the youngsters identified. She compared all the various career routes and options with the sophisticated functions of the latest phone model. In this way, she bridged the gap from the advisor to the student and found a way to develop a more compelling talk. Thanks to the appealing metaphor, she discovered a fresh approach to enliven her story and inspire the young people.

To practise creating metaphors and have a little fun at the same time, try this exercise. You need three people: Person A has a subject (like writing a book, for example) that they want to communicate in a different way. Follow these steps:

1. **Person A says: '[The topic] is like. . . .'**

   Using the book-writing example, Person A may say, 'Writing a book is like. . . .'

2. **Person B thinks of an object – any object at all to complete the sentence 'Writing a book is like. . . .'**

   Person B, for example, may say, '. . .an apple.'

3. **Person C makes the connection.**

   For example, they may say: '. . .because you can get your teeth into it.'

This exercise makes a good suppertime game. And you can use it to find a metaphor to help you communicate a message in a more memorable way.

Applying metaphors to find new solutions

In his book *Sleight of Mouth*, Robert Dilts relates the story about a young man in a psychiatric ward suffering from the delusion that he's Jesus Christ. He spends his days unproductively, rambling around, annoying and being ignored by the other patients. All attempts by the psychiatrists and their aides fail to convince the man of his delusion.

One day, a new psychiatrist arrives on the scene. After observing the patient quietly for some time, he approaches the young man. 'I understand that you have some experience as a carpenter,' he says. 'Well . . . yes, I guess I do,' replies the patient. The psychiatrist explains to him that they're building a new recreation room at the facility and need the help of someone with the skills of a carpenter. 'We could sure use your assistance,' says the psychiatrist, 'that is, if you're the type of person who likes to help others.'

And so the story ends well. The patient has been respected for his beliefs and becomes open to communicating with people once more. Now his therapeutic healing can begin.

In this story, the new psychiatrist connects with the client by working with his own metaphor of carpentry. The patient believes that he's Jesus Christ, and so the psychiatrist accepts that and doesn't attempt to contradict. Instead, the psychiatrist works with the patient's belief and adopts the same metaphor – Jesus the carpenter – to set the patient on the road to recovery.

Symbolic Modelling

James Lawley and Penny Tompkins, authors of *Metaphors in Mind* (2006, Developing Company Press) have developed a process called Symbolic Modelling. This process enhances the ability of those trained in NLP and other methods to work at a symbolic level with clients. 'Metaphor is particularly valuable with those who find it difficult to describe what is happening for them because of trauma, lack of self-awareness or embarrassment,' says James. 'For example, in a business meeting, a senior leader may not want to say that he's scared about the way the organisation is going. However, by getting into the symbolic domain, he can readily admit that it's "like a rough sea getting more turbulent". This enables him to express his fears without exposing himself to judgement.'

Working with symbols and metaphors allows clients to feel more resourceful when dealing with challenging topics. As psychotherapists, Penny and James are experienced at working symbolically with clients who've been through severe trauma. Sometimes a client may find that speaking about the details of the event is too painful. 'Working with clients' personal metaphors,' Penny says, 'honours their unique experience and creates a context in which change can take place organically. This can happen because the Clean Language of David Grove prevents therapists from unwittingly adding to or changing a client's symbolic experience.'

We provide the Clean Language question set in Chapter 18 and you can find more on Clean Language and Modelling in Chapter 19.

Permission from James Lawley and Penny Tompkins.

Skilled therapists of all disciplines frequently work with the client's own metaphors to help shift problems. In the same way, you can work with other people's metaphors to aid communication in everyday conversation. For example:

- To convey bad news like project delays or job changes
- To calm down an anxious teenager facing exams
- To explain a complicated subject to a group of people
- To encourage confidence or courage in a young child

You can use word-play to defuse tension, through themes such as the weather and nature – moving from rain and storms to sunshine and calm, or comparing a challenging situation with climbing a mountain or crossing a river. Also, relating a message in terms of a friend's favourite sports – golf, tennis, sailing, or football – can help elicit shifts in thinking.

As an example, when your colleague at work tells you that 'this project is a real nightmare,' you can gently drop words connected to sleep and dreaming into the conversation to gain more information or lead the person to a more positive state of thinking. So you may feed some of the following types of language into the discussion: 'What aspects of the project are keeping you awake at night?', 'Are there some scary bits?', 'Perhaps people need to sleep on this for a while?', 'How would you like to get this put to bed?', and 'So in your wildest dreams, what would you see happening?'

Anthony is a therapist who works with clients with addictive behaviours. He told us:

> *I had a client who told me about the pleasure she derived from her drinking until it got out of control. Initially she described the delight of her favourite tipple – the anticipation and smell of the first glass, how appealing it looked in the bottle, beautifully packaged and presented. But as she went on to describe the feelings of helplessness as the addiction overtook her, the alcohol was transformed into an ugly spirit that haunted and frightened her. Over a period of time, we were able to work with her story, develop the plot and rework it to have a happier ending. She could then believe in a future where she could break free from the addiction that was overwhelming her life.*

Employing direct and indirect metaphors

NLP distinguishes between direct and indirect types of metaphors:

- A *direct* metaphor compares one situation with another that has an obvious link in terms of the type of content. For example, it may compare learning a new computer software application with learning to drive: both are about learning.

- An *indirect* metaphor makes comparisons that aren't immediately obvious. For example, it may compare learning new computer software with cooking a meal or planning a holiday. Such indirect metaphors form the basis of the most creative advertising campaigns.

Building Your Own Stories

In her 'Passion to Publication' writing workshops, Kate encourages budding authors to create their own Origin Stories and then develop them into an article or book. These stories are the personal ones that have fired up the person's passion for what they're writing about and relate the times when the writer felt the extremes of emotion – from peaks of excitement to troughs of anxiety. As each person in the group shares a story, it inevitably fires up new stories for the other writers as they connect the writer's experience with similar ones of their own. The most convincing writing tells compelling stories, just as the most compelling tales are those told from the heart.

Strong communicators recognise the power of story to achieve rapport more readily and entrance their audience – whether that is with one person or many. Indeed much therapeutic work depends on the narrative form of communication. In this section, we gather together ideas for you to develop your own repertoire of stories and build your skills as an engaging storyteller. Even if you never thought of yourself as a storyteller before, you can soon see how to capture your own story ideas and organise your thoughts for maximum effect.

Using the Personal Story Builder Journal

Everyday experiences can form the basis of your own compelling stories. Here's a way to capture and record storylines that you can adapt later.

1. **Find a situation that generated an emotion: write the emotion down (was it joy, contentment, pride, fear, anger, shock, confusion, guilt, and so on?).**

2. **Name the characters of the people involved.**

3. **Tell what happened by giving three key points of the storyline.**

4. **Relate the outcome: in other words, how did it end?**

5. **Describe something funny or interesting that was communicated.**

6. **Explain what you learned from this story.**

7. **List your ideas for developing this story: identify where, when, and to whom you're going to tell it.**

Stories develop and change over time. Come back to the journal at regular intervals to extend your repertoire of stories that you can create. As you listen to speakers who inspire or entertain you, notice that their storylines are quite simple. Feel free to record interesting stories you hear others tell and put your spin on them to make them your own.

As you begin to create your own favourite stories, think about the following aspects:

✔ How are you going to *start* the story and how will you *finish*? Some great starts lose their way (and their readers) long before the finishing post.

✔ What happens in the *middle* to give the dramatic interest – what are the interesting landmarks, battles, dilemmas, or conflicts on the way?

✔ Who are the *characters* – who's the hero and what about the supporting cast? How can you make them memorable?

✔ How can you make sure that you build the content around a strong framework?

Discovering more ways to flex your storytelling muscles

Effective storytelling is a fabulous skill that is worth developing – a well-told story captures the audience and remains with the people long after the other details of an event are forgotten. Here are some suggestions for you to hone your technique:

- ✔ Start with simple stories and then get more adventurous as your skills grow.

- ✔ Head for the children's library for all sorts of examples of folk and fairy tales that you can adapt well to any context. One of our clients describes *Alice in Wonderland* as the best business book ever written.

- ✔ Remember that when you tell a story the focus is on you. Practise and live with your story so that when you perform, you can command the audience's attention and take everyone with you. Know the first lines and last lines by heart and simplify the structure to a few key points.

- ✔ Tell a humorous story with a deadpan serious face and you can make much more impact than when you smirk all the way through. The element of surprise is powerful.

- ✔ Hold on to that essential ingredient of rapport to keep people listening (head to Chapter 7 for more details on creating rapport).

- ✔ Arrange the time, place, and setting in which you tell the story. Make sure that people are relaxed and comfortable. Campfire settings and flickering log fires make for perfect storytelling moments – as do seats under shady trees on a lazy summer's day.

- ✔ Think of your voice as a well-tuned musical instrument. Notice how your breathing affects your voice and practise a range of sounds and volume. Enjoy exploiting all your skills to perform to the full range of expression.

- ✔ See what you can discover from other people's stories and the way they tell them. You may adapt part of their story to make it your own or notice how they work with their voice, the audience, and the stage.

- ✔ Speaking from the heart rather than reading from a book or script is more powerful . . . and people allow you to be less than word perfect.

- ✔ Stimulate your audience's senses so that they can see vivid pictures, hear the sounds, get in touch with feelings, even smell and taste the delicious tale you're concocting for them.

- ✔ Have a great beginning. For examples of memorable openers, head to the later sidebar 'Hooking people in'.

Hooking people in

Once upon a time. . . . Have you noticed how every great story intrigues the reader with its opening? Think about how you're going to begin your story to attract attention and retain interest. Here are some introductory lines for starters:

'Whether I shall turn out to be the hero of my own life, or whether that station will be held by anybody else, these pages must show.' Charles Dickens, *David Copperfield*.

'It might have happened anywhere, at any time, and it could certainly have been a good deal worse.' Elizabeth Jane Howard, *The Sea Change*.

'"Take my camel, dear," said my Aunt Dot as she climbed down from this animal on her return from High Mass.' Rose Macaulay, *The Towers of Trebizond*.

'José Palacios, his oldest servant, found him floating naked with his eyes open in the purifying waters of his bath and thought he had drowned.' Gabriel Garcia Marquez, *The General in His Labyrinth*.

'In the beginning, there was a river. The river became a road and the road branched out to the whole world. And because the road was once a river it was always hungry.' Ben Okri, *The Famished Road*.

'I am doomed to remember a boy with a wrecked voice, not because of his voice or because he was the smallest person I ever knew or even because he was the instrument of my mother's death, but because he is the reason I believe in God.' John Irvine, *A Prayer for Owen Meaney*.

Adding loops to your story: And this reminds me of. . .

Have you noticed how, in a novel, a writer may open up a number of loops or storylines that run in parallel throughout the book?

In one of the greatest storybooks of the world, *The Thousand and One Nights*, a collection of a tales tells how King Shahriyar had an unpleasant behavioural problem. He'd got into the habit of killing a succession of his young virgin brides after their first night of marriage.

At the rate he was demolishing the female population, the source of potential brides began to run dry. Thanks to the cleverness of Shahrazad, the daughter of his senior statesman and the king's potential next victim, the pattern was broken. Shahrazad is said to have collected a thousand and one books of histories and poetry, fascinated as she was by the lives of kings and past generations.

On her marriage night, she entertained the king with a tale that hung in the air unfinished at dawn. The king's curiosity got the better of him awaiting the completion of the tale and he spared her life – again and again and again – as the thousand and one tales unfolded. And he broke the habit of killing his new brides!

You too can build story loops into your storytelling skill set. This advanced device can help with the stories you tell, whether in a presentation, training, or social setting.

You begin one story and then before you complete it, you say 'ah that reminds me of. . .', or 'have I told you the one about. . .'. The stories hang in the air, incomplete; people are left uncertain, wondering what happened and how the story's going to end. This technique enables you to keep the audience's attention and concentration as they try to create order out of the confusion. You can build story loops naturally as you wander from subject to subject. Be sure to close the stories off eventually, however, or you simply end up annoying your audience.

And finally, sit back, relax, and enjoy another story from the Sufi tradition

There was once a small boy who banged a drum all day and loved every moment of it. He wouldn't be quiet, no matter what anyone else said or did. Various people who called themselves Sufis, and other well-wishers, were called in by neighbours and asked to do something about the child.

The first so-called Sufi told the boy that he would, if he continued to make so much noise, perforate his eardrums; this reasoning was too advanced for the child, who was neither a scientist nor a scholar. The second told him that drum-beating was a sacred activity and should be carried out only on special occasions. The third offered the neighbours plugs for their ears; the fourth gave the boy a book; the fifth gave the neighbours books that described a method of controlling anger through biofeedback; the sixth gave the boy meditation exercises to make him placid and explained that all reality was imagination. Like all placebos, each of these remedies worked for a short while, but none worked for very long.

Eventually, a real Sufi came along. He looked at the situation, handed the boy a hammer and chisel, and said, 'I wonder what's *inside* the drum?'

Chapter 18

Asking the Right Questions

. . . .

. . . .

*W*hen you know the 'right' questions to ask, you get the results you want much faster. Throughout this book, in the true spirit of NLP, we deliberately aim to be non-judgemental, and so you can quite legitimately say that no 'right' or 'wrong' questions exist, only different ones.

So, we need to be more precise. When we talk about asking the 'right' questions, we're looking specifically for incisive questions – those that put your finger precisely on the nub of an issue, those that have a positive effect in the shortest possible time. In this context, the 'wrong' questions are those that send you off-course, meandering down dead ends, and gathering interesting but irrelevant information.

In this book, we explain and demonstrate that your language is powerful; it triggers an emotional response in you, as well as others. Therefore, you can make a difference as you begin to choose your language with increasing awareness. In this chapter, we bring together some of the most useful questions you can ask in different situations to make things happen for yourself and for others. Knowing the right questions to ask may make a difference for you when you want to do the following:

✔ Set your life going in the right direction

✔ Make the best decisions

✔ Help others to take more responsibility

✔ Select and motivate people

✔ Coach others to overcome their limitations

Question-Asking Tips and Strategies

Before rushing on to the critical question you probably want answered – 'what are the magic questions that do make a real difference?' – take a quick breather and consider *how* to ask questions when you're working with people, which is just as important as *what* to ask.

In this section, we encourage you to challenge your personal style and assumptions and adapt your own behaviour in order to function at your best, whether you're the client or in the coaching seat.

Cleaning up your language: Removing bias

Have you ever wondered how many questions you ask that make assumptions based on what *you* want, and *your* personal map of reality, rather than what other people want? Human beings find that not projecting their ideas, needs, wants, and enthusiasms on to others is difficult – especially on to those closest to them. You influence other people all the time; you just can't help it. For that reason, most questions aren't what we call *clean* – in the sense that they assume something, as in the famous 'when did you stop beating your wife?' question.

Even the one small word *beating* has different meanings for different people. Did you think of *beating* in the context of physical violence, or in the competitive sense of winning at a sport or game, or something else entirely?

Therapists go through many years of training in order to work with their clients like a clean mirror, which can simply reflect the issues back to clients so they can deliberate on them. Some mirrors get to shine brighter than others! After all, you know how much you can communicate just through one raised eyebrow or a suppressed giggle. (This is the reason why Freud had his clients lying on a couch while he, as the therapist, sat behind the client's head!)

If you want to be respectful of other people's views, make a point of noticing how well you can avoid prejudicing the result of a discussion. Are you telling somebody else what to do based on what you would do yourself?

Beware of making the kinds of generalisations or limiting decisions that we talk about in Chapter 15. Listen to what you say, and if you hear yourself issuing instructions that begin with words such as you 'must', 'should', 'ought to', and 'can't' – the time is right to stop directing the action and imposing your stance on others.

Fishing for answers

A therapist was working with a client who told her that she'd had a dream. All the client was able to remember was that it was raining and she'd been to a restaurant. Then she woke up feeling hot and anxious:

Therapist: 'Oh, so your dream was about fish, was it?'

Client: 'I don't know.'

Therapist: 'But you know that you were in a restaurant?'

Client: 'That's right.'

Therapist: 'And it's likely fish was on the menu?'

Client: 'Yes, most restaurants have fish on the menu.'

Therapist: 'And it was raining, so that could represent water and fish swimming in water?'

Client: 'Well, yes, you're right.'

Therapist: 'Sounds like we're getting closer. Perhaps you were feeling like a fish that had been caught and then cooked, even? What's that all about?'

Of course, this story is fiction and reality is quite different. But the story shows how easily you can find yourself listening to one point and then leading somebody into your subjective interpretation of the facts.

Imagine that you're a manager coaching or mentoring a colleague or employee at work. In a coaching session, beginning with a clear aim in mind is essential. Therefore, you may quite reasonably ask 'What do we want to work on today?'

The question is simple, direct, and focuses attention on the shared understanding that you're *working* on something. Your words set out the intention for the type of interaction you're sharing: this isn't just a friendly chat, we have work to do today. This question is a 'better' opening in the context of this section than asking 'Shall we work out why you haven't finished the project as fast as Fred?', because you're giving the other person some space to think and bring real live challenges to the discussion.

Coaching is about exploring and challenging clients, leading them on to take responsibility and commit to action. Clean questions help you achieve these aims. Any suggestions you include must be phrased in such a way that people think for themselves, instead of being influenced by your own bias.

So, an even cleaner opening question that directs a client to think carefully for themselves may be: 'What would you like to have happen?'

Curiosity may have killed the cat, as the saying goes, but a different perspective may be that curiosity is the pathway to understanding. You choose which saying suits you best.

Discovering Clean Language questions

The counselling psychologist David Grove created a body of knowledge known as Clean Language, in which he perfected the art of asking clean questions. This work continues to be developed and now forms part of some NLP practitioner training modules. (You can read more about David Grove's work and the people who patiently modelled him for a number of years, James Lawley and Penny Tompkins, in Chapter 19.)

Grove created a set of questions that can be used in a variety of applications; in psychotherapy and coaching, of course, but also in health, business, and education. The questions come in three types and work in different ways:

- ✔ **Current perception questions:** Expanding the client's understanding of a situation.

- ✔ **Moving time questions:** Working with the client's sense of time.

- ✔ **Intention questions:** Concentrating on the outcome the client wants.

ANECDOTE

Making decisions with Clean Language

A student was having great difficulty trying to describe why making decisions was such a problem for her. Penny Tompkins shared this dialogue of working with Clean Language questions with the student:

'"And, making decisions is like what?" I enquired.

She thought for a moment and replied: "You know, it's like going to the dentist. I'm in the waiting room and I'm dreading going in."

After a couple more clean questions, I could tell she was deep inside her metaphor by the amount of time she took to answer and in the way she finally said, "I really need courage."

"And what kind of courage is that courage?" was my next question.

"A courage that will help me go through it rather than delay any longer."

"And when courage will help you go through it; where is that courage?"

She touched her chest with her right hand and said, "Inside me. In my heart."

I continued asking Clean Language questions so she could develop her resource metaphor for courage, "a strong energy filling my heart".

At the end of our time together she said, "If you had told me when we started that a comment like 'going to the dentist' could link so directly with my decision making, I wouldn't have believed it. In fact, you couldn't have told me, I had to experience it for myself."'

Thanks to Penny Tompkins and James Lawley for providing this anecdote.

The overall aim of Clean Language is to remove the bias inherent in the questioner's language by exploring people's model of the world from their own perspective. Although the questions can look strange out of context, just consider the subtle difference between asking a really clean question such as 'And is there anything else?' compared with 'What are you going to do now?' The latter question clearly includes the expectation from the questioner that the person must do something.

Starting the Clean Language process

Penny and James suggest that one way to begin the Clean Language questioning process is to put the client into a resourceful state, by developing a *resource metaphor*. You can start the process of developing a resource metaphor by asking the following question:

> And when you're at your best, that's like what?

You can ask this question generally, as it stands above, or you can make it more specific by placing it in a specific context, as we do by adding the following words in square brackets:

> And when you're [working] at your best, that's like what?

> And when you're [collaborating] at your best, that's like what?

> And when you're [focusing] at your best, that's like what?

Or try adding a personal quality:

> And when you're most [patient], that's like what?

> And when you're most [loving], that's like what?

> And when you're most [content], that's like what?

When the person has created a resource metaphor, you can then ask the following clean question that begins the process of developing a desired outcome (goal, objective) metaphor:

> And what you would like to have happen, is like what?

When the person has spoken, written, or drawn a metaphor in answer to these questions, you can ask the first five developing questions listed in the next section, so as to bring the metaphor to life. We want the person to be living in their personal metaphorical landscape (to use several metaphors!).

Developing current perception questions

Here are some examples of asking clean questions that increase a person's understanding of a situation:

> ✔ **Attributes:** And is there anything else about. . . ?
>
> And what kind of. . . ?
>
> ✔ **Location:** And where/whereabouts is. . . ?
>
> ✔ **Relationship:** And is there a relationship between . . . and. . . ?
>
> And when what happens to. . . ?
>
> ✔ **Metaphor:** And that's . . . like what?

Trying out moving time questions

These clean questions are great when working with a person's sense of time:

> ✔ **Before:** And what happens just before. . . ?
>
> ✔ **After:** And then what happens/what happens next?
>
> ✔ **Source:** And where does/could . . . come from?

Working on intention questions

The following clean questions are useful to explore a person's desired outcome:

> ✔ **Desired outcome:** And what would you like to have happen?
>
> ✔ **Necessary conditions:** And what needs to happen for their desired outcome?
>
> And can . . . ?

In order to work well with these questions, you can benefit from formal training in Clean Language. However, you can begin to make small adjustments to clean up your questions yourself, so that you act as an unbiased facilitator instead of unwittingly influencing another person's thinking.

Imagine that someone describes a problem to you, such as having too much work, and requests your help. If you ask the person 'And that workload is like what?', you're inviting them to work with their own metaphor. The person may come up with a metaphor such as, 'It's like a brick on the back of my neck.' You can then simply ask, 'And what would you like to have happen when there's a brick on the back of your neck?', so that you pace the person's experience and lead them towards coming up with their own solutions.

As with all the suggestions in this chapter, just try it and see how it works.

Recognising that the way you behave is what counts

Own up now . . . have you ever shouted at someone, 'Stop shouting at me!'? Nonsense, isn't it, expecting someone else to do what you clearly aren't demonstrating in your own behaviour. Yet people do it all the time. You can easily see in someone else the negative qualities that you want to change in yourself.

The art of encouraging somebody else to change is to model that behaviour yourself. If you want somebody to become curious, be curious yourself. If you want someone to be positive and helpful, you too need to model that behaviour. If you think that someone just needs to lighten up, inject some fun into the proceedings.

Instead of expecting other people to change, lead the way yourself. One of the best lessons we can pass on is 'The way you behave with other people determines the way people behave with you.'

So when you ask questions, do so with awareness of how you're behaving as much as what you say.

Pressing the pause button

Silence is golden. Pausing for a moment when one person has finished speaking is helpful, and in turn lets you think before you speak.

Alan Whicker, presenter of the fascinating *Whicker's World* television series, has a unique style of interviewing people. He asks a question and leaves a long pause after he gets an answer. The interviewees, feeling the need to fill the silence, elaborate with details that give far greater insights into their personality than the initial answer did.

Pauses give other people critical space to process what you said and to consider their reply.

Simply giving people unhurried time to think within a structured framework of questioning is a huge benefit in business and family situations. Listening to others is a generous act and an undeveloped, undervalued skill in most organisations, which is why coaching is so powerful. Trained coaches understand the power of listening and the importance of powerful questioning combined with silence so that clients can process their thoughts. They listen not only to what's being said, but also to the message beneath the words, paying acute attention to what they see as well as recognising the importance of getting clients into the most resourceful state to solve their own issues.

Great listeners create productive meetings, build strong relationships, and find the insights to solve complex issues.

Testing your questions

If you have any doubts about whether your question is appropriate to help a person or situation move to a better place, stop and ask yourself the following:

- ✔ 'Is my next question going to add value in this conversation? Is it taking us closer to where we want to go? Is it going to move us further apart?'
- ✔ 'What is the outcome or result I'm looking for here?'

If in doubt, stay silent until a more powerful question comes into your head. You may then find yourself asking the person to take the lead by asking something like 'What's the most useful question to ask yourself here?' or even 'Can you tell me the most useful question I could ask you?'

Making positive statements the norm

When we say to you, try really hard and don't think of a pink elephant, what happens? Yes, of course, you immediately think of a pink elephant, you just can't help it! Similarly, if you say to a child 'Don't eat those sweets before tea.' What happens? The child is compelled to *eat the sweets* – you've inadvertently issued a command.

The brain doesn't distinguish the negatives – it ignores the 'don't' and thinks 'do'. Better to say to the child 'Tea's coming, so save your appetite for just two minutes'

Figuring Out What You Want

Knowing what you want can be the greatest challenge, because it's a constantly moving feast. Sometimes you can get what you *think* you wanted and yet be disappointed, because in fact that wasn't what you really wanted at all! To figure out what you really want, you have to ask yourself two questions: 'What do I want?' and 'What's that going to do for me?'

What do I want?

If one great question comes out of NLP, it's 'What do I want?'

Sometimes you know very clearly what you don't want, which is a good starting point. When you know what you don't want, flip it over and ask yourself what's the opposite. And then check with yourself again, 'So, what is it that I do want?'

As you begin to articulate your answers, explore some details and allow yourself to dream a little. Imagine yourself in the future; fast forward your personal movie to a time when you have what you want and maybe more besides. Employ all your senses and ask yourself what that feels like, sounds like, and looks like? Are any smells or tastes associated with getting what you want? Check inside with yourself as to whether it seems right. Does it energise and excite you? If you feel anxious or exhausted, that's a clue that something's wrong.

What's that going to do for me?

When you've thought about what you want, and some words and ideas have come to you, the next question is 'What's that going to do for me?' Perhaps you have a goal to achieve – to bid for a new business project, take up a new sport, or quit your work and go trekking in Nepal.

Ask yourself what achieving that aim is going to do for you. And ask the same question three times – really drill down until you hit some core values that make sense for you. Otherwise you may be choosing to do things that take you meandering down side roads, instead of staying on track for where you want to get to.

Keith was a successful, high-flying salesman evaluating his performance in his job. When he first worked with an NLP coach, his priority was to focus on developing specific skills he needed in place. His primary focus was to pave his succession route to becoming the next sales director in his company.

After a few sessions in which his coach asked him what he wanted and what that would do for him, Keith delved further into what he really wanted, taking into account all aspects of his life and work. He realised that if he achieved this career goal, he would have to give up much of the freedom and flexibility that his current role gave him. He realised that much of the new desirable role meant that he'd be commuting into town in the rush hour, and stuck most of the day at a desk in the corporate headquarters agreeing targets, budgets, and sorting out the legalities of the company pension schemes. ('I'd be like a puppy chained to a desk,' he said.)

In fact, Keith thrived on being out with customers and winning deals. The promotion wasn't going to provide what he really wanted. With this realisation, he chose to reset his career direction and take his skills into another department of the corporation. From there, he was able to use his initiative to open up new international sales territories.

Over a longer period of getting into the habit of asking himself what he wanted, he made more significant life changes, leaving corporate life to set up his own software company. This move allowed him time to be with his young family in a way that his own father hadn't been able to do: Keith wanted to watch his children growing up.

Asking Questions to Help Make Decisions

You make decisions all the time: whether to go to work or stay at home; what to have for lunch and supper; whether to accept an invitation to see a film; how much you should spend on a new computer or holiday; whether to lay on a Christmas party with your family or not.

Imagine that one sunny day you're happily working at your job and a call comes in from a business head-hunter: a new job is on offer, you're the person the company wants, and by the way, it means moving your home to a town by the sea 300 kilometres away. You weren't even considering a change, but you're flattered, and so you go and talk to the company. The deal looks pretty attractive and you think, wouldn't it feel good to be working near the sea in hot weather like this? But a niggling little voice inside you is saying: 'Is this the right thing to do? Are you sure?'

Should you go for it or should you stay doing what you know best? How can you decide this one?

Here are four key questions that you can ask yourself, or someone else, to guide in making a decision – a life-changing one or something smaller:

- ✔ What will happen if you do?
- ✔ What will happen if you don't?
- ✔ What won't happen if you do?
- ✔ What won't happen if you don't?

These four questions are based on Cartesian logic and you may find them referred to as *Cartesian co-ordinates*. All you need to remember is that they offer some powerful linguistic patterns that enable you to examine a subject from different angles.

We often talk clients through these questions, and the decisions can be major – shall I leave my wife, move house, change career direction, have a baby, recruit a new team? The questions focus your attention and challenge your thinking. When you reach the last question, you may stop and think, 'that's confusing'. Good. This reaction means that you're arriving at a breakthrough in your thinking.

If you make a change in one area of your life at the expense of another area, the chances are that the change isn't going to last. So, for example, if you move jobs but have to give up important interests or friendships where you currently live, the change isn't going to make you happy in the long term and you probably won't stick with it. Don't take our word for it; try the questions out now on something about which you're deliberating. You can see that the questions encourage you to check out your decision based on the impact on the whole of your environment, in a healthy way – what we call an *ecology* check (we talk more about this aspect in Chapter 4).

Challenging Limiting Beliefs

When someone's thinking is stopping them from achieving a much sought-after goal, you can ask three simple questions in order to challenge such thinking. To help others (or yourself) overcome a limiting belief, ask the three questions set out in this section.

When asking the questions, give the person plenty of time to talk about an issue, and move on only when you sense that they've 'got it off their chest':

✔ **Question 1: 'What do you assume or believe about this issue that limits you in achieving your goal?'**

Ask this question three times until you're sure that you've reached the heart of the matter – what NLP describes as a limiting belief. As you delve deeper, you may say: 'That's right, and what else about this limits you?'

For example, the person may be thinking 'I'm not good enough,' or 'Nobody will let me,' or 'I just don't know how.' When you hold a negative position like these ones, you stop yourself from doing what you need to do to achieve what you want.

✔ **Question 2: 'What would be a more empowering belief, one that's the positive opposite of the one holding you back?'**

This question flips the limitation over to the positive side. For example, the positive opposite of the assumptions and beliefs above would be stated positively as 'I am good enough,' or 'Somebody will let me,' or 'I do know how.'

With this second question, your colleague or client may get confused or even cross because it's challenging to answer. Yet, this question's critical to hold on to if you're going to get a switch in perspective and come up with a more empowering belief that helps someone shift forward. So stick with it.

✔ **Question 3: 'If you knew that [your new freeing belief] . . . what ideas do you now have to help you move towards your goal?'**

This question completes the process. At this point, the person comes up with their own ideas on how to move forward: 'Oh well, if I knew that I was good enough, I'd do X, Y, and Z.'

This questioning works by putting somebody into an 'as if' way of thinking. If you act with the belief that something can happen, you can then find the behaviours to achieve the aim.

Kate worked with a managing director who wanted to be successful in her business and yet was struggling to make a decision on having a child. Her limiting belief was 'It's not possible to be a good mother and a successful businesswoman at the same time.' By working through the three questions, she evaluated the new opposite assumption that 'It's possible to be a good mother and a successful businesswoman at the same time.'

By working in this 'as if' framework – that is, operating as if it was possible to do both well – she opened up many ideas on how to run the company differently in order to pursue motherhood at the same time as being successful in business. Not only did she go on to have two healthy well-adjusted children, she also put in place more flexible policies that benefited the men as well as the women in the company.

Finding the Right Person for the Job: A Question of Motivation

Getting the right people in the right jobs at the right time can be a tricky problem. Asking the right questions can help you to match people to the qualities needed to succeed in particular roles.

To get somebody lined up in the right job, you need to ask yourself about the *personal qualities* that are necessary to do that job well, as well as the *technical skills* involved. How is that person going to behave? The following questioning begins before you recruit:

✔ What are some of the essential criteria for someone to perform this job well? Come up with about five key words, which may include things such as teamworking, self-starter, clear processes, creativity, customer service, learning, variety, stability, flexibility, well organised, intellectual challenge, good product, attractive environment, travel.

✔ Does the person need to be motivated to achieve results or sort out problems?

✔ Does the person need to be primarily self-motivated or get consensus from customers or a team?

✔ Does the style of working mean that the person must follow processes or does the person have freedom in how things get done?

The next four sections contain questions that you can ask at the interview in order to gain specific information on how people are likely to behave in a given context, as well as their technical skills to do the job you have in mind. The questions are based on the NLP meta programs that you can read about in Chapter 8.

The same questions apply when you check in with members of your team to see how things are going and what adjustments you can make to keep people motivated.

What do you want in your work?

This question enables you to match the criteria or hot buttons that you're looking for with those that are important for the individual. When you hear that someone wants lots of freedom and flexibility, they may do well in a creative environment but not if required to tightly project-manage an implementation of a new system. If they thrive on change, they may be good for a short-term contract, but are unlikely to stay more than a year or two unless you can provide new roles.

Why is that important?

Taking each of the applicant's criteria in turn, ask 'Why is that important?' This question enables you to identify the direction in which the person is motivated: *away from* a problem or *towards* a solution. A person with an *away-from* preference may say that 'Salary is important so I don't have to worry about not being able to pay my mortgage.' A person with a *towards* preference may say that 'Salary is important so I can buy my own home easily.'

The clues to understanding people are in the language style they adopt, for example:

- ✔ If someone is motivated *towards*, you may hear words such as attain, gain, achieve, get, include.

- ✔ If someone is motivated *away from*, you may hear words such as avoid, exclude, recognise problems.

How do you know that you've done a good job?

This question enables you to identify the source of a person's motivation.

If people are *internally focused* – that is, they pay more attention to what's happening for themselves than for other people – you can motivate them by using phrases such as 'only you can decide', 'you may want to consider', and 'what do you think?'.

If they're *externally focused* – that is, they need to be convinced by other people and through gaining facts and figures – you can motivate them by using phrases such as 'others will notice', 'the feedback you'll get', and 'so and so says so'.

If you're employing somebody in customer service, that person needs to value external approval, instead of being internally focused. However, if you want to give a person a project to get on with on their own, someone with a strong external focus is likely to struggle without regular approval from others.

Why did you choose your current work?

This question is a great one to ask when you want to know whether someone is motivated by having options or by being told what to do. If somebody has an *options style*, you're going to hear words such as opportunity, criteria, choice, unlimited possibilities, and variety. On the other hand, if somebody has a strong *procedures style*, they're likely to give you a step-by-step response, the story of how they got into their current line of work. You're likely to hear such people talking about processes and using phrases such as 'the right way' and 'tried and true'.

Both styles can work in the same team quite happily together. To motivate your options people, build in as many choices as you can offer them. Get them to brainstorm new ways to do things. To motivate your procedures people, get them to focus on the necessary systems and processes to bring more structure and controls to the team.

Checking In with Yourself

In order to keep on track to where you want to get or what you want to achieve, on a daily basis or longer term, questioning yourself can be very helpful. Therefore, check out the following list of questions to ask yourself every day:

- ✔ What do I want?
- ✔ What will that do for me?
- ✔ What's stopping me?
- ✔ What's important to me here?
- ✔ What's working well?
- ✔ What can be better?
- ✔ What resources will support me?

If you accept the NLP presupposition that 'There's no such thing as failure, only feedback,' you aren't going to be afraid of asking questions from the fear that you may get answers you'd prefer not to hear. Tune into the feedback you get for yourself as well as others as you ask the right questions.

Part V

Integrating Your Learning

In this part . . .

You put all your NLP knowledge together in two chapters on modelling and change. Ever wondered how somebody else can be so good in an area where you want to raise your game? Here you discover how to use your NLP tools to model anybody who excels at anything from public speaking to housework to building relationships.

You also find out how to harness the power of NLP at transition points in your life and work. In the chapter on change, we encourage you to make light work of difficult times.

Chapter 19

Dipping into Modelling

In This Chapter

▶ Finding out how to replicate excellence

▶ Bringing your new NLP skills together

▶ Uncovering the deeper structure of experience

▶ Discovering the unexpected bonuses of modelling others

Here's a popular NLP story. A group of NLP master practitioners head off to a remote location to study a shaman at work, a healer renowned for the results he achieves in extraordinary circumstances. Their mission is to look for 'the difference that makes the difference', the essence of the shaman's skill, as they study his behaviour while working with a sick patient.

A lot of apparent mumbo-jumbo surrounds the shaman's work: incantations, dramatic posturing, and potions that characterise the external aspects of his work with a patient. After their period of observation, the NLP practitioners take the opportunity to question the shaman. One asks, 'So at what point did the healing actually begin?' Anticipating an answer such as 'When I placed my hands on the wound,' the practitioner is surprised to hear the answer, 'When I went up to the mountain top several days ago and *set my intent*.'

You can take various messages from this story. One is in the power of setting your intent in any situation and noticing the effect that intent has on the results you get. Another is to recognise that what you see on the surface isn't always the whole story. As you read through this chapter, we invite you to set your own intent to find someone who excels at something you're interested in doing well and have yet to master, and to begin modelling that person by paying attention beyond the obvious external behaviours. We show you how to get started.

We don't expect you to become an expert NLP modeller just from reading this chapter – that takes many years of patient observation. Instead, we want you to have fun as you increase your powers of sensory acuity using NLP as we take you further on the journey. You never know about the great places that modelling can lead you to, as several modellers we mention in this chapter have found out. You gain the most from modelling when you're already comfortable with the fundamental concepts of NLP that we explain in Part I and you'll also find it helpful to get familiar with the logical-levels model that we explain in Chapter 11.

Developing New Skills through Modelling

When most NLP Master Practitioner courses come towards a conclusion, students are invited to engage in a *modelling* project that integrates their knowledge of the previous months and years of learning about NLP. The projects vary in their level of complexity and can range from modelling someone who successfully gets themselves listed on an online dating website to another who excels at running sales meetings.

NLP modelling is the ability to replicate fully the desirable competence of another person by getting to the unconscious behaviours beneath that skill and coding those behaviours into a model that you could teach to other people, in order to replicate the results.

You can acquire new skills by going to class, reading books, listening to CDs, or watching DVDs. These processes take time as you take the material, try it out, adapt it, and incorporate it in your life. Modelling offers you a way to accelerate your skills in leaps and bounds. At its heart, NLP is about understanding what it is to be human – how people do what they do – and from the outset the NLP developers adopted techniques of modelling human behaviour in order to further their understanding and share it with others.

NLP attracts people who are interested in finding out about people. Your own modelling of others begins with a deep desire to learn and be curious about how other people function and get results. Richard Bandler and John Grinder created the original Milton and Meta Models thanks to their fascination with the communication skills of therapists. Other leaders in the NLP community – including Robert Dilts, Judith DeLozier, Todd Epstein, David Gordon, Stephen Gilligan, Tim Hallbom, Leslie Cameron-Bandler, Suzi Smith, and many others – applied modelling principles from the comprehensive study of fields such as leadership, genius, organisational development, creativity, health, wealth, and relationships.

Modelling involves an *exemplar* – who's competent in a particular field – and a *modeller* – who studies the exemplar. Through a process of study and observation, the modeller creates a *model*: an explanatory framework of how the exemplar functions.

To see what's really possible through modelling, you may like to take a look at www.nlpu.com and Robert Dilts's work on the strategies of genius. Dilts studied a range of exemplars, many of whom weren't actually alive – such as Mozart and Leonardo da Vinci. From his study of Walt Disney, Dilts created a model of creativity (known in NLP as the Disney Strategy) that explores Disney's ability to turn dreams into real projects.

When you begin modelling, you look to identify explicit underlying patterns in the way your exemplar operates, listen for their beliefs and values, and get curious about how people think and behave. Ultimately, the test of the model you then create is whether it stands alone so that you can teach it to someone else and they can then replicate the results your exemplar achieves.

Like any field of intellectual enquiry, modelling involves wanting to solve a problem, answer a question, discover something new, and gather the information to present an informed and valuable hypothesis that stands up to scrutiny when tested. NLP literature abounds with interesting studies of modelling, including what you find in this chapter and much more besides. Modelling is the crux of NLP.

Have you ever looked at someone with a touch of admiration and asked yourself, 'How do they do that?', 'How do they manage to have such a good life?', or 'I wish I could. . . .'

If so, that's good; you're ready to learn from others. However, to make things simple for yourself, take a small chunk size or aspect of their skill to model. Instead of looking at someone's whole life, identify something they excel at, such as how they negotiate a pay rise or how they speak to their children without getting cross. Begin by considering an area of your life in which you want to improve your skills or transform your experience, and ask yourself the following questions:

- **What would I like more of in my life and work?** For example, do you want more fun, more challenge, or a partner to share your life with? Do you want more holidays or a better paying job?

- **What would I like less of?** Perhaps you want to be less involved in office politics, not have to nag your teenage children so much to get their coursework done, or get rid of some household chores. Do you want to spend less time travelling on business?

- **Who do I already know who's achieved a specific capability that I can learn from?** As you look around, you're likely to spot someone fairly close who has a skill that you've not been able to gain just yet.

Keep this information in mind as you choose your subjects for your personal modelling activity. Ideally you should choose three different exemplars so that you develop a robust model.

Modelling reminds you of the power of having a range of exemplars in your life to show you the way in all kinds of activities. Kate had been attending yoga classes for many years, studying with many teachers, and just assumed that she was unable to stand on her head and achieve other more advanced postures, because she lacked the natural flexibility of her more bendy teachers. When she positioned her mat alongside Yvonne, a lady of similar age, Kate found a better exemplar. By watching how Yvonne moved slowly and gracefully into the more difficult postures, Kate tuned into Yvonne's approach to health (both in and beyond the classes), noticed her belief that it was fine to take years if necessary to perfect her skill, watched the tiny postural adjustments, and realised that she too could master the headstand and feel relaxed in the posture.

This small success changed Kate's belief about what her body was able to learn. She paid more attention to the fine detail of other moves, relaxed into developing her own practice, and let go of the belief that she had to compete with other people in the class.

If you want to become competent at a relatively simple behavioural skill, such as a dance move, find someone who's recently learnt to do what you want to do as one of your exemplars. Such a person offers a good starting point because they're *consciously competent*: that is, still aware of the learning process they've been through and able to give you practical tips.

Modelling is a natural human talent

Modelling doesn't have to be complicated. As a human, you're a natural modeller from the time you first look into your mother's eyes as a baby and recognise the power of a smile or gentle word, to when you follow in the footsteps of teenage friends by wearing similar clothes or work colleagues hooked on the latest technical gadget.

In meta-program terms (turn to Chapter 8 for more details), you're continually sorting for similarities and differences among the people you mix with, moving towards some behaviours and away from others, testing out options and looking for procedures to follow. You have extraordinary talents; walking on two legs, eating, speaking, and reading this book, and all these everyday behaviours require a multitude of unconscious microprocessing elements. When you come to model an exemplar, you unpack, recognise, and model the minute details of such processes in human behaviour, thought, and feeling.

Think about when you discovered a new skill: learning your alphabet, riding a bike, driving a car, playing a sport, running a meeting, cooking a meal, how to choose clothes that suit you, managing your finances. Most likely, everything that you can now do well involved you learning from some kind of role model who showed you how it was done. You may not have been taught consciously, but you absorbed the knowledge by hanging out with someone who did that thing already, such as your big brother and his friends who rode two wheeler bikes round the neighbourhood while you followed behind with stabilisers fixed on your cycle.

Sometimes obvious _role models_ such as parents, friends or people you spend time with, are less competent than you once believed them to be. What you learn by being with them doesn't increase your capability for the better, so you need to choose more suitable role models who demonstrate the excellence you seek. For example, if your father was someone who believed he was unable to make a meal without burning it, you may have modelled his habit of nipping to the local shop and buying ready meals to pop in the microwave. Or, what if your mother was unreliable with money, wasting every last penny, you may have unconsciously modelled her habit of leaving your bank account overdrawn. Your role model of parenting may have been less than helpful and you need to find a new one to save you repeating their mistakes. As you pick your own new _exemplars_, choose the best ones to whom you can get access.

In Chapter 4 we look at well-formed outcomes and the resources you need to achieve your goals. Finding appropriate exemplars whom you can model can be a valuable way of accelerating your ability to reach your outcome. For example, if your goal is to learn hang-gliding, yet you are held back by your fear of heights, then find three people who have the capability to hang-glide in spite of any fears. By modelling these exemplars you too may build your confidence.

Getting to a deeper structure

NLP modelling seeks to bring the intangible to the surface. The model you create of the other person seeks to extract the essential thought processes and strategies in a certain context, yet it will always be a partial description of the whole complexity of that human being. Just like when you visit the site of an historical ruin, and a miniature model clarifies the pile of dusty rubble and broken mosaics in front of you, an NLP model seeks to get beneath the skin of a human being who excels in a particular field to identify the essence of what's going on inside.

In Chapter 2, we introduce you to the essential NLP presupposition that 'the map is not the territory'. Like all humans, you have your mental maps and modelling seeks to understand those maps. NLP modelling enables you to find the deep structure underlying a successful person's behaviour, so that you can then make your processing explicit to other people and allow them to get the opportunity to replicate the exemplar's successes. Modelling attempts to make conscious what's happening at a deeper unconscious level.

NLP distinguishes the deep structure of your experience from the surface structure of your language. You can find more on this in Chapter 15.

Even within NLP, no agreement exists on the best way to dig down to the deeper structure through modelling, and as you explore modelling in more depth you find many approaches based on the preference of the modeller. In this way, much of modelling is done on an intuitive basis rather than by a well-documented and logical approach.

You glean much information from watching and listening to the exemplar in action, of course, but if you don't have easy access to your subject you also discover plenty from documents and recordings.

Assume that what you see and hear on the surface in terms of someone's behaviour and words is only part of the story. Be patient and observe what may be really going on for that person in terms of assumptions, beliefs, and values.

If you're modelling an entrepreneur, for example, you may notice the fiery temper that someone like Alan Sugar demonstrates in the popular *Apprentice* TV series. What you may not understand so easily is how to generate the drive to create something from nothing, the enduring motivation, or the mental strategies to negotiate a complicated deal. When you take two other exemplars of successful entrepreneurs, and look at how they operate, you can decide whether or not an attribute such as temper is an essential factor for success, or just a characteristic that one exemplar has.

Discovering Modelling Case Studies

Some of the modelling undertaken by NLP leaders involves incredible patience to understand complex skills and build the detailed behavioural maps that benefit others. Many skills are made up of subsets of other skills. For example, an experienced therapist can react appropriately in highly sensitive situations and a business leader can make successful decisions under pressure while maintaining rapport with a network of stakeholders. Great salespeople do much more than get a contract signed. In this section, we take a look at some informative case studies.

The Reluctant Exemplar

One of the biggest challenges when modelling an expert is that experts aren't consciously aware of what they do: they are *unconsciously competent* and hence you need to spend time just being with them. The problem can be compounded when your exemplar isn't interested in being modelled or doesn't want any intrusion in their work? Penny Tompkins and James Lawley faced this dilemma when they set out to model New Zealand therapist David Grove, originator of Clean Language (check out Chapter 18 for more details).

Grove's early work was in the area of trauma, where he had exceptional results working with a client base that included Vietnam war veterans and adults who suffered severe childhood abuse. From the 1980s until his death in 2008, his work went through a number of innovations covering four major themes: Clean Language, Metaphor, Clean Space, and Emergent Knowledge.

Says Penny: 'We realised how valuable David's ideas would be outside the therapeutic field, yet there was nothing written about that. At first, David was reluctant to be modelled.'

When Penny approached him with the idea of being an exemplar he replied, 'I don't care what you do, but I don't want you to ask me any questions, I don't want to know you're in the room.' Luckily this restriction didn't alter Penny and James's determination to go ahead with the project. The only question was, 'How?'

One of the mysteries of NLP is the lack of description about how the originators, Bandler and Grinder, modelled the first experts from which NLP was born. To figure this problem out for themselves, Penny and James took the first five books that were the result of the modelling of Bandler, Grinder, and others, and 'reverse engineered' what they most likely did to arrive at these models. Through trial and error, Penny and James created their own model for modelling for which David Grove was to be the first exemplar.

Thus began a painstaking period while they tried to figure out how to model David when he was in the UK only periodically. The project took them four years and involved attending David's therapeutic retreats as participants, getting hold of recordings of David's early work, and spending hours and hours going through transcripts of sessions. As a result of their modelling, Penny and James developed *Symbolic Modelling*, an approach that enhances an NLP practitioner's ability to work with people's metaphors, at the symbolic level. (Flip to Chapter 18 for more on Clean Language and Penny and James's work.)

Their work resulted in the influential book *Metaphors in Mind*. Over the years, David Grove's attitude changed, and in the foreword to their book he praised 'Penny's tenacious "won't take no for an answer" style'. He went on to say, 'My life continues to be enriched by your ongoing interactions.'

Meeting her match on the river

As a keen recreational rower, Gillian Burn's modelling project focused on understanding how to achieve a positive inner state in order to row effectively for optimum performance. She chose three exemplars: the club rowing coach; the most improved female rower; and Olympic rower Greg Searle. Her project culminated in presenting her research to fellow master NLP practitioners, at the end of their course.

Her presentation began by lining up groups of people as if they were in a rowing boat. She then taught them a combination of strategies involving the senses of what they would see, feel, and hear, and their breathing, posture, and movement when in the best state to compete. She incorporated the TOTE model – test, operate, test, exit, described fully in Chapter 12 – into the learning process. The test was whether the rowers were still with every muscle poised for action and a strong inner smile. If so, they were ready; if not, they had to refocus and repeat a visual, auditory, and kinaesthetic strategy.

From modelling the rowers, Gillian was able to identify some common themes for everyday life to create an appropriate inner state, a positive feeling, and a belief that you can achieve what you want with the right preparation, inner thoughts, and self-confidence.

In addition, however, Gillian discovered an extra and very special unexpected benefit from interviewing the club coach in depth and discovering much more about his personality. 'Through the modelling process and subsequent conversations, we became exceptionally good friends and now share our life together and the joys of bringing up our young daughter,' says Gillian. 'Who knows what opportunities people can find if they give themselves the time to listen and find out about another person without any prejudice or barriers or even thinking they're trying to find a partner. It was in not looking for a partner, when John and I got together: it was the result of a deep conversation about a common interest.'

The Rainmaker's Dance

As someone with a 24-year career in sales management, Rob Biggin was fascinated by meeting senior managers who excel at creating sales opportunities and yet have had no formal sales training: people who are known as 'rainmakers'. He invited his several exemplars to teach him how they sell and learnt much that now informs his training programmes in service organisations.

He was intrigued by the words he heard from his first exemplar:

The chap told me that when he goes into a sales meeting with a prospect, he has in mind that he may well be going on holiday with this person in the future. [In fact, the exemplar was about to go on holiday with a client.] This frames how he handles the meeting and treats the person with the utmost interest because he wants to get to know them well. This was definitely not something I could have predicted and yet I saw that it made a huge difference in his attitude towards a prospect.

In the seven-step model that Rob now teaches, he suggests that delegates approach every meeting by setting their intent to be very interested in the client, and shares the story of the successful manager who behaves 'as if' he's going on holiday with that person in the future.

Rob also tried a simple fun exercise based on the sameness and difference meta program, and found that all his exemplars sorted the coins for sameness and did the same thing in business – identifying the things they had in common with their prospects. (See Chapter 8 for more on meta programs.) They very quickly looked for ways in which to connect and build rapport, as in 'I see we both have two sons' or 'I like to read *The Economist* too.'

As a result of his modelling work, Rob developed his training programmes and the way he now coaches professionals to hone their business-generation skills.

Key Stages in Modelling

We're confident that you can identify someone in your life who has demonstrated specific skills that you'd like to have at your disposal. In this section, we lead you through a generic process of simple modelling so that you can take on aspects of your exemplar's skills.

The key stages are as follows:

1. **Knowing your outcome.**

2. **Identifying your exemplar.**

3. **Finding a modelling method you can work with.**

4. **Gathering your data.**

5. **Building your model.**

6. **Testing the prototype.**

7. **Refining for simplicity.**

We describe these steps in the following sections to give you some tips on how to get started on your own modelling project.

Knowing your modelling outcome

NLP takes you from being stuck in a problem to achieving outcomes. When you know your outcome in any scenario, you focus your attention on what you want, for example 'I want to be a better dad' or 'I'd like to appear confident when I go speed dating.' Being specific about the capability that you want to model is helpful; for example, 'playing with my children when I come home from work' or 'taking a keen interest in a person when I meet them'. This focus is especially useful in modelling to help you know when to stop, because you recognise that you've achieved your outcome. You always learn more when you practise what you discover about, and from, your exemplar. This attention to the outcome is much more important than being overly precious about your methodology at this stage in your learning.

Create a well-formed modelling outcome by going through all the steps we outline in Chapter 4 and summarise in Appendix C. You may be modelling as part of an NLP training course or to develop your own NLP knowledge, to be better at your job, develop a skill such as a new language, or become better at your business.

Identifying your exemplar

When choosing an exemplar, you're looking for one and often several examples of people who do precisely what you'd like to do well in the same or similar context. Your exemplars may well have reached the stage of being *unconsciously competent* at whatever they do well: they're so skilled at what they do that they find 'unpacking' the details when others ask for advice hard; they simply say 'I just do it,' so you need to do some detective work to retrieve the information. For example, for your exemplar you may choose someone who is successful at the following:

- Building an active social network
- Coaching clients through divorce
- Creating a warm and welcoming home environment
- Displaying an aptitude for learning new languages
- Finishing DIY projects
- Formatting clear documents
- Franchising businesses
- Raising money for charity
- Staying healthy while looking after others

Keep your modelling simple at first: the more clearly defined the skill that you want to replicate and the more accessible your exemplar, the easier you are going to find your task. Trying to model Picasso or a very private celebrity is going to be extremely tough, even though some keen NLP modellers have done exceptional work on modelling public figures.

Consider one specific desired behaviour or skill the exemplar has that you want to replicate. You don't want to capture all the person's behaviours.

You're surrounded by people who can do things that you can't do so well. Often somebody in your close network has valuable expertise that you can tap into, even within your family. While attending her NLP Master Practitioner programme, Rachel was chosen as an exemplar for five separate modelling projects by fellow students who were keen to model different aspects of her approach to business and health. They were intrigued at how she had set up a successful business as well as changing her career at various points from a chef to an events manager to become an independent health and fitness guru and author with a strong brand and exuberant personality. Some were interested in specific behaviour changes such as her success in giving up smoking and weight loss.

'It was actually humbling to be chosen by my peers as an exemplar. Just the fact of being modelled made me pay closer attention to things that I now take for granted in how I carry out my business,' she says. The act of modelling has potential benefits for the exemplars as well as other people, because you can make people consciously aware of their experience and changes they may make.

Finding a modelling method you can work with

Modelling is about finding out, at a deep level, how exemplars experience their world that enables them to do what they do so successfully, and about creating an understanding of what they're thinking, feeling, and behaving in any one moment. You're trying to get inside someone's head and need to acquire the most appropriate tool for the job. Inevitably, the quality of the information-gathering tool that you adopt has a crucial effect on the process.

This aspect raises the fundamental chicken and egg question in modelling. Do you create the structure for your model first or does that develop later? Our view is that having some framework or hypothesis as a beginner in modelling is helpful, as is letting go of the model if appropriate. For this reason, Robert Dilts's clear and practical logical levels structure (which we describe in Chapter 11) is a popular starting point for both information gathering and analysis of your exemplars.

Here are some initial points to consider about each of your exemplars at the different levels:

- **Environment:** Where, when, and with whom do they spend their time?
- **Behaviour:** What do they do? What are their habits and strategies?
- **Capabilities:** What skills do they have?
- **Beliefs and values:** What do they believe to be true? What is important to them?
- **Identity:** What is their sense of themselves? Who are they in this context?
- **Purpose:** What is their sense of purpose and connection to how they fit into the bigger picture?

You're human so you come to modelling with your own knowledge and preconceived ideas. Your model itself acts as a filter on what information you observe and collect.

Gathering your data

To prevent yourself getting overwhelmed by data, we suggest that you begin with a mix of two information-gathering approaches:

- **Unconscious uptake:** In this approach, you hang out with your exemplar as much as you can so that you can intuitively get a sense of how the person operates. Arrive with no fixed agenda other than to emulate their breathing and physiology and get a sense of what being in the person's shoes is like. Ideally, you start without a model in your head and move into the second perceptual position where you have deep rapport with your subject. Notice what you see, hear, and feel. Check out Chapter 7 for more on rapport and understanding other points of view.

- **Analytical information gathering:** In this approach, you can structure your entire data collection around tools such as the logical levels explained in Chapter 11. This process is an effective way of building information, especially when you have limited time and access to your exemplar.

The NLP tools and techniques that we outline throughout this book can assist you in developing your information gathering. Your analysis of data and modelling is an opportunity to refresh your knowledge and hone your skills. Here's how:

- **Assumptions or presuppositions:** From what assumptions does your subject operate? See Chapter 2 for more details.

- **Beliefs and values:** What beliefs do you notice in your subject – what are the person's key drivers? Chapter 3 helps you here.

- **Emotional-state management:** What can you discover about your exemplar as regards this aspect, which we describe in Chapter 9.

- **Metaphors and stories:** What stories does your exemplar tell or respond to? Chapter 17 guides you in this area.

- **Meta programs:** Can you spot meta programs in the person's language: for example, detail versus global, towards and away from, options and procedures, internal and external focus? Chapter 8 has more about meta programs.

- **Perceptual positions:** Does your exemplar take the different perceptual positions explored in Chapter 7? Try stepping into three or four perspectives yourself as the modeller.

- **Strategies:** Can you identify the strategies your subject adopts, and code them as we explain in Chapter 12?

- **Time:** What is this person's sense of time as explained by time-line work in Chapter 13? Do they operate in the moment or are they good at planning?

- **Visual, auditory, and kinaesthetic predicates:** What do the language patterns tell you about how this person communicates in this particular context? We discuss these items in Chapter 6.

Your exemplar is going to be good at some things that you're already competent at yourself, so concentrate your investigation on areas that are most unfamiliar to you, to save your time and energy.

Building your model

When you've gathered your data, you have all you need to build a model that demonstrates the patterns you uncover in your exemplar. This structure is the coherent description of the essential patterns, and demonstrates to other people what they need to copy in their attempts to get the same results as your exemplar.

You can take an existing framework, such as the logical levels model, and be willing to build the model in your own way, adding your unique knowledge to it just as the modellers did in the earlier section 'Discovering Modelling Case Studies'.

When Kate wrote her book *Live Life. Love Work* she was curious about the lessons to be gained from numerous professionals about times when they achieved a flow state of contentment with their lives. When she first began the modelling, she built a framework to focus her attention and questioning on some core principles about how professionals steer a course in their lives, and worked with an acronym that she thought would be memorable for her readers. As she began writing up the research, and using the approach within her own coaching practice, she realised that if she kept to her precious model, it would be contrived. So she simplified the model to one that more usefully encompassed what she heard in her interviews. This one became a clearer, more valuable framework for her readers to follow.

Testing the prototype

When you have your model, be willing to test and continuously improve upon it. The NLP TOTE model encourages you to Test, Operate, Test, Exit to test your prototype (see Chapter 12 for more info). The way to test is to teach the model to others and see how it works. Do they get the same results?

As NLP-trained coaches, Kate and her colleague Rob were invited into a global IT corporation to model Robin, an internal professional development manager at work and observe how he guided his large team of consultants to take ownership of their careers. Robin was interested in NLP and knew that he was extremely successful at what he did, recognising aspects of his work, and yet he found that fully documenting what he did and how was difficult.

As a result of modelling Robin at work, Kate and Rob were able to capture the essence of Robin's approach. Together, the trio converted Robin's work into a career coaching model and taught his approach to other senior managers in the organisation. Kate and Rob made Robin's original model more robust by incorporating fundamental NLP concepts such as using rapport building to improve business relationships, perceptual positions to enhance personal brand development, and time lines and logical levels in order to capture information about the career journey. In this way, the modeller supported the exemplar to become even more capable, as often happens.

As the training programme became popular, those attending realised that they now had a simple lifelong methodology to manage their own careers as well as those of the people who worked for them. What was particularly powerful about Robin's approach was his use of metaphor and stories to get the message across to fellow managers in a way that was creative and inspirational. However, other people didn't have to tell the same stories; room was left for them to tell their own. Each of the managers attending the training took the essential structure of the model and applied it in their own way. The key proof of the model was that they all got results.

Refining for simplicity

The question for the modeller to decide is which elements of the exemplar's behaviour are an essential part of the model, and which are just an interesting piece of information. Does the golfer's pre-match ritual make the difference to the winning shot? You need to isolate at least three occasions when the desired behaviour is present, so that you can spot common patterns between them. This approach may mean choosing at least three exemplars, or if you want one person's particular way of doing something, at least three separate instances.

You have to be willing to stay for longer than usual in the space of 'not knowing', absorbing the details you've gathered, and then to 'chunk up' to the essential elements of what needs to be your model (you can read more about chunking in Chapter 16.) When you have your model, try it on for size to work out what is essential to have and what you can safely leave out. You also need to check that someone else's model fits with your values and whether you may need to do some work on your own beliefs. Here, you could enlist the support of an NLP coach if you're developing a model to make changes in your own life.

Fran Burgess of the Northern School of NLP suggests that writing a book is just like the process of modelling. You have all the data and are left with the question of how to sort the data and the structure has to emerge. Modellers, like writers, need to be willing to delve into a tremendous amount of detail in order to find the apparent simplicity of what finally emerges in their work.

Writers work in their unique way and the actual writing part – of words to paper – is a tiny part of the overall publication process. Yet many people don't realise this fact when they attempt to model an author and extract the essential core elements to the model. When Kate writes books, she starts with gathering masses of information, reading other books on and around the subject, surfing the net, going to events, interviewing people, and creating flipcharts of ideas and visual computer maps that break down the structure of chapters, before getting into a project plan with dates and deliverables. The neat finished product often belies the volume of books, paperwork and computer files involved in her office and home.

When Romilla writes, she does some things in the same way as Kate, going out and meeting people and brainstorming ideas to a flipchart, and others in a very different way. She likes to listen to CDs and tapes, and prefers to tape conversations, absorbing the information before she writes. Both of us have our antennae tuned for months and plenty of unconscious processing goes on when a book is in our heads.

Our ways of getting a book to completion are quite different, though. Kate's more likely to outline her ideas and illustrate them with stories. Romilla drops her ideas into her visual maps on the computer, using the same software as Kate, yet with the facility to see ideas as floating topics rather than connected to a central idea, because this approach gives her the flexibility to slot headings together as she expands on them. She uses a voice-capture program to 'engage with and talk to' her imaginary audience. She learnt this process from her good friend, Rintu. When she started by typing, completing her work took ages because she felt compelled to edit as she went along. Now she is a much faster 'writer' and her language is more natural.

From our two exemplars, you could create a model that would include some core stages for how to write a book chapter, although differences do exist between the exemplars. A description of the core model (in other words, the bits that are the same) that you might get when modelling Kate and Romilla would look like this:

1. **Gather background information – surf the net, meet people, read, or listen to CDs.**

2. **Create a visual map of ideas.**

3. **Draft text in Microsoft Word.**

4. **Revise text.**

5. **Deliver computer files to editorial deadline (90 per cent of the time!).**

As you spend more time with the exemplars, you're likely to need to take one specific aspect of their process and break that into sub-processes, and dwell on the details for a while. You might also begin to notice things not made explicit, such as strategies for mulling over ideas and the part that less obvious activities such as walking and meditation play in working to get clarity of thought. You might also notice the fact that one writer also scribbles lots of long hand-written notes in a café while another records ideas into a tape recorder as part of their drafting process. If you were to model a third writer, you may notice their habit of spending a whole morning rearranging one page of text with infinite patience at the editing stage. Each writer works in their own way; the test is whether the model takes you to the desired end result of delivering an acceptable manuscript on time.

A book may be in an author's head for many years before it reaches publication. As an expert in modelling who's currently refining her own work for publication, Fran suggests that modellers need incredible patience. She has been working with modellers for over ten years and only now feels she has identified the many structures behind the process of modelling. Incidentally, she also recognises that every modeller she has met finds being modelled themselves in any modelling methodology other than their own very difficult. 'They don't respond to it. Modellers tend to live their model and they are wedded to it,' she says. Your mental models are central to your identity.

The difference that makes the difference is unlikely to be immediately visible. Great modellers have tremendous patience and boundless curiosity. Stay curious!

Modelling gives you the ability to raise your game in any field of learning. It doesn't promise that you can become an expert and win at everything: clearly not everyone can be number one in a particular sport or a celebrity film star. However, if you can identify the strategies of excellence in your exemplar and replicate them for yourself, you're likely to get similar results. Most encouraging, modelling gives you a practical method to get better and better at what you want to do or be; to open up options for your life and learn in the way that you know best – simply by being with competent people and keeping all your senses awake.

Chapter 20

Making Change Easier

In This Chapter

▶ Understanding the structure of change

▶ Discovering the mindset for avoiding change fatigue and staying productive

▶ Maintaining employee engagement through change

▶ Bringing NLP tools together

'Nothing endures but change' is an oft-quoted truism. Change can happen in one of two ways:

✔ You can initiate and plan for change. This type of change can be something relatively minor such as buying a new car or getting a new kitchen, or it can be life-changing – for example, when you decide to get married, move house, have kids, or change jobs: in these cases, you feel as if you have some control, although external agencies can throw a spanner in the works and leave you feeling helpless and stressed.

✔ You can have change imposed on you, for example, by your employer or through events such as an unexpected pregnancy or loss of a loved one: change is harder to accept when you feel as if you're the victim.

The NLP approach is that no single correct map of change exists at any one time. To survive and thrive, you need to acknowledge and embrace the fact that change is happening and put strategies in place to work with change rather than against it.

Because NLP is about how people think and behave, this chapter focuses on the *people aspect* of change and not on the project management of change in the workplace. We aim to show you how to deal with change in a way that allows you to maintain your equilibrium through choppy times, whether you initiate the change or a change is imposed on you. Should you come across someone for whom change isn't going as smoothly as they would like, we hope the insights you gain here enable you to ease their way a little. You could do this as simply as listening sympathetically, by lending a helping hand, or just explaining what they are experiencing.

To do all this, we pull together NLP tools and techniques from the rest of the book to illustrate how you can apply NLP to the changes that happen in your everyday life, be they relatively small or life-changing and whether they are created by you or other people. For example, think about the presupposition, 'if what you're doing isn't working, do something different' (Chapter 2 covers NLP presuppositions in more detail). Change is all about doing something different when what you're already doing isn't working.

The premise in writing this chapter is that whatever the change, you can handle it humanely and compassionately – for example, when dealing with redundancies in a corporation. This chapter is also about enabling you to make change easier for yourself by understanding what you experience. Instead of beating yourself up, if you think you could have done better at something, you can show yourself some kindness and focus on what you've done well.

Keep a notebook to hand, and as you read through this chapter note what you're going through or how you're anticipating change, and think about how the change can be made easier by applying specific NLP techniques.

Finding Clarity and Direction

Knowing where you want to go is crucial, because without clear direction you can end up expending a lot of energy chasing what you don't want and waste a lot of time achieving nothing.

For maximum results, you need to be sure about exactly what outcome you want from the change you choose to create. For example:

- ✔ I want to weigh 57 kilograms (126 pounds) by 30 September 2010.
- ✔ Our attrition rate is 27 per cent and we want to reduce that to 15 per cent.
- ✔ We want to outsource our services.
- ✔ I want my wedding day to be perfect.

Chapter 4 takes you through the process of getting clarity about your goals and uncovering hidden fears. The examples we use in Chapter 4 are aimed, primarily, at people wanting to create goals in their personal life using the NLP well-formed outcome approach. This useful process is also great, however, for change involving a team or a work department.

Imagine that you're experiencing change in your work life. You're a manager who needs to keep a change process on track while making sure that your staff are engaged and motivated (so that productivity loss is kept to a minimum), and also ensure that you can keep yourself upbeat and healthy. The big problem when change like this happens in an organisation is that people feel powerless. The perception of lack of control leads to negative stress and lack of motivation. Very little room exists for manoeuvre in big-change objectives set by top management. The people who have to implement the change can get some sense of control and stay engaged in the change process if they can decide the steps of how to actually put the change in place. Teams and individuals can apply the goal-setting techniques of Chapter 4 and experience less stress.

Take some time out to sit your team around a table and brainstorm any impending changes (and team in this sense can be your family or a larger social group). This process is a good way for the whole team to find out what each other's concerns are as regards the change. If the team is too big to fit around a table, break the team into several groups and allocate one point to each group. The team then comes together and one group talks about what it discussed, thus bringing more valuable insights.

Understanding the Structure of Change

In order to make change easier to understand, we use two models to illustrate what you may be experiencing and what you may allow for when you find that change is making you feel uncomfortable or making you behave in a way that's out of character.

The Kübler-Ross Grief Cycle

Dr Elisabeth Kübler-Ross wrote about the 'Five Stages of Grief' in her famous book *On Death and Dying*. Although originally designed to deal with death, her model is useful in helping to understand change.

You don't come across this model in standard NLP courses. However, people are fairly familiar with the Kübler-Ross 'Five Stages of Grief' as applied specifically to corporate change. The reason we include it here is to pace anyone who doesn't know much NLP but who has used this model for organisational change, as a lead-in to applying NLP to change.

When change strikes, people try to maintain the status quo because it's secure and stable. When a change occurs in the status quo of any system, even when it's expected, people can experience the different stages shown in Figure 20-1. This model can forewarn and forearm you to deal with change more effectively, and help other people in the organisation manage change better. Understanding what you're going through helps you to manage yourself by managing your emotional state, so Table 20-1 examines these stages further. It offers ways of helping you to behave more resourcefully by having rapport with other people through an awareness of how change is affecting them.

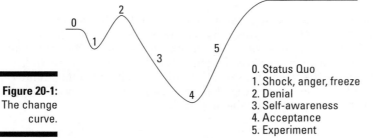

0. Status Quo
1. Shock, anger, freeze
2. Denial
3. Self-awareness
4. Acceptance
5. Experiment

Figure 20-1:
The change
curve.

When involved in corporate change, the manager's job is to keep the dip of the curve as low as possible and to keep the time frame from point 1 (the start of experiencing change) to point 5 (a new status quo begins to emerge) as short as possible, because that gets people back into full performance mode as soon as possible.

Table 20-1	The Stages of Grief in the Change Curve for Change in the Workplace	
Stages in the Change Curve	**How People May React**	**What Actions Help**
1. Shock and anger	People may procrastinate when they experience shock. Feelings of shock and anger can be fleeting or last for a long time, depending on how resilient someone is. People feel trapped and respond fearfully.	Allow people to let off steam and reassure them that the change is temporary and things are going to get better. *Stress that the change is not personal.* Subtly work to help people change their map of the world, because people react based on their existing map and the depth of their reaction depends on what their map tells them to do or how to react.

Stages in the Change Curve	How People May React	What Actions Help
2. Denial	People may have a false perception about their ability to cope. They may think they can handle things. They think everyone else is to blame. People can stay here and become dinosaurs who can't cope with change, which can result in their losing their job or being sidelined.	Coaching helps. The tool is to give feedback, because without feedback people don't realise that they're in denial and deluding themselves.
3. Self-awareness	People feel worse as they realise their toolkit of skills and knowledge isn't good enough to cope with the change. They go into survival mode. The state of feeling bad and inadequate can spill into other areas of people's lives.	Here people need support and to know where they are on the curve and why they're feeling bad. People feeling like this need to tell their spouse, colleagues, and manager and ask for leeway to be grumpy and scared. They need to be given permission to feel bad and behave unresourcefully.
4. Acceptance	People start to take personal responsibility for dealing with change as they realise they have finally stopped resisting the change. People's perception of their abilities is incorrect because they feel useless.	This stage is where people are shown how other people coped with change by giving them case studies, providing coaching and exemplars to model.
5. Experiment	This stage is the learning and integrating of new tools, so people start modelling others to see how they deal with change. They feel more capable and competent.	Training people to acquire new skills and give them room to make mistakes. At this stage, managers must have done sufficient risk analysis and contingency planning, so that mistakes aren't detrimental to the company. A high-risk management is necessary at this point so that mistakes can be handled and dealt with appropriately. A blame culture only kicks people back to stage 2.

As you emerge from the change, *integration* then follows. You settle into the new way of doing things and are more flexible because you've had to learn to cope with a new environment. Your perception of your own competence rises and is likely to be measured more accurately. The change can be incorporated into the identity of the company by constantly referring back to it, until it becomes unconscious.

People react differently to change. Each person spends different lengths of time at each stage and each person has to be dealt with differently by team-mates and manager. A manager's role, therefore, needs to change as they deal with the different stages that different people are at.

When you're leading or facilitating a team, experiencing the team's emotions is quite normal. For this reason, managers can feel a rollercoaster of frustration, fear, and anxiety as they experience the different phases themselves. So they may need coaching, mentoring, going for a beer, or whatever their release mechanism is, to gain space and perspective.

When people are under stress, their behaviour may need to be excused. Before reacting to someone, adopt the second position to, metaphorically, 'walk in that person's shoes' in order to get a better understanding of how the person is feeling (check out Chapter 7 on understanding other people's perspective). This process gives you the ability to move up and take the bird's eye view when 'trouble's on the ground'.

NLP logical levels

The *NLP logical levels* are a powerful way to think about change by breaking it down as a model into different categories of information. (Turn to Chapter 11 for more on logical levels, which are sometimes known as neurological levels.)

As you begin to consider the kind of changes that you experience, you find that logical levels can help you to find a route forward in confusing times. To do this, having alignment through all the logical levels of identity, belief and values, capabilities and skills, behaviour and environment is particularly important, because having an incongruity at one or more levels stops the desired result from happening. This model can be as useful when experiencing personal change as for understanding corporate change. The model's key value is that it provides a structured approach for understanding what's happening. This enables people to make a decision about choosing how they want to feel about the change and how they're going to behave.

In whichever case, changing at the lower levels of the diagram (see Chapter 11) is easier than at the higher levels. So, for example, a company may find making changes to the building (environment), such as painting the walls a brighter colour, is easier than changing the culture or creating a new identity for itself. Changes like these at a higher level have an impact on people below it; changes at lower levels can impact people above, but this isn't a given.

Jas, a very bright, well-educated 30-something, booked herself on to a programme of Relationship Wizardry® coaching, as she'd had a series of relationships but she couldn't settle into anything permanent. Jas is the daughter of very successful parents, and as a result of the coaching, she realised that she'd modelled herself on her strong, very independent mother. Unfortunately, her identity as a strong, independent woman prevented her from accepting anything from people, and this affected all areas of her life. She admitted that some of her relationship problems were because she found it hard to accept love and would push her partner away (behaviour) if they came too close emotionally. Jas also realised that she had some self-esteem issues (beliefs) because she didn't feel she measured up to the success her mother had achieved by the time she was Jas's age, and she didn't feel she deserved a successful, dynamic man like her father.

Romilla helped Jas to 'design' her ideal relationship using the well-formed outcome process (see Chapter 4). One of the first steps Jas incorporated was to change the environment where she met people. She joined groups where she was more likely to meet people with whom she had interests in common. Before the coaching, the misalignment through Jas's logical levels stopped her attaining her goal of a long-term relationship.

Creating alignment in logical levels

Alignment in any venture makes things flow more smoothly and helps you to attain your target more quickly. When you think about the logical levels (see Chapter 11), if you have alignment through all levels, you're going to find success easy.

Elaine is 45, married with young children, and climbing the IFA (UK's International Financial Advisors) ladder. She's extremely bright and very ambitious (one aspect of identity). She's also passionate about women having an understanding of how to attain financial security (values) and believes in educating women to this end, because she 'knows' (belief) that every woman has the right to financial independence.

Elaine has a string of letters after her name (capabilities and skills) but is striving to get more qualifications. This aim is completely congruent with her ambition of where she's taking her business, and the way she acts and talks about women's finance (behaviour) engenders complete trust. She has a lovely office at home (environment) where she can keep an eye on her children. When she needs to think, she goes into the garden for a spot of meditation. Because all the areas for her business are aligned, she's making good progress.

Although this second anecdote is an example of what Jim experienced when his wife died, it can apply to anyone who goes through loss: of a marriage when a split occurs or the loss of a job due to redundancy, sacking, or retirement.

Jim, an accountant, and Alicia had been married for almost 30 years. The first couple of weeks after Alicia died were tied up with making the funeral arrangements and Jim functioned on autopilot, but then he went through huge change:

✔ **Environment:** Jim found that he was rattling around their bedroom after he took Alicia's clothes to the charity shop. A bed that had been comfortable for two felt very big and the king-size quilt was too heavy.

   Obviously, depending on the loss, different aspects apply when adjusting to or creating a new environment for a new life.

✔ **Behaviour:** Jim had always been very playful and men and women enjoyed his company because he was such fun. In fact, Alicia would tease him for being an outrageous flirt. Some months after Alicia died and life began to stabilise, Jim realised that his sense of humour had started to return. He was surprised to notice that his interaction with the women he was meeting had changed dramatically. Although he was his playful self with women who were Alicia's and his old and trusted friends, he was much more reserved with women he was meeting for the first time. He realised that he'd seen Alicia as a guard against women who may misconstrue his playfulness.

✔ **Capabilities and skills:** Alicia had managed all the household affairs because she enjoyed the element of control and juggling funds and utilities to get the best rates and deals. Jim didn't want to think about numbers when he was at home. Suddenly, Jim had to organise the running of the home as well as manage his work.

   Jim was extremely organised at work but both Alicia and he had given him tacit permission to be less than organised at home. Jim decided to bring his organisational skills into his life at home; he modelled his time keeping and organisational behaviour at work to manage himself at home (for more on modelling, go to Chapter 19).

Jim also found himself at a loss with leisure time and holidays. He slowly developed new strategies (check out Chapter 12 for more on this area) for deciding where to go and how to organise trips. Initially, he took holidays where he was able to acquire new skills. Jim had always enjoyed cooking and so his first holiday was to book a week in Tuscany to learn authentic Italian cooking and discover the flavours of Tuscan wine. Eventually, he was able to go on tours and see parts of the world Alicia and he hadn't got around to seeing.

Jim had to force himself to do things on his own, like going to the cinema. He took up hobbies that kept him interested in life, but his biggest thrill was to help a charity with its accounts.

✔ **Beliefs and values:** Jim found his beliefs around the future were shattered. Initially, all he saw when he looked into his future was darkness and loneliness. As the weeks became months, Jim began to see small glimmers of light as he forced himself to keep busy and engage with people. Interestingly, he says, on re-examining his values around his work and relationships he found that they hadn't changed although his values around 'life' had shifted dramatically. Before, they had focused on what was important to him about his life with Alicia – companionship, love, laughter, fun. He discovered that although he believed intellectually in love, he was too frightened to even contemplate the consequences of finding it again. He decided his highest value is leaving a legacy that's going to help people live more joyfully and 'add happiness to the collective unconscious'.

✔ **Identity:** What frightened Jim most was the loss of part of his identity. For 30 years, he'd been Alicia's husband. His role in life was to look after her. He said he felt adrift, rather like Scarlett O'Hara saying, 'Where shall I go? What shall I do? Whom do I look after now?' This stage is the hardest part of rebuilding his life but he has discovered that he has to do this a piece at a time. Two years on, holes still exist and can catch him out, but he recites the litany he found that gives him comfort, 'This too shall pass.'

We offer Jim's anecdote to help you understand what you're likely to experience when you encounter change in your life, so that you find it easier to work through the change instead of fighting it and making change harder.

Make a copy of Table 20-2 and use it to record the insights you get as a result of change that is happening in your life and to write down things you could do differently to make change easier.

Table 20-2	The Effects of Change on Your Logical Levels	
Logical Level	*Insights*	*What You Can Do to Facilitate the Change*
Identity		
Values and beliefs		
Capabilities and skills		
Behaviour		
Environment		

Identifying the strongest level for change

Depending on your journey and circumstance, changing one of the logical levels may have the greatest impact on what you're trying to achieve.

Tom was highly ambitious but found himself living a life of mediocrity; he was extremely frustrated and blamed everyone and everything for his bad luck. In fact, he was lucky to have a manager who engaged a coach to work with Tom. During a coaching session that involved a time-line exercise, Tom discovered that he was carrying a lot of emotions around the death of his mother when he was 11 years old. He realised he had very deep-seated beliefs around life being unfair and him being unlucky. Doing some work on his time line (see Chapter 13) to let go of limiting beliefs worked at the level of Tom's beliefs and changed his life dramatically.

When Tom shifted his beliefs around the unfairness of life and reviewed his sense of being unlucky, he discovered that his identity shifted from that of a person who saw himself as a victim to someone who was successful. He felt brave enough to ask to go on a management training programme (capabilities and skills) and he engaged his manager and colleague to share ideas (behaviour), which was something he'd felt too fearful of doing in the past.

Although you may need to strengthen a level, perhaps by adding new skills, or redecorating your office, you may find that you need to remove something too. For example, if you're always late for meetings, you may need to improve your time-management techniques but, more importantly, you may have to remove unconscious, emotional blocks, causing the unhelpful behaviour, as in Tom's case.

Where are you experiencing change in your life? Do you want to make a big change but keep putting it off? Think about Elaine in the above example. She had five opportunities presented to her where she could have become an IFA, but she held on to her job as project manager because it felt safe. She eventually took the plunge when her environment didn't support her circumstances. She had a baby and wanted to work from home to have more time with him. Doing the following exercise helps you to get clarity about which of the logical levels you may need to develop or change:

1. Make a note of the change you're going through or want to make.

2. Copy out and complete the logical level matrix (Table 20-3).

3. Identify the logical level that will have the most impact.

4. Write down the change you're going through or the change you want to make.

Table 20-3	The Logical Level Matrix	
Logical Level	*How This Level Supports the Change*	*How This Level Doesn't Support the Change*
Identity		
Beliefs and values		
Capabilities and skills		
Behaviour		
Environment		

Now make a list of what you're going to do differently in order to make change easier or to instigate change. For example, Elaine (see the earlier section 'Creating alignment in logical levels') realised that she needed to add IFA qualifications to her capabilities and skills. She realised that, as a woman working from home, she was at a disadvantage in relation to other IFAs who could travel easily to clients and some of whom had offices and an infrastructure to support them. She wanted to stand out by being one of the most highly qualified IFAs.

Holding On to Values

Your values are important because they support your identity; a value of honesty and kindness may result in you knowing that you're a 'good person'. The way you measure your values is by the criteria you give them. People can share a common value but can measure them differently. For example, two managers who espouse efficiency as a corporate value may measure efficiency with different criteria. One may see efficiency in purely monetary terms and only look at the bottom line. The other manager may measure efficiency in terms of people engagement.

Because values lie in the realms of the unconscious mind, until you understand them consciously, you hold on to them with a fervour, verging on the religious, which leaves very little room for manoeuvre. You may think that this strength is good, perhaps when training puppies, husbands, and children! However, as regards the workplace, some flexibility can be efficacious. The criteria for measuring the effectiveness of values can give room for negotiation.

In the example of the managers with the efficiency value, a mediator may be able to show how employee engagement benefits the bottom line or how a healthy bottom line gives job security and leads to employees engaging more fully. Understanding how to address people's values makes any change easier, be it getting all the members of a team to pull together or a husband and wife to work towards a common goal.

Grasping the Importance of Clear Communication

You can't impose change, change has to be bought into.

—Jayne Reddyhoff

The success of any change programme depends on everybody in a team pulling together; the team can be the whole corporation or part of a department, or indeed, a family. In this situation, rapport really comes into its own. The person with rapport can influence and bring on-board the people who can make or break the change process. The idea is that your communication reaches out to everybody so that they understand very clearly what you want from them. This section pulls together techniques given throughout this book to build rapport, especially in the written form.

If you think about the perceptual positions (which we discuss in Chapter 7) and remember to create communication from the perspective of the person you're addressing, you find that carrying people along with you is much easier. This process is where you need to understand at least some of the values of the people involved in the change process. (Turn to Chapter 3 to discover more about values.)

Knowing your own values is important in choosing a job or a partner, be it a business or life partner. You need to understand other people's values when trying to succeed in achieving a common goal. You can make an assumption about common values in a company if you're careful in choosing who you employ. If the corporate values are repeated time and again, the people who stay and flourish understand these values and are in tune with them. As a manager or an individual wanting to build a long-lasting relationship, knowing the values of the person you want to motivate is very useful; sometimes, you simply need to ask, 'What's important to you about x?', where 'x' can be, 'working for this company', 'a relationship', or 'working together'. Having everyone working to fulfil common values makes change so much easier than if individuals work to their own agendas dictated by their individual values.

Using visual, auditory, and kinaesthetic (VAK) language allows your audience to more easily understand your message. Chapter 6 tells you more about these aspects.

Like values, the meta programs (which we describe in Chapter 8) are some of the most abstract filters that you use to filter the data your senses pick up about your world. Because of their abstractions, using the meta programs with a person shows a preference, and helps you to build rapport more easily. We suggest you start with the 'towards/away from' and 'big picture/ detail' meta programs'.

When creating any communication, keep a cheat sheet to hand with points for remembering how to write. It may look something like this:

- ✔ Values
- ✔ VAK
- ✔ Towards/away from
- ✔ Global/detail

Leave space to insert anything that you think may be a good addition to your aide mémoire.

Keep in mind that some people feel overwhelmed if they're given too much information, and so a useful practice may be to provide a short overview followed by more detail. For example, if you're easily overwhelmed by too much detail, buying a new car or washing machine, or even choosing a holiday, can be difficult. A useful strategy is to ask someone you trust who understands your needs to give you a list of two or three cars, washing machines, or holidays that fit your 'must-have' criteria. Having fewer options from which to choose makes decision-making quicker and easier.

During an IT department restructuring, the well-meaning management wanted the change process to be an inclusive experience for the department so kept everyone apprised of the smallest detail regarding the change. Productivity hit rock bottom, however, because the programmers were extremely distressed by the barrage of information they were being sent several times a day. Productivity rose only when the manager realised he needed to filter the incoming flood of information to only that which would affect the programmers.

Creating the Mindset for Change

We introduce you to the concept of behavioural flexibility as one of the pillars of NLP in Chapter 1. This idea is crucial in dealing with whatever life throws at you. When you can develop the mindset that allows you to do deal with these variables, you have the means to maintain equilibrium for most of the time. Why most of the time? Well, we're very conscious that when, with something like bereavement, life gets very tough, perhaps all you can do is go into survival mode. But remember, even managing to crawl through the day is a testament to your ability to be flexible in the face of such a harsh reality.

Every day remind yourself of something that you have achieved, however small it may seem to you.

Letting go of fear

Fear incapacitates. People aren't so much afraid of making a mistake; really, the fear is about the consequence of an action. Fear is people reacting to their existing model of the world (turn to Chapter 2, which covers NLP presuppositions). So if you've been in an environment where you were constantly criticised or mistakes weren't tolerated, you're likely to be fearful of being criticised if your actions aren't in line with what is expected. This may force you into a state of procrastination or inactivity.

An urban legend pertains to a top salesman at IBM who reputedly lost a very large amount of money on a project. When the salesman was summoned to see Thomas J Watson Snr, one of IBM's most influential leaders, he offered his resignation, which was rejected. Watson said that IBM had just spent a vast amount of money on the salesman's training and didn't want to waste it.

If you're holding yourself back because you're afraid to do something, for example, you may be afraid to move to a different job, accept a marriage proposal, move house, accept a promotion, and so on, the following exercise may help you to uncover your hidden fears.

This exercise helps you with your decision-making. Even if afterwards you decide to do nothing, you've still made a conscious decision. This process itself can dispel a lot of your fears:

1. **Ask yourself the questions from the well-formed outcome exercise that we describe in Chapter 4. Here 'x' relates to taking some action, such as the ones we mention above.**

    What will happen if I do x?

    What won't happen if I do x?

    What will happen if I don't do x?

    What won't happen if I don't do x?

2. **Make a list of the pros and cons of making your decision.**

3. **Make a list of everything that you think may go wrong and how you'd deal with the arising problems.**

4. **Decide that you're going to learn from the situation, no matter what happens.**

5. **Release any fears that haven't gone away using submodalities (see the following anecdote about David).**

In the world of business, the fact is that companies sometimes set up change programmes to improve efficiency for survival – which often means cutbacks in hours or people – or to improve the bottom line. Departments can be merged or closed down or a problem – such as strong competition, high attrition rates, low morale, or low productivity – may need to be addressed. NLP techniques can help you through such difficult times.

When David and his colleagues faced another swathe of cuts at work, he felt the old dread of losing his job dogging his waking moments. He'd been through several changes and states of feeling 'not good' and realised that his motivation and well-being had both suffered. He decided enough was enough and adopted the following strategies to stay productive:

1. **David applied the 'what if' reframing process (which we explain in Chapter 14) and asked himself, 'What's the worst that can happen?'**

David knew that he may be out of work for several months but because he'd built a financial 'war chest' after the last cuts, he could survive for six months without work. This realisation went a long way to alleviating the feeling of dread he felt when he thought of being made redundant; the frequency declined but the intensity was still there. David decided to release the fear that he felt each time he thought of the changes that were being incorporated (see point 3 below).

He decided he didn't like his work defining his identity, as in 'I am a salesman.' He asked himself what he'd do if he didn't have to work to pay his mortgage and remembered how much he'd loved working with wood at school. David decided that regardless of the outcome at work, he'd take classes in woodwork.

2. **He recognised he had a choice about how he dealt with the change.**

Instead of letting the change get to him, he decided to treat each day as a learning experience. At the end of each day, he listed what had been difficult. He then reframed the difficulty by asking himself, 'What can I learn from this?' and 'How can I use it in the days ahead?'

3. **Most importantly, David decided to take charge of the way he reacted to the negative conversations around him and the fear he felt.**

He began employing a pattern interrupt (see the NLPjargonalert icon that follows this list). Each time his colleagues began talking about the problems they were experiencing. He discovered how to differentiate between when the talk was negative, simply because his colleagues felt good about feeling bad, and when a need arose to solve a genuine problem. When the talk was meaningless negativity, David held his hand up and said something along the lines of 'Let's stop wallowing; we know things are tough and they're likely to get tougher but we've got to stay strong.' After a while, just having David hold his hand up switched his colleagues into problem-solving mode.

David found out that dread, for him, had two components. He felt the fear as heaviness descending, sliding down from his shoulders, and saw a solid, black cube encasing his torso. The cube was a metaphor for the way he felt in his body (see Chapter 17 for more on metaphors). Each time the dread returned, David changed the picture of the cube by introducing pockets of silver into it. The cube turned into a honeycomb of grey and then silver until it disappeared. (Check out Chapter 10 for more on submodalities.) While he worked with the image, David also did some breath work with an affirmation that he said out loud, if he was by himself. He drew a breath deep into the centre of the cube and on each exhalation he said, 'I'm relaxed, strong, and confident, and I feel good.'

A *pattern interrupt* is when a break occurs in a pattern of thought or behaviour. For example, when a coach asks a client, 'How can I help?', the client may take a deep breath, link into feeling bad about a problem, and burst into tears. These steps constitute part of the sequence in the programming that the client has with regards to the problem. The coach may break the flow in the pattern by doing or saying something unexpected. Anecdotally, Richard Bandler has been said to have tipped water over a client to break her pattern. The aim of the unexpected interruption is to break the neurological links that a person has built into a sequence.

The sword of Damocles of job cuts is still hanging over David, but he no longer allows himself to become incapacitated. He realises that he has a life away from work and that he'd rather have a 'whole life' than put his life on hold until he can get away from work at the end of the day.

One rather interesting side-effect occurred as a result of David's acceptance of the change. His manager noticed that he was far more productive than other members of staff and decided to offer him a promotion when the cuts were done. Now David feels that he's more secure if/when future cuts are announced and is more engaged with his work. His productivity is better now that he doesn't feel the dread that was his constant companion before he decided to change the way he thought. He gets more recognition for his work, and so he's more engaged and finds himself in an upward spiral.

Being willing to experiment

When a section of an IT department was being outsourced, some of the people who were going to lose their jobs buried their heads in the sand and waited for the inevitable. A couple of people, however, were willing to experiment with new ways of working and developed their hobbies into potential businesses. The difference in mindset gave this pair the flexibility to move forward. The other group was stuck in inactivity and helplessness because they were unable to think beyond 'I've always worked in IT' and hope they'd find work in a diminishing market.

Part of this healthy mindset is accepting that nothing's permanent and that the person with the most flexibility in a system survives and may even thrive. Being fearful stops you experimenting and creating options for yourself.

Getting Help on the Way

You may find that managing simple change on your own is easy. For introducing bigger changes, however, getting help facilitates the process. For personal change, you can get relevant help, such as that of a coach, a nutritionist, a financial advisor, an estate agent, or if you think of a holiday as a temporary change, you may employ the services of a travel counsellor.

For making change at work, using *change champions* is essential. A department of 500 people was being restructured. The staff were broken up into groups of 20. Each group was assigned a staff manager and all information was funnelled through that manager. The 20 managers bought into the change and went out and sold the change to their teams. They were in effect the 'change champions'. This reorganisation turned out to be one of the more successful, with minimum disruption and loss of productivity. Another reason given for the success of the project was that the management team and the top 200 people out of 500 all had individual one-on-one coaching sessions. Management placed a high value on clear communication and timely support systems for employees.

Strengthening resources

Throughout this book, we talk about the need to be flexible. Being willing to experiment is an aspect of being flexible and you're more likely to experiment if you're in a resourceful state. When you feel resourceful, you can find ways around problems more easily. This mindset, in turn, makes change a lot easier for you to deal with than if you were to feel resentful.

Alan, a salesman, was unstoppable when he felt well and energetic. Other days he just couldn't cut the mustard. He decided to make a memory of himself on one of his unstoppable days. To do this, he picked a day on which he'd been really successful and wrote down, in graphic detail, exactly what he'd seen, heard, and done to make himself feel so energetic and unstoppable. He used his notes to create an anchor of being unstoppable (Chapter 9 has all the info on how to use anchors). Initially, Alan did the exercise with a friend who helped him follow each step of the exercise correctly. When he could remember the steps, he was able to do the exercise by himself. His sales went up by 15 per cent in the first three months after he started employing his 'unstoppable anchor' before seeing a sales prospect.

Future pacing

Even when you've chosen to introduce some change into your life, you may at times find that your resolve wavers. A useful exercise for staying on track is to mentally take yourself into the future to the time when you've achieved your goal to remind yourself of what you want to achieve. This technique is particularly good when you start a programme of healthy eating and are being tempted by a chocolate bar whispering your name. You can use this process to break the unhelpful strategy (turn to Chapter 12 to discover more on breaking habits) of instant gratification by building an extra step into developing a strategy for developing awareness of what you eat; in fact, being mindful of all your actions.

Planning the road map

As Billy Wilder is reputed to have said, 'Hindsight is always twenty–twenty.' One way of achieving your goals is to know where you're at, where you want to go, and then logically work out the steps you have to take to get to your goal. An even better way to do this is to pretend 'as if' you've achieved your goal and work backwards, with hindsight, following the steps in this exercise (see Chapter 14 for more about 'as-if reframing'). Chapter 13 tells you in detail how to 'time travel'.

This exercise is a variation on the 'Getting rid of anxiety' exercise in Chapter 13 and can show you a different way of using time lines:

1. **Find yourself somewhere safe and quiet to relax deeply and think about your goal.**

2. **Draw a line and write down the starting point and endpoints for your goal at each end of the line.**

3. **Think about what the steps are for getting you from start to finish and jot these down on the line.**

4. **Float way above your time line so that you can see your past and your future stretching below you.**

5. **Still above your time line, float forward along your time line until you're above the time where you have successfully achieved your goal.**

6. **Turn and look back to now and allow your unconscious mind to fill in any gaps you hadn't thought of for your road map and add these to the sheet you've created.**

7. **Allow all the events along your time line to align so that they support your goal, noting any actions you may have to take along the way.**

8. **When you're ready, float back to your present and back down into the room.**

Taking One Step Forward

The decision to make a change takes just a moment, but the change itself can take anywhere from a few minutes to a lifetime. What's important to recognise is that in order to incorporate change you have to do something actively. This section looks at the importance of the first and last steps in a change project.

Making that initial move

The first step is the most important because it starts the momentum that takes you to the second and subsequent steps of your journey. Often, breaking down a goal into smaller, manageable chunks keeps you motivated on the path to success.

Susan, a drug addict for 24 years, was walking home from a nightclub very early one morning, when an encounter with an acquaintance turned her life around. When she tried to talk to him, all he said to her was, 'Go home, look in the mirror, and make some different choices.' Susan went home and looked in the mirror and saw that she looked terrible. Her skin was grey, she had dark shadows under her eyes, she was bedraggled and emaciated, and she acknowledged that she looked and felt dreadful.

She decided then and there, 'I don't want to do this anymore. I don't want to look like this anymore.' This decision, although all stated in the negative (check out Chapter 4 on how to create well-formed outcomes) was the first step Susan took in taking back control of her life. She had a strong 'away-from' motivation pattern, recognising what she didn't want. (See Chapter 8 for more on the 'away-from' motivation pattern.)

The next thing she did was to change her environment. She stopped seeing her drug-taking friends and got a job. During her clean-up phase, a neighbour suggested that Susan attend teacher-training college. This suggestion started Susan on her path to learning to become an excellent coach and get her MA degree in humanistic psychology.

Celebrating and closure

Many goal-setting processes go into great depth, talking about well-formed outcomes, planning the road map, and taking the first step. Not many talk about the last step or *closure*. Admittedly, closure isn't the last step in the grand scheme of things, but integrating a last step to signal the end of a phase in a project or the project itself can be very useful.

Any change requires focus and the expenditure of huge amounts of physical and emotional energy and puts people under considerable stress. This stress can be *distress* (bad stress) or *eustress* (good stress, what Mihaly Csikszentmihalyi, the author of several inspirational books, calls *flow*). In either case you need a period to recharge your batteries. Getting closure releases the tension of concentrated work, signals the end of a phase, and gives you permission to move on to the next challenge.

End a project – which could be work at home (such as having your garden landscaped) or at work (where you're involved with improving productivity within a team) – with a debrief. You could examine the following:

- ✔ What went well?
- ✔ What could have been better?
- ✔ What lessons were learned?
- ✔ What will you do differently next time?

Remember to congratulate the team (even if that team has only one member – you) and finally make sure that you *celebrate*!

Part VI
The Part of Tens

The 5th Wave   By Rich Tennant

"It's called that because we feel that people are entirely free and therefore responsible for what they make of themselves and for themselves. Now, do you still want the double anchovy with the fried mozzarella strips?"

In this part . . .

You see why the famous *For Dummies* Part of Tens is so well loved as we put more information quickly and simply at your fingertips. This part gives you a taste of the broad impact of NLP on everyday life, from parents and teachers to sales success and personal development. We provide something for everyone: ten applications of NLP, other books to read, online resources to use, and films to watch. And you see just how much more you can find out now that you've become curious.

Chapter 21

Ten Applications of NLP

*W*e find daily applications for NLP in our work as professional coaches, consultants, and trainers. Also, at home with family and friends, NLP influences how we think and behave. So, how can you use NLP in your life? In this chapter, we present ten practical suggestions that we hope get you curious about how you can apply the contents of this book right now. Remember that these points are only suggestions: you choose what makes a difference for you and the people you connect with.

Developing Yourself

Personal development is a massive arena, because people are searching for meaning and contentment in an unpredictable world. When you read this book, we hope that you take away this one lesson: NLP offers a means for you to learn, grow, and develop yourself, and you can choose whether the ideas fit for you, or not. In addition, you can use NLP to coach and help others too, in which case you need to stay strong and healthy yourself so that you can be an authentic role model.

The NLP toolkit offers a collection of models and exercises, as well as encouraging an inquisitive mindset, which allows you to do the following:

✔ Choose your most resourceful emotional state and use *anchors*, a mental technique to access and hold that good state when you're feeling challenged. You progress best when you feel safe enough to have a go at something new. To explore how to set and fire anchors, look at Chapter 9.

✔ Guide your thinking in different ways using the assumptions on which NLP is based: check out Chapter 2 for more on these NLP presuppositions.

✔ Find out what makes you function at your best – gathering information about how you reflect your experience through your senses, what NLP calls *representational systems*. You can get to grips with representational systems (sometimes called *modalities*) in Chapter 6.

✔ Take responsibility for your own learning instead of waiting for someone else to do it for you.

✔ Increase clarity on what you really want in all aspects of your life. The well-formed outcomes we introduce in Chapter 4 are fundamental to looking at what you want. Also check out the checklist in Appendix C.

✔ Find out how to make changes at the most appropriate logical level of experience to improve your ability and self-confidence – whether that confidence is about your environment, behaviour, capability, beliefs, identity, or purpose. This aspect is discussed further in Chapter 11.

✔ Pay attention to what is happening for you in terms of your energy levels, to ensure that you don't push yourself too hard and burn-out.

✔ Discover how to build rapport more easily: we devote the whole of Chapter 7 to developing this important skill.

Managing Your Personal and Professional Relationships

'Help. This relationship isn't working!' Having a bad relationship with someone can be a horrible, stuck experience. The door is closed in your face. One statement you hear a lot in NLP is 'If what you're doing isn't working, do something different.' Fortunately, NLP offers many ways for you to get unstuck and open the door to more possibilities. Here are a couple of methods you can start with:

✔ **The Meta Model:** This model provides a way for you to delve below the surface of vague everyday language like 'I'm not happy with this,' with useful questions that gather specific information and challenge assumptions that get in the way of happy and rewarding relationships. When you know how to communicate more precisely, you can get to the heart of what you and other people really mean to say. The Meta Model is described in detail in Chapter 15.

✔ **The NLP meta-mirror:** This technique encourages you take different perceptual positions. The meta-mirror is a favourite method for exploring challenging situations through the act of examining how you relate to other people. By taking different viewpoints into account, you come away with fresh ideas to move your relationships forward – or say a polite goodbye. The meta-mirror is described in detail in Chapter 7.

Negotiating a Win–Win Solution

Suppose that you're going to enter into an important negotiation in your life: perhaps you've spotted the home of your dreams. NLP can help you to get the best deal when you're confronted with estate agents pushing you to buy the new house at the highest price while selling your current one as low as possible. NLP helps accomplish your aim by providing principles and strategies you can use to everybody's advantage. Take a look at the techniques in the following list, which although we relate to buying a house you can apply whether you're negotiating for a job, buying a car, hiring contract staff at work, or involved in any conflict resolution:

- ✔ Go for the positive outcome – begin with your desired result in mind. Use positive language. Always focus on what you want rather than what you don't want. For the full story on outcomes, see Chapter 4.

- ✔ Engage your senses – make your outcome more specific by noticing what it looks like, sounds like, and feels like when you achieve a successful negotiation. You can get a sense of this technique in Chapter 6.

- ✔ Note down your *hot buttons* (your preferred criteria) – focus on five key elements that are important to you in making the move. Put them in order of priority and keep returning to them to check that you're getting what you want.

- ✔ Note down the hot buttons from the point of view of the sellers – what's important to them? Imagine what being in their shoes would be like and remind yourself of what they want every time you have contact.

- ✔ Keep in mind what positive by-products you get from the house you already have that you don't want to lose. These positive elements may be the number of bathrooms, the sunny south-facing garden, or the good local transport.

- ✔ Know your bottom line. Be prepared to walk away with no deal instead of getting carried away in the moment just to complete a deal that's disappointing for you.

- ✔ Manage your state of mind. Staying calm and relaxed when the negotiation gets to you helps you to make the best next move. Take a look at Chapter 9 about dropping anchors.

- ✔ Use the technique of *chunking* – the ability to be able to shift someone's view to the big picture or focus down to specifics confidently. Chunking is a key skill in any negotiation. If you're disagreeing on details, chunk upwards from the specifics of your contract to gain common agreement on key points, and then you can chunk downwards to smaller issues when you've achieved that common ground. Chapter 15 helps you to get specific when necessary, while Chapter 16 shows you how to speak in general terms that are easy to agree with. With this flexibility in your approach, you increase the chances of the other person hearing your message loud and clear.

> ✔ Maintain rapport with everyone in the sale chain. Even when you disagree with the content of what they're saying, match and mirror their body language and tone of voice. Things progress more smoothly when everybody listens! We cover the all-important NLP skill of rapport building in Chapter 7. Also, Chapter 6 gives you more ways of building rapport by recognising whether someone has a visual, auditory, or kinaesthetic preference, and then using language to match that person's preference.

Meeting Those Sales Targets

You may have met two types of salespeople. Some just want to sell to you regardless of whether you want to buy: their goal is to hit their targets and you may be just an enemy – the budget holder – to conquer along the way. They want to get their commission and then get the hell out of there in their new car, lights flashing, horn tooting at anyone in their way. Fortunately, some salespeople take the longer view, and approach their profession by building good relationships with clients. They're probably very well-focused on targets and yet they take their time, and they listen carefully to what the other person wants before they attempt to share knowledge. Selling the product comes further down the line.

NLP principles apply to creating strong sales relationships. They allow you to build rapport, get clarity on what other people want, understand their values and criteria, and be flexible along the way until you close a deal or decide to walk away because you know the fit isn't right. NLP reminds you to listen not only to the words being spoken, but also pay attention to the physiology. Where do the eyes move, or how does the colour of someone's skin change according to their feelings.

Taking the NLP approach leads to a winning situation that's highly considerate and respectful. Integrity is the key word that comes to mind here. Good salespeople are able to take the customer's perspective and match the benefit of the product to the customer's need. People don't want to be blatantly sold to: they want to be listened to and find solutions to their issues. They want products and services that help them run a business or enjoy life more; they want the 'feel-good' factor. NLP deals with influence and how people make decisions, and successful sales are ones that match the customer needs at many levels.

Here's a saying to bear in mind: 'People buy on emotion and justify with fact.' Whether you're selling a product or an idea, you connect primarily with people on an emotional level. People buy *you* first, before they buy what you're selling.

Creating Powerful Presentations

The ability to communicate well is fundamental to your success. In fact, you may find that it's the single most important skill that affects your future. When you can present well you have the leading edge in so many areas of life, whether your passion is to be a politician, sportsperson, teacher, TV presenter, cheerleader, or business leader of the year. Have you got the self-confidence to go out and stand up for what you believe in? Do you really want to sit through a celebration dinner scared because you have to give the vote of thanks at the end? If you can present well, you can get ahead. Or simply relax and have a good time.

So what's stopping you making powerful presentations? In one word – you!

Sadly, so many people we meet are terrified of presenting. And if they're not terrified, they certainly prefer to hang around backstage than get out front and sock it to an audience.

NLP can make a difference for you in three ways:

- ✔ It shows you how to make your purpose in presenting crystal clear.
- ✔ It shows you how to touch everyone in an audience through your use of language.
- ✔ It shows you how to feel confident about standing up in front of any group.

Imagine that you've been invited to do a talk at the annual meeting of your local gardening club. (For gardening, substitute your own hobby from hamster-training to glider-flying.)

Using NLP, your first task is to engage your brain to decide on the outcome of your presentation. What result, or action, do you want to happen, when people have been so inspired by your speech? Map out this outcome clearly for yourself, bearing in mind what the audience would like to discover from you.

As you begin to build the content of your talk, think VAK – visual, auditory, and kinaesthetic (head to Chapter 6 for tips on engaging with people's dominant senses). How are you going to connect with people who like pictures, those who hear the words, and those who just go with their gut feelings? As you develop your script, remember that some people just need the headlines and others like the nitty-gritty details.

Remember that NLP gives you the tools to prepare mentally for any presentation. Get clear about how you want to appear at the presentation – laughing and jovial, full of deep and meaningful gravitas, or perhaps somewhere in between? Find a time when you were like that in the past, so that you can hold, or anchor, the previous experience and regain that feeling for yourself. Turn to Chapter 9 for all about setting stage anchors.

Here's the most important tip – the Holy Grail: don't get hung up on other people's tips and techniques. We all present differently, and being yourself can be refreshing. When you speak from the heart about something you care passionately about, people connect with your authenticity and sense of purpose.

Managing Your Time and Precious Resources

Everybody has the same amount of time in the week: 168 hours. So why do some people spend their lives racing against the clock while others gently amble along? The difference is in how people use that time.

Understanding how you relate to time makes a big difference to your daily experience. NLP distinguishes between people who operate *in time* – where you live in and for the moment – and people who operate *through time* – where you step back to view past, present, and future as an onlooker. Being in the moment is easier when you're *in time*. Planning time is much easier when you're *through time*. Time-travelling tips are waiting for you in Chapter 13.

As an NLP coach, Kate encourages her clients to notice how they relate to time, and to spend it wisely, in order to understand the impact of spending time on what they don't want to be doing and freeing up their energy for what really motivates them. Your time is precious, and when you've spent it, you can't reclaim it.

Taking on too much to please others has the opposite effect when you let them down. NLP shows you how to say 'no' while maintaining rapport with friends and colleagues.

Being Coached to Success

Do you want to do something, something in particular that you've thought about for a long time but have yet to start or to achieve? If so, NLP coaching can help you make that leap from the idea – the initial desire to make a change – to making it happen.

When you work with a coach who embraces the principles of NLP with skill, that person uses the NLP presuppositions and believes in your unlimited potential. The coach supports you in achieving goals that seemed impossible, by getting you clear on your values and beliefs and changing the interference that gets in your way. And that can be seriously liberating and fun. No joking.

NLP coaching focuses your attention on getting the results you want – the outcomes – and stops you dithering along the way, dissipating energy on all the things that you don't want. NLP helps you to jump over or remove the barriers that stop you. Coaching closes that gap from where you are now to where you want to get to – from your *present state* to your *desired state*.

Action turns the dream into reality. One key reason why coaching gets you results is that you make a commitment to action. Another reason is that you break down your goals into bite-sized, realistic chunks. When you work with a coach you make a commitment to somebody else, as if somebody's standing beside you with the stopwatch and clipboard and checking in at regular intervals to make sure that you're on track.

The principles of NLP can apply to achieving success in sports, and so you often find sports coaches using the anchoring techniques of NLP to help a client get into a confident state before a big match or performance.

Coaching is often about enabling people to restore their balance and harmony. We believe that coaching is about much more than simply excelling on the golf course or in boardroom battles. Taking a holistic view – considering all aspects of your life – enables you to create your own future. We coach highly successful executives who want to be outstanding in their work. By examining the whole picture of their lives as well as their work patterns, these people unleash their own energy and direction to get what they want.

If you excel in one aspect of your life to the detriment of other aspects, say your work, life at work may be great but your home life becomes miserable. You then have an unbalanced and potentially unhealthy existence. Clients who succeed at the extreme heights in business can damage their health or important relationships along the way. And those who have a very comfortable home life can neglect their professional potential. If these scenarios describe you, finding an NLP coach can help you restore balance and harmony to your life.

Using NLP to Support Your Health

'Stressed' spelled backwards is 'desserts'. Little wonder that dieting is so stressful when you keep seeing those puddings in front of your eyes – puddings can be very attractive when you're stressed!

Seriously though, NLP has much to offer you if you want to stay healthy, because it recognises the inextricable connection between mind and body. NLP views a person like a system that needs to stay balanced in order to be healthy.

Have you ever had a time when you had too much to do, not enough time to do it, and not much say about when and how it was done? Perhaps you've felt like a hamster on a treadmill going nowhere? Most people go through tough times – peaks and troughs are normal. The danger zone hits when people don't recognise what's happening and their lives spiral out of control. When this happens, the body steps in with a braking mechanism. Chronic fatigue, tension headaches, neck and back pains, as well as outbursts of anger and anxiety, can all be warning flags from your body that you're not in control of your own life.

NLP helps people to stay centred and focused on their core values and self-awareness, and so remain in tune with their health.

Using tools such as the Milton Model (see Chapter 16), metaphors and stories (see Chapter 17), and anchors (check out Chapter 9) can help in reducing stress and fears around illness. Unless you have medical training, however, be very sensitive when using NLP with anyone with chronic health issues. Never attempt to 'fix' someone or override the physical symptoms, which are important messages that need professional attention.

A delegate on Romilla's 'Beyond Di-Stress' workshop, named Cassy, had worn herself to a frazzle, trying to meet her commitments at work where she had been recently promoted, and trying to satisfy the demands of her family. During the workshop, Cassy realised that she was pandering to the demands of her boss and her family because she had a deep need for love that stemmed from the fact that she'd been adopted. Despite loving adoptive parents and a very stable and happy childhood, Cassy had always felt as if she was one of life's rejects, because her biological mother had given her away.

Another delegate heard Cassy's story and reframed her perspective as 'but you're really one of the chosen'. The change in Cassy was palpable and pleasant to see, as she processed this positive slant on her identity. After the workshop, Cassy was able to say 'no' to a lot of people in her life, and one of the unforeseen benefits was that her children became more responsible for their own lives.

Connecting to Your Audience: Advice for Trainers and Educators

NLP has expanded its reach into education with specialist NLP programmes for teachers and educators. In addition, people who want to lead business workshops can also benefit from NLP training.

NLP recognises that individuals learn in very different ways, and only the pupil really knows the best way. Good teachers take responsibility for teaching so that the pupils can profit – they truly connect and inspire. NLP moves the emphasis from teaching to learning and gets people to begin to notice how they learn in the best way. Work currently being done with simple techniques such as the Spelling Strategy, explained in Chapter 12, is transforming education for children, and ultimately the quality of their lives for the long term.

The learning process involves many rich dimensions beyond just being taught facts or given the right answers. For learning to connect and last, people need to be put into a positive and receptive state. Getting the trainer and the group into a receptive state is far more important than covering all the curriculum.

When you're discovering a new skill, become curious about how to make that work for you. Think of your best learning experience; a time when you felt good about learning. For example, Kate knows that she learns best when having fun, being with people, and feeling okay to experiment and make mistakes. These items aren't going to be the same for other people and when she runs workshops, she pays attention to the needs of her delegates and adapts her training accordingly.

NLP shows you how to discover people's preferences for taking in information – and so as a teacher, you need to recognise that some people respond to pictures, some to words, and others to touch or feelings. Using highly general language at the beginning of a session enables you to connect with the different levels of expertise in a group. So your introduction may go something like the following:

> *We cover many aspects of the subject today. Some of you will already have a lot of knowledge in this area and have your own ideas, opinions, and experiences to contribute.*

> *For some of you, the concepts will just reinforce what you already know and give you time to sit back and consider the implications of what you do already.*

> *For others, there will be new perspectives and, during the course of the day, we will have the opportunity to explore some new ways to add value and power to what you're currently using.*

> *You will make up your own minds on how these ideas will be applied.*

Also keep in mind the various stages of learning. When you take on a new skill, such as driving a car, you move through different levels of competence. When you start out you're blissfully ignorant – *unconsciously incompetent*. You don't know what you don't know. Then you move to *conscious incompetence* and you've woken up to what you don't know. As you build your capability you become *consciously competent* until you become *unconsciously competent* when, as an expert driver, you forget what being a learner was like. This process can make learning from experts difficult, because they can be so far removed from being a beginner that they say 'just do it' and are unable to break down the skill into easy stages.

Getting the Best Job for You

Huge competition exists for good jobs in challenging economic times, which means that approaching your career change and job interviews strategically is more important than ever. Shifting jobs merely because you're bored – like changing the wallpaper or going shopping and coming home with yet another blue shirt – can be counterproductive. You may change jobs and then realise that the change was what was attractive and not the job itself.

Working with an NLP-trained career coach can guide you towards obtaining the job that takes your life in the best direction (instead of just a different job) and presenting yourself at your very best in an interview. Career planning needs to be done proactively or you can end up like Alice in Wonderland: not too bothered about where you get to, just so long as it's somewhere. Making informed decisions, based on your values and desired future, ensures that you don't leave a perfectly good job only to end up somewhere where you're very unhappy or at best just as unsettled as you were in your previous job, and still searching for the greener grass.

Make your job search a well-formed outcome using the checklist in Appendix C. Do your homework about the person with the power to appoint you to your dream job and decide how that person's map of the world operates. Chapter 7 contains a checklist to help you think about the people you need to influence.

Be creative about making yourself stand out from the crowd. To gain perspective, shift into second and third positions (which we describe in Chapter 7) and think of yourself as a product; what would your features and benefits be? In front of a mirror, practise being the person your dream employer wants to employ – check out the communication information in Chapter 7 to ensure that your words, gestures, and tone of voice present a consistent view. How would you dress and talk? What would you be saying about yourself and your capabilities? Remember, you need to believe in yourself for others to feel confident in you – and buy you.

Chapter 22

Ten Books to Add to Your Library

*W*e read voraciously. This trait enabled us to expand our knowledge of personal development and NLP. Here we offer you ten NLP-related books that had a major impact on our development; use them as a shortcut to your growth. We hope they enrich your life and the lives of those around you.

Changing Belief Systems with NLP

Robert Dilts, the author of *Changing Belief Systems with NLP* (Meta Publications, 1990), is one of the most creative trainers and authors in the world of NLP and one of the people who really walks his talk. In this book, he describes how your beliefs can prevent you from achieving what you want and living a totally fulfilling life. The book helps you explore your beliefs and gives you exercises to change them in order to get alignment at all levels of your personality for permanent change.

The User's Manual for the Brain

In *The User's Manual for the Brain* (Crown House Publishing, 2001), Bob G Bodenhamer and L Michael Hall, two of the most prolific writers in the field of NLP, have produced a book for someone who wants to get to the NLP practitioner level without going on a course. Unlike some other NLP books for beginners, this one is very easy to follow and gives you a really good foundation prior to attending a practitioner course. In addition, master practitioners of NLP are sure to find this a brilliant book to revise their existing knowledge.

Core Transformation

Core Transformation (Real People Press, 1996) offers techniques in NLP, discovered and developed by Connirae Andreas, and designed to bring greater wholeness to the reader in order to facilitate personal change. The technique for *Core Transformation* is based on the premise that conflicting parts exist in every person's unconscious, yearning to reach a core state and thereby wholeness. This book is a breakthrough in the field of personal development because it enables you to use limitations as a springboard to reaching core states such as inner peace.

Frogs into Princes

Frogs into Princes (Real People Press, 1979) is one of the seminal books in the field of NLP. The book is actually the transcript of a live training session conducted by the founding fathers of NLP, John Grinder and Richard Bandler, and beautifully edited by Steve Andreas. Although further developments have occurred in NLP since this book was first published, this title is a must-read for starting you on the path of discovering NLP.

Influencing with Integrity

In *Influencing with Integrity* (Crown House Publishing, 1984), Geine Z Laborde makes use of lots of line drawings and cartoons to create a book that's easy to read and understand. She simplifies a complex subject to give the reader a set of state-of-the-art skills to use in all areas of communication. The straightforward approach, with its focus on business applications, makes this book especially useful for people in the corporate world.

Manage Yourself, Manage Your Life

If you want to discover the theory of NLP, *Manage Yourself, Manage Your Life* (Judy Piatkus Publishers, 1999) by Ian McDermott and Ian Shircore isn't for you. However, if you want to experience NLP while you 'plan to make change happen on your terms', this book is just the one to read and practise. Experiencing NLP with this book, prior to going on an NLP practitioner course, provides an invaluable basis for your learning.

Persuasion Skills Black Book

Rintu Basu's *Persuasion Skills Black Book* (Lean Marketing Press, 2009) is a practical book, written to help you master the language of persuasion in bite-sized chunks. The techniques are given further clarity by the use of everyday examples. This book is useful to a cross-section of people, from teachers to salespeople or parents trying to deal with recalcitrant teenagers.

Presenting Magically

If you're a trainer or presenter, this elegantly written book by David Shepard and Tad James is a must for you. The techniques in *Presenting Magically* (Crown House Publishing, 2001) use NLP and accelerated learning and show you how to captivate your audience from the start. Practise the exercises in the book to model 'natural-born' presenters and raise your presentation skills to mastery level.

The Magic of Metaphor

In *The Magic of Metaphor* (Crown House Publishing, 2001) as well as its sequel *More Magic of Metaphor*, Nick Owen puts together a collection of stories designed to transform the reader, with nuggets that motivate you and provide you with strategies for excellence. The stories uplift you and promote positive feelings and confidence while challenging the very foundations of your ideas, attitudes, and beliefs. This book is extremely useful to people in professions as diverse as counselling, psychology, professional speaking, management, and teaching.

Wordweaving: The Science of Suggestion

Wordweaving: The Science of Suggestion (Quest Institute, 2003) is one of two books by Trevor Silvester; the second being *Wordweaving Volume II – The Question is the Answer*. The author writes about the complex subject of trance in a very easy-to-follow style. The book moves away from the constraints of hypnotic scripts and instead addresses the relationship with the client presenting an issue. This approach gives the reader the flexibility and creativity to get results more effectively through trance. Anyone working with therapeutic issues, including NLP practitioners, hypnotherapists, and coaches, as well as novices, is going to find this book a very interesting read.

Chapter 23

Ten Online NLP Resources

*W*here else would you go these days for more information than the Internet? Exploring for NLP information online can lead you to a wealth of interesting material not only on NLP, but also on related areas of personal development. In this chapter we offer ten websites that offer relevant resources to further your NLP learning.

Anchor Point

Anchor Point is at www.nlpanchorpoint.com. This site is crammed full of very informative articles on NLP dating back to its early days; a mix of personal experiences with NLP and more scholarly articles. Anchor Point Publications also publishes an excellent NLP magazine. Visit this site for a variety of classic books, audio and video tapes, and products on NLP and related topics.

Association for Neuro-Linguistic Programming (ANLP)

The Association for Neuro-Linguistic Programming (UK) is at www.anlp.org. This site offers information for the newcomer and details of NLP events, as well as access to NLP practitioners and trainers if you need help to resolve issues, and some frequently asked questions.

Clean Language

On the www.cleanlanguage.co.uk site set up by James Lawley and Penny Tompkins, you find a wealth of articles, and not just about Clean Language. This website is a rich source of material that connects therapy, health, education, and coaching with metaphors and symbols. The site uses the analogy of a building to guide you to the separate rooms, where you can find the information you need generously laid out.

Crown House Publishing

Crown House Publishing – www.crownhouse.co.uk – has a wonderful selection of personal development books on some fascinating subjects stretching from 'Mind Body Spirit' to business, education, and psychotherapy. They offer titles that you may not find elsewhere and are the publishing arm of the excellent Anglo-American Books, who also organise the annual NLP Conference in the UK.

Encyclopedia of Systemic NLP and NLP New Coding

If you access only one NLP resource, make sure that it's this one. nlpuniversitypress.com contains an encyclopaedia of NLP, created primarily by Robert Dilts and Judith DeLozier. Details of the NLP University set up by Robert, Judith, and other leaders in the field can be found at www.nlpu.com. The encyclopaedia is a fabulous resource, given freely in the collaborative spirit that shows NLP at its best. This site enriches the knowledge of both starters and experienced NLP practitioners.

John Grinder

www.quantum-leap.com is the website for John Grinder, one of the co-creators of NLP. The site gives you a flavour of Grinder's work and information on books by John and his partner Carmen Bostic St Clair, the current presidents of Quantum Leap, as well as links to other NLP sites.

Michael Gelb

NLP encourages creativity in your life by tapping into unconscious processes. For some more ideas on creativity, visit www.michaelgelb.com. Gelb, author of *How to Think Like Leonardo Da Vinci*, encourages people to use all their senses to realise their potential for optimum individual and corporate growth. This site is a good one if you're interested in improving your creativity.

Richard Bandler

News about the work of Richard Bandler, co-creator of NLP, can be found at www.richardbandler.com. Visit this website if you want to know what he has developed, and for opportunities to train with him. This site provides links to other sites and gives lots of information on articles and what to buy in the way of books, tapes, and CDs, and what seminars and training programmes are available to extend your knowledge.

Shelle Rose Charvet

You can find details about Shelle Rose Charvet, author of the very accessible book on meta programs *Words that Change Minds*, at www.successstrategies.com. This site is useful for NLP beginners and practitioners alike, with humorous articles illustrating the principles of NLP. Some very useful products are available from this website on the business and personal world, with particular emphasis on business relationships, including sales and customer service.

The International Society of Neuro-Semantics

Find Bob G Bodenhamer and L Michael Hall, two of the most prolific writers on NLP, at www.neurosemantics.com. Their site is packed full of information by way of articles introducing you to 'self-mastery and success' and has a good review of books for increasing your knowledge of NLP and NLP-based applications as well as its relationship to the field of Neuro-Semantics. An excellent site for beginners and practitioners interested in the history of NLP, with a particularly useful glossary of terms.

Chapter 24

Ten Films That Include NLP Processes

*I*n this chapter, we select ten films for you to watch. We found these films uplifting and often thought-provoking, but most of all we spotted aspects of NLP in each of them. In the following sections, we identify some NLP features in each film to illustrate the sorts of things you can look out for as you hone your NLP skills, even when relaxing at the cinema.

Avatar

Before talking about the NLP features in the film, we want to suggest that James Cameron is a very unreasonable man, because as George Bernard Shaw said: 'Reasonable people adapt themselves to the world. Unreasonable people attempt to adapt the world to themselves. All progress, therefore, depends on unreasonable people.'

Avatar shows James Cameron's dedication and focus in bringing this film to life. It took more than ten years of keeping hold of the vision in his head. Even more amazing is that he and his team developed a virtual camera that took the process of performance capture to a new level – creating and adapting the film world to his needs and progressing the science of film-making not just for themselves but for future film makers. If you have a visual preference (as we describe in Chapter 6), this film is a real treat, especially if you watch it in 3D. Here are the two main themes that we want to point out:

✔ Life is much more fulfilling when all your logical levels are aligned (check out Chapter 11 for all about logical levels). Especially effective is when whole communities have this alignment because this situation leads to a powerhouse for change that's fast and for the good of all. The Na'vi people are the indigenous inhabitants of a moon, Pandora. Their spiritual connection to the moon and all her inhabitants have them treading carefully, only taking what they need for their survival. The Na'vi are aligned through this spiritual identity all the way to the environment of Pandora, which provides the strength to defeat their human foe, despite the humans' superior fire power.

✔ Values (turn to Chapter 3 for details) are a very powerful driver. As Jake Sully (Sam Worthington) begins to understand the richness of the culture on Pandora, his values conflict with those of his compatriots, the other human visitors who just want to exploit Pandora's resources. In this case, Sully is willing to die for his values.

Starring: Sam Worthington, Zoe Saldana, and Sigourney Weaver. Director: James Cameron. Studio: Twentieth Century Fox Film Corporation (2009).

Ferris Bueller's Day Off

A thoroughly entertaining film about a teenager, Ferris Bueller, played by Matthew Broderick who believes that 'Life goes by so fast, if you don't stop and look around, you might miss it.' With this belief in mind he decides to play truant and persuades his best friend, Cameron (Alan Ruck), to join him. An agenda for the day is for Ferris to help Cameron gain some self-esteem. This film is all about beliefs and taking responsibility for your actions. Ferris believes in himself and is adored by everyone, from his parents, class and school mates, to the town's folks in general. The only exception is his principal, Ed Rooney, performed with manic intensity by Jeffrey Jones and his sister, Jeanie Bueller, played brilliantly by Jennifer Grey.

The interesting point is to notice what people focus on and how it affects their lives. Ferris focuses on enjoying life, helping Cameron, and beating the system, and he sails through his day, achieving his goals. By contrast, Ed Rooney and Jeanie Bueller are consumed with hate for Ferris, and Rooney certainly ends up having a terribly painful day, in more ways than one. Jeanie overcomes her angst during a hilarious conversation with a boy in the police station, played by Charlie Sheen, in which he suggests that Jeanie needs to focus more on sorting herself out and less on what her brother's doing.

The biggest transformation takes place in Cameron. At the start of the film Cameron is a victim, completely at the mercy of the people in his life; his father, of whom he is terrified, and particularly Ferris, to whom Cameron can't say no. By the end of the film when Cameron has 'killed' his father's sports car, he admits that he allowed himself to be led by Ferris and could have said no at anytime. The best part is that Cameron has the courage to stand up to his father when he tells him about his car.

Starring Matthew Broderick, Alan Ruck, Mia Sara, Jeffrey Jones, and Jennifer Grey. Director: John Hughes. Studio: Paramount Pictures (1986).

UP

UP is an animated film that appeals across generations, although adults rather than youngsters may relate more to some particularly poignant moments in the first 11 minutes . Ultimately, this film tells a love story about Carl (Edward Asner) and Ellie (Elie Docter) and how he finally fulfils a youthful dream after being propelled into the adventure of a lifetime.

Ellie is utterly charming as a gap-toothed youngster with a shock of red hair. She's loud, extrovert, with strong proactive tendencies (check out Chapter 8 on meta programs) and completely bowls over the quiet, introverted, reactive Carl. Carl's helium balloon floats to the ceiling when Ellie pounces on him at their first meeting. In her 'gung ho' way, Ellie decides they should retrieve Carl's balloon and pushes him across a board on the first floor of a derelict house with no thought of any risk, resulting in poor Carl breaking his arm.

When Ellie visits a recuperating Carl because 'you may need cheering up', she shares a secret she's never shared with anyone: her diary that's labelled, 'My Adventure Book'. One page has a picture of Paradise Falls where Ellie has decided she's going to live. She shocks the timid Carl when she exuberantly announces, 'I ripped this right out of a library book,' with no thought to the consequences of her deeds.

One page is labelled 'STUFF I'm Going TO DO' and is followed by several blank pages. She then tells Carl, 'I'm saving these for all the adventures I'm going to have.' The interesting point about Ellie's Adventure Book is that, although she shares its details with Carl in the beginning, he isn't aware that she has kept it updated. He looks very sorrowful when he finds her 'Adventure Book' years later because he thinks she missed out on getting to Paradise Falls. He's very surprised when he sees the pages are full of photographs of their life together. Carl's idea of an adventure focused on visiting Paradise Falls: Ellie lived each moment as an adventure.

The film is a reminder to take pleasure in the 'little moments' of life, and that although having a road map for your life is useful, you shouldn't fixate on goals to the exclusion of simple pleasures. You need to review your road map to fit in with your changing values and life experiences.

And in Ellie's words. . .

> *Thanks for the adventure – now go have a new one.*

Starring: Edward Asner, Christopher Plummer, Jordan Nagai, and Elie Docter. Directors: Pete Docter and Bob Peterson. Studios: Walt Disney and Pixar (2009).

Dune

Dune follows a hero's journey story line where Paul Atreides (Kyle MacLachlin), the son of Duke Leto (Jürgen Prochnow), travels from his familiar world to Arrakis, a world that's almost supernatural by the standards he has known. He encounters the indigenous, 'blue-within-blue' eyed people who are indigenous to Arrakis and discovers the secrets of the worms and the spice Melange – 'the greatest treasure in the Universe'.

With this knowledge, Paul Muad'dib, as he's now known, frees the people of Arrakis from the Emperor's corrupt rule, avenges his father, and fulfils his destiny. The special effects of this film seem dated in the 21st century, but they were superb for 1984. Apart from being thoroughly entertaining, you can take some very useful lessons from this film: change is inevitable, especially for growth to take place:

> *. . .but a person needs new experiences . . . they jar something deep inside, allowing him to grow. Without change, something sleeps inside us . . . and seldom awakens . . . The sleeper must awaken.*

—Duke Leto

Jessica, the Duke's beloved concubine and Paul's mother (Francesca Annis), demonstrates her sense of personal power by taking complete responsibility for her choices, whatever the consequences:

> *I vowed never to regret my decision. I'll pay for my own mistakes.*

—Jessica

Dune demonstrates the power of the mind and how it can conquer fear. In particular, when Paul Atreides is tested by the Reverend Mother Gaius Helen Mohiam (Sian Phillips), he has to consciously control the fear gripping him in order to survive the test.

Starring: Kyle MacLachlin, Jürgen Prochnow, and Francesca Annis. Director: David Lynch. Studio: Universal Studios (1997).

As Good as it Gets

Jack Nicholson's portrayal of a curmudgeonly, obsessive–compulsive recluse, Melvin Udall, is hilarious. This film has lessons about rapport – or rather, how not to do rapport!

Udall behaves horribly. He doesn't care about the way he treats people and he's an ace at breaking rapport, even when he doesn't know it. Greg Kinnear plays a gentle, gay artist, Simon Bishop, who bears the brunt of Melvin's unpleasantness. Unfortunately, Simon gets beaten up and ends up in hospital and Melvin is forced into looking after Verdell (Jill the dog), Simon's pet. The way Verdell trains Melvin in rapport building will delight animal lovers. One of Melvin's behaviour patterns is to avoid cracks in the pavement. The bond between man and dog is sealed when Verdell follows Melvin's example and daintily avoids the cracks in the pavement too.

In Chapter 2, we discuss an NLP presupposition that 'every behaviour has a positive intention'. Melvin ends up doing kind deeds that are really appreciated by the recipients, however, the positive intention is usually to keep Melvin stuck in his obsessive–compulsive behaviour. One example is when Carol Connelly (Helen Hunt), a waitress who works in the place where Melvin has breakfast, is off work because her son is sick. Melvin gets a private doctor to treat the boy so that Carol can come back to work to serve him because he can't abide anyone else serving him.

Starring: Jack Nicholson, Helen Hunt, and Greg Kinnear. Director: James L Brooks. Studio: Columbia/Tristar Studios (1997).

Bend it Like Beckham

This delightful film is about girl power, friendship, and fulfilling dreams and aspirations in spite of obstacles, and also shows how 'isms' can trap you in a prison of unhappiness until you have the courage to break out of the restrictions that are imposed on you.

Jess (Parminder Nagra) a British girl of Indian parents only wants to play football; unfortunately she's trapped by a cultural background that frowns on such unladylike activities and has to sneak off to play the beautiful game, leading to some interesting subterfuges. Jess is miserable until she comes out into the open and admits her passion for football. She becomes close friends with a Caucasian, English girl Juliette 'Jules' Paxton played by Keira Knightly, which causes hilarious misunderstandings. When Jules leaves Jess at a bus stop and they're spotted giving each other a hug by an Asian family, the family immediately see the innocent embrace through prejudiced filters and assume that the white, short haired person is a boy, which really sets the cat among the pigeons.

Juliet Stevenson plays Jules's homophobic mother, Paula Paxton. She's a total and utter delight as she struggles to understand and accept Jules's tomboyish ways and what she misunderstands to be a homosexual relationship between Jess and Jules. Her attempts at trying to be politically correct and pretending to understand Asian ways in order to make Jess comfortable in her home are extremely touching and will have you shedding tears of laughter.

Chapter 14 examines some of the conflicts that arise when the logical-level hierarchy (see Chapter 11) is misaligned, whether it is within an individual or groups of people. Conflict is present in *Bend it Like Beckham* because Jess's family and community have certain beliefs about the role of girls. The girls who do conform to the norms of being able to cook and produce offspring are accepted into the bosom of the family and community. In a way, the community's identity is threatened by the behaviour of Jess's non-conformity. Paula Paxton, too, allows Jules's behavior to affect her feelings.

Starring: Parminder K Nagra and Keira Knightley. Director: Gurinder Chadha. Studio: Twentieth Century Fox Home Video (2002).

Field of Dreams

This classic film is about the fulfilment that comes from manifesting one's dreams and the yearning that's left when dreams aren't fulfilled. When you focus on what you love, rather than what you think you 'have' to focus on, your ambitions are more easily realised.

Kevin Costner plays Ray Kinsella, a farmer who decides to build a baseball field in the middle of nowhere because he hears a voice say, 'If you build it they will come.' The film employs a host of sensory references to heighten the atmosphere – sounds, smells, and feelings, the importance of which we discuss in Chapter 6 – as well as using metaphors to the *n*th degree.

Kinsella and his family are a metaphor for you and the people you may experience in your life: the doctor, the relatives you have to tolerate, the conflicts you encounter in life, and how you deal with them. Notice how Ray talks about his father. He seems angry that his father grew old because he allowed himself to get worn down by life. His response to the voice is almost a reaction to the mediocrity of his father's life and the fear that this chance may be his last to achieve something. Interestingly, Kinsella is running an *away-from* meta program in order to move *towards* his own dream (Chapter 8 has more on these meta programs).

Starring: Kevin Costner and Ray Liotta. Director: Phil Alden Robinson. Studio: Universal Studios (1989).

Gattaca

This inspiring sci-fi film concerns the situation in which determination overcomes genetic 'flaws' and proves that having everything handed to you on a silver platter doesn't ensure success. This film illustrates how your focus on your goal can help you overcome even the most insurmountable odds. Vincent Freeman, played by Ethan Hawke is an 'invalid', a God child, meaning he was a love child, not genetically engineered. He's left handed, considered a shortcoming, and has a risk of heart failure, and so has to live with everyone else's belief in his vulnerability. According to the hand that Vincent is dealt, the only way he can get close to the space programme is as a cleaner. Therefore, Vincent 'borrows' Jerome Eugene Morrow's (Jude Law) identity in order to gain access.

This film demonstrates the power of beliefs. Everyone sees Jerome when they look at Vincent because that's the person they've been programmed to see. Vincent's unshakeable belief in his own abilities helps him to fulfil his dreams, as does his refusal to buy into what the world at large doesn't consider possible. Some poignant moments revolve around Jerome's acceptance that even with everything going for him, he was still second best, and that he really found a real purpose in life, even for a short time, when Vincent 'lent him his dream'. Vincent's focus and determination gave Jerome a purpose in life, which he hadn't had, despite being given all the advantages Vincent hadn't. Despite all the advantages, Jerome was on a path of self-destruction until he started to work with Vincent.

Starring: Ethan Hawke, Uma Thurman, and Jude Law. Director: Andrew Niccol. Studio: Columbia/Tristar Studios (1997).

The Matrix

A thrilling sci-fi exploration of reality and what you can come to see and achieve when you begin to believe in yourself. This film has many NLP lessons to offer, from the use of language to the beliefs that lie behind the action.

At one point, agent Smith (Hugo Weaving) says 'we are willing to wipe the slate clean' and emphasises the metaphor in his words by sliding Neo's (Keanu Reeves) file to the end of the desk: auditory words to a kinaesthetic action. The really interesting scene is where Morpheus (Laurence Fishburne) explains that reality is simply interpretations the brain makes of electrical impulses that are produced from what you take in through your senses. Elsewhere in the film, Morpheus and Neo are sparring and Morpheus tells Neo to stop 'trying' to hit Mopheus and actually hit him. To try to do something can actually give a clue to a doubt, because if the doubt didn't exist, you'd carry out an action instead of just trying.

Another point to notice is after Neo fails to make a jump in virtual reality but finds himself bleeding in actual fact; Morpheus points out that the mind makes the injuries a reality. Initially, Neo is just another person retrieved from the matrix, but gradually, as his confidence builds, his self-belief grows and he achieves feats that surprise even himself.

Starring: Keanu Reeves, Laurence Fishburne, and Hugo Weaving. Directors: Larry Wachowski and Andy Wachowski. Studio: Warner Studios (1999).

Stand and Deliver

Nothing to do with Adam and the Ants, but instead a terrific film based on a true story of a high-school teacher motivating his class of East Los Angeles barrio youngsters to believe in themselves and overcome stereotyping. What's really interesting, and adds to the humour, is how Jamie Escalante, played by Edward James Olmos, paces his students to lead them to learning calculus (check out Chapter 7 for more on pacing people successfully). He uses similar gestures and body language to those of the students and uses rap to teach them simple mathematics. With a well-formed outcome in mind, Escalante shows considerable flexibility in his behaviour.

When Jamie can't teach computing because of a lack of computers, he chooses to teach maths instead. As the class comes under suspicion for cheating, because they've done so well, Jamie demonstrates flexibility in his behaviour and persuades his class to re-sit the test. Curiously, other teachers are against the students being taught maths or to aspire to better themselves. They are driven by fear of failure. The other teachers are afraid that if the students fail, it will knock what little self-esteem they have.

One key lesson to take from this film is to be careful of trying to protect people from what you may see as their weakness. You may in fact be colluding in keeping them trapped in their comfort zone and stopping them from growing due to the filter you're applying to the situation (turn to Chapter 5 for more on communication).

Starring: Edward James Olmos. Director: Ramón Menéndez. Studio: Warner Studios (1988).

NLP at the Cinema

The preceding sections give you a taste of the NLPisms to look for in a film, so why don't you now try your hand at sharpening your own NLP skills. Whenever you watch a film, see whether you can spot the items from the following list of suggestions:

- ✔ Which NLP presuppositions are demonstrated in this film?

- ✔ What do you notice about rapport in this film?

- ✔ What maps of the world are depicted – how do they match up to your reality?

- What do you notice about the words the characters say, their use of language, and the meta programs they run?

- What's the effect of the soundtrack at different points in the film on your *state of mind*?

- What message does this film contain about dreams, goals, and outcomes?

- Are the characters victims of circumstances, and if so, what's the process by which they take control of their lives?

- What are the beliefs and values demonstrated in the film?

- How do the characters pace and lead each other?

- Which characters, if any, display flexibility in their behaviour?

- What's the visual impact of the film? How do you experience the kinaesthetic dimensions of feelings and touch, plus a sense of taste or smell?

Part VII
Appendixes

In this part . . .

We pull together a resource list to get you started with some addresses for further NLP contacts and training, plus two of the most useful everyday templates from the book. Use these templates to help you build relationships with people and set well-formed outcomes in everything that you do.

Appendix A

Resource List

. . . .

*I*n this appendix, we draw together a selection of the wealth of resources available on NLP, to help you when you've read everything you want to in this book. This list is by no means exhaustive and you're sure to find many more worthy people and organisations as your interest deepens.

Contacting the Authors

Romilla Ready
Ready Solutions Ltd
phone 0845-6444759 (UK local rate)
(+44) 0118-9547744
(+44) 0118-9547722
email enquiries@ready
solutionsgroup.com
website www.readysolutions
group.com

Kate Burton
Creativity in Communication
phone (+44) 0118-9734590
email info@kateburton.co.uk
website www.kateburton.co.uk

United Kingdom

Association of NLP (ANLP)
Arlingham House
St Albans Road
South Mimms
Hertfordshire
EN6 3PH
phone (+44) 020-30516740
website www.anlp.org

Awaken Consulting
phone (+44) 0845-8732036
website www.awakenconsulting.co.uk

Beyond Partnership Ltd
2 Holbrook
Bromham
Wiltshire
SN15 2DH
phone (+44) 01380-859106
website thebeyondpartnership.com

Frank Daniels Associates
103 Hands Road
Heanor
Derbyshire
DE75 7BH
phone (+44) 01773-532195

International NLP Trainers Association
PO Box 187
Gosport
Hampshire
PO12 9AE
phone (+44) 02392-588887
website www.inlpta.co.uk

International Teaching Seminars (ITS)
ITS House
Webster Court
Websters Way
Rayleigh
Essex
SS6 8JQ
phone (+44) 01268-777125
website www.itsnlp.co.uk/

Lazarus Consultancy
phone (+44) 020-83492929
website www.thelazarus.com

Mind for Business
phone (+44) 01604-881581
website www.mindforbusiness.com

NLP Conference, London
website www.nlpconference.co.uk

NLP Research Conference

website www.nlpresearchconference.com

Northern School of NLP

Station House Training Centre
Station Road
Whalley
BB7 9RT
phone (+44) 01254-824504
website www.nlpand.co.uk

Performance Partnership

11 Acton Hill Mews
310 Uxbridge Road
Acton
London
W3 9QN
phone (+44) 020-89929523

PPD Learning Ltd

17 Cavendish Square
London
W1G 0PH
phone (+44) 0870-7744321
website www.ppdlearning.co.uk

The NLP Company

Ground 2
50 Hopehill Road
Glasgow
G20 7JP
phone (+44) 0141 5608714
email info@thenlpcompany.com
website www.thenlpcompany.com/

USA and Canada

Canadian Association of NLP (CANLP)

website www.canlp.com/welcome.htm

Michael Neill

phone (+1) 818-340-4464
email michael@successmadefun.com
website www.successmadefun.com

NLP Comprehensive
PO Box 648
Indian Hills
CO 80454-0648
phone (+1) 800-233-1657
email learn@nlpco.com
website www.nlpco.com

NLP Institute of California
1534 Plaza Lane, #334
Burlingame
CA 94010
phone (+1) 800-767-6756
website www.nlpca.com/

NLP University – Robert Dilts and Judith DeLozier
phone (+1) 831-336-3457
website www.nlpu.com

Robbins Research International
9191 Town Centre Drive
San Diego
CA 92122
phone (+1) 800-466-7111
website www.tonyrobbins.com

Success Strategies
1264 Lemonville Road
Burlington
Ontario
Canada
L7R 3X5
phone (+1) 905-639-6468
website www.successstrategies.com

Denmark

Mind Stretch, Copenhagen
Lindevangs All 3
2000 Frederiksberg
phone (+45) 7020-4401
website www.mind-stretch.dk/

Appendix B
Rapport Building

••

*T*his form is a copy of the one in Chapter 7. You can use it when you have important people with whom you want to build stronger relationships – at home or at work. We ask you to keep a written record so that you take time to think about these individuals. In turn, this process gives you the opportunity to focus on what you want from the interaction in order to achieve a win/win outcome. Feel free to photocopy and complete this form as and when you please.

Fill out this form for anyone with whom you want better rapport.

Name: _____

Company/group: _____

What's your relationship to this person? _____

Specifically, how would you like your relationship with this person to change?
_____
_____

What impact would this change have on you? _____
_____
_____

What impact would this change have on the other person? _____
_____
_____

Is this change worth investing time and energy? _____
_____
_____

What pressures does this person face? _____
_____
_____

What's most important to the person right now? _____

_____

_____

Who do you know that you can talk to who has successfully built rapport
with this person? And what can you discover from this other person? _____

_____

_____

What other help can you get to build rapport? _____

_____

_____

What ideas do you have now for moving this relationship forward? _____

_____

_____

What's the first step? _____

_____

_____

Appendix C
The Well-Formed Outcome Checklist

*T*he checklist below is a summary of the process of creating well-formed outcomes that we describe in full in Chapter 4.

Feel free to photocopy this list and complete the questions whenever you want to set very clear goals for yourself.

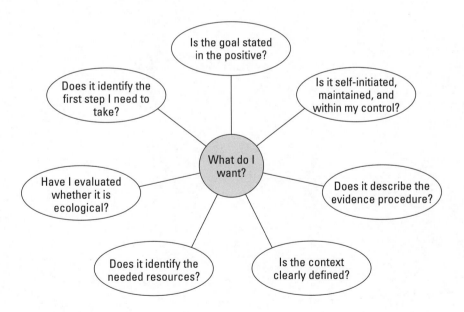

Index

external behaviour, 76
external meta program, 134–135
extrovert meta program, 82–83
extrovert personality type, 128
Eye Movements Game, 101–102
eye-accessing cues
  described, 99
  diagram of, 100, 199
  Eye Movements Game, 101–102
  in love relationship, 204
  reversed, for left-handed people, 100, 199
  strategies revealed by, 198–199
  table summarising, 99–100

• F •

fables. *See* stories
facial expressions. *See also* body language
  eye-accessing cues, 99–102, 198–199
  lying indicated by, 101
failure, 22–24
family tales, 267
fears
  of change, letting go, 326–329
  of success, 34
feedback, 22–25
feeler personality type, 128
Ferris Bueller's Day Off (film), 356–357
Field of Dreams (film), 361
films including NLP processes, 355–364
filtering. *See also* Reticular Activating
  System (RAS)
  by attitudes, 85
  awareness of others', 85
  beliefs affected by, 44
  data remaining after, 35, 78–79, 125
  deletion of information with, 79
  distortion of information with, 79–80
  generalisation with, 81
  map of the world affected by, 20–21
  by meta programs, 81–83, 125
  in NLP model of experiencing, 239
  projections affected by, 57
  of sensory data, 57, 79
  VAK, 91
  by values, 44, 83–85
  values affected by, 44

first impressions, in rapport building, 111–112
first perceptual position, 120, 121, 122
flexibility. *See* behavioural flexibility
Ford, Henry (industrialist), 45, 85
forgiveness, finding, 219
fourth perceptual position, 122
frames, 58–60
Frankl, Viktor (*Man's Search for Meaning*), 188
Freud, Sigmund (psychotherapist), 131
Frogs into Princes (Andreas, ed.), 348
fun, 18, 103
function switch for resolving conflicts, 232
future. *See also* goals; time line
  better, creating, 222
  daydreaming the reality of, 52–53
  designing, dream diary for, 70
  directing brain toward, 60
  direction of, 211–212
future focus, 141–143

• G •

Galanter, Eugene (psychologist), 194
Gattaca (film), 361–362
Gelb, Michael, website for, 353
generalisation
  defined, 81
  downside of, 81, 243
  in everyday encounters, 238, 244
  exploring your thinking, 245–246
  Meta Model patterns, 241
  meta programs combined with, 82
  Milton Model patterns, 254
  in NLP model of experiencing, 239
  overview, 81–82
  questions including, avoiding, 279
  questions to ask about, 241, 244–245
  self-fulfilling prophecies due to, 81
  usefulness of, 81, 243
  values leading to, 85
  verbal cues of, 244
generosity in use of power, 88
Gestalt, 211, 225
global meta program, 135–138, 325

Q

R

FOR DUMMIES

Making Everything Easier! ™

UK editions

BUSINESS

Marketing Kit For Dummies
978-0-470-74490-1

Business Plans Kit For Dummies
978-0-470-74381-2

Consulting For Dummies
978-0-470-71382-2

FINANCE

Investing For Dummies
978-0-470-99280-7

Reading the Financial Pages For Dummies
978-0-470-71432-4

Sorting Out Your Finances For Dummies
978-0-470-69515-9

HOBBIES

Growing Your Own Fruit & Veg For Dummies
978-0-470-69960-7

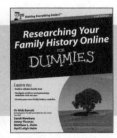

Researching Your Family History Online For Dummies
978-0-470-74535-9

Electronics For Dummies
978-0-470-68178-7

British Sign Language For Dummies
978-0-470-69477-0

Business NLP For Dummies
978-0-470-69757-3

Competitive Strategy For Dummies
978-0-470-77930-9

Cricket For Dummies
978-0-470-03454-5

CVs For Dummies, 2nd Edition
978-0-470-74491-8

Divorce For Dummies, 2nd Edition
978-0-470-74128-3

eBay.co.uk Business All-in-One For Dummies
978-0-470-72125-4

Emotional Freedom Technique For Dummies
978-0-470-75876-2

English Grammar For Dummies
978-0-470-05752-0

Flirting For Dummies
978-0-470-74259-4

Golf For Dummies
978-0-470-01811-8

Green Living For Dummies
978-0-470-06038-4

Hypnotherapy For Dummies
978-0-470-01930-6

IBS For Dummies
978-0-470-51737-6

Lean Six Sigma For Dummies
978-0-470-75626-3

Medieval History For Dummies
978-0-470-74783-4

Available wherever books are sold. For more information or to order direct go to www.wiley.com or call +44 (0) 1243 843291

14652 (p1)

FOR DUMMIES®

A world of resources to help you grow

UK editions

SELF-HELP

Healthy Mind & Body ALL-IN-ONE For Dummies

978-0-470-74830-5

Emotional Healing For Dummies

978-0-470-74764-3

Improving Your Relationship For Dummies

978-0-470-68472-6

STUDENTS

Learning English as a Foreign Language For Dummies

978-0-470-74747-6

Student Cookbook For Dummies

978-0-470-74711-7

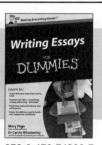

Writing Essays For Dummies

978-0-470-74290-7

HISTORY

British History For Dummies

978-0-470-99468-9

Twentieth Century History For Dummies

978-0-470-51015-5

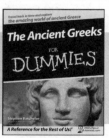

The Ancient Greeks For Dummies

978-0-470-98787-2

Origami Kit For Dummies
978-0-470-75857-1

Overcoming Depression For Dummies
978-0-470-69430-5

Positive Psychology For Dummies
978-0-470-72136-0

PRINCE2 For Dummies, 2009 Edition
978-0-470-71025-8

Psychometric Tests For Dummies
978-0-470-75366-8

Raising Happy Children
For Dummies
978-0-470-05978-4

Reading the Financial Pages
For Dummies
978-0-470-71432-4

Sage 50 Accounts For Dummies
978-0-470-71558-1

Self-Hypnosis For Dummies
978-0-470-66073-7

Starting a Business For Dummies,
2nd Edition
978-0-470-51806-9

Study Skills For Dummies
978-0-470-74047-7

Teaching English as a Foreign
Language For Dummies
978-0-470-74576-2

Teaching Skills For Dummies
978-0-470-74084-2

Time Management For Dummies
978-0-470-77765-7

Work-Life Balance For Dummies
978-0-470-71380-8

FOR DUMMIES®

The easy way to get more done and have more fun

LANGUAGES

978-0-470-68815-1
UK Edition

978-0-7645-5193-2

978-0-471-77270-5

Art For Dummies
978-0-7645-5104-8

Bass Guitar For Dummies, 2nd Edition
978-0-470-53961-3

Christianity For Dummies
978-0-7645-4482-8

Criminology For Dummies
978-0-470-39696-4

Forensics For Dummies
978-0-7645-5580-0

German For Dummies
978-0-7645-5195-6

Hobby Farming For Dummies
978-0-470-28172-7

MUSIC

978-0-470-48133-2

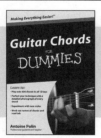

978-0-470-66603-6
Lay-flat, UK Edition

978-0-470-66372-1
UK Edition

Index Investing For Dummies
978-0-470-29406-2

Knitting For Dummies, 2nd Edition
978-0-470-28747-7

Music Theory For Dummies
978-0-7645-7838-0

Piano For Dummies, 2nd Edition
978-0-470-49644-2

Physics For Dummies
978-0-7645-5433-9

Schizophrenia For Dummies
978-0-470-25927-6

Sex For Dummies, 3rd Edition
978-0-470-04523-7

Sherlock Holmes For Dummies
978-0-470-48444-9

Solar Power Your Home
For Dummies, 2nd Edition
978-0-470-59678-4

SCIENCE & MATHS

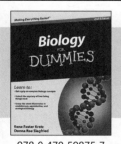

978-0-470-59875-7

978-0-470-55964-2

978-0-470-55174-5

The Koran For Dummies
978-0-7645-5581-7

Wine All-in-One For Dummies
978-0-470-47626-0

Yoga For Dummies, 2nd Edition
978-0-470-50202-0

FOR DUMMIES®

COMPUTER BASICS

978-0-470-57829-2

978-0-470-46542-4

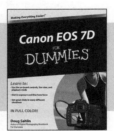

978-0-470-49743-2

DIGITAL PHOTOGRAPHY

978-0-470-25074-7

978-0-470-46606-3

978-0-470-59591-6

MICROSOFT OFFICE 2010

978-0-470-48998-7

978-0-470-58302-9

978-0-470-48953-6

Access 2007 For Dummies
978-0-470-04612-8

Adobe Creative Suite 5 Design
Premium All-in-One For Dummies
978-0-470-60746-6

AutoCAD 2011 For Dummies
978-0-470-59539-8

C++ For Dummies, 6th Edition
978-0-470-31726-6

Computers For Seniors For Dummies,
2nd Edition
978-0-470-53483-0

Dreamweaver CS5 For Dummies
978-0-470-61076-3

Excel 2007 All-In-One Desk Reference
For Dummies
978-0-470-03738-6

Green IT For Dummies
978-0-470-38688-0

Macs For Dummies, 10th Edition
978-0-470-27817-8

Mac OS X Snow Leopard For Dummies
978-0-470-43543-4

Networking All-in-One Desk Reference
For Dummies, 3rd Edition
978-0-470-17915-4

Photoshop CS5 For Dummies
978-0-470-61078-7

Photoshop Elements 8 For Dummies
978-0-470-52967-6

Search Engine Optimization
For Dummies, 3rd Edition
978-0-470-26270-2

The Internet For Dummies,
12th Edition
978-0-470-56095-2

Visual Studio 2008 All-In-One Desk
Reference For Dummies
978-0-470-19108-8

Web Analytics For Dummies
978-0-470-09824-0

19546 p4